Howard Barker's Theatre

Methuen Drama Engage offers original reflections about key practitioners, movements and genres in the fields of modern theatre and performance. Each volume in the series seeks to challenge mainstream critical thought through original and interdisciplinary perspectives on the body of work under examination. By questioning existing critical paradigms, it is hoped that each volume will open up fresh approaches and suggest avenues for further exploration.

Series Editors

Mark Taylor-Batty
Senior Lecturer in Theatre Studies, Workshop Theatre,
University of Leeds, UK

Enoch Brater
Kenneth T. Rowe Collegiate Professor of Dramatic Literature &
Professor of English and Theater, University of Michigan, USA

Brecht in Practice: Theatre, Theory and Performance
by David Barnett
ISBN 978-1-4081-8503-2

Postdramatic Theatre and the Political
edited by Karen Jürs-Munby, Jerome Carroll and Steve Giles
ISBN 978-1-4081-8486-8

Theatre in the Expanded Field: Seven Approaches to Performance
by Alan Read
ISBN 978-1-4081-8495-0

*Ibsen in Practice: Relational Readings of Performance,
Cultural Encounters and Power*
by Frode Helland
ISBN 978-1-472-51369-4

*Rethinking the Theatre of the Absurd: Ecology, the Environment
and the Greening of the Modern Stage*
edited by Carl Lavery and Clare Finburgh
ISBN 978-1-472-59571-3

The Contemporary American Monologue: Performance and Politics
by Eddie Paterson
ISBN 978-1-472-58501-1

Howard Barker's Theatre

Wrestling with Catastrophe

Edited by James Reynolds and Andy W. Smith

Series Editors
Enoch Brater and Mark Taylor-Batty

Bloomsbury Methuen Drama
An imprint of Bloomsbury Publishing Plc

B L O O M S B U R Y
LONDON · NEW DELHI · NEW YORK · SYDNEY

Bloomsbury Methuen Drama
An imprint of Bloomsbury Publishing Plc

Imprint previously known as Methuen Drama

50 Bedford Square
London
WC1B 3DP
UK

1385 Broadway
New York
NY 10018
USA

www.bloomsbury.com

BLOOMSBURY, METHUEN DRAMA and the Diana logo are trademarks of Bloomsbury Publishing Plc

First published 2015

© James Reynolds, Andy W. Smith and contributors, 2015

James Reynolds and Andy W. Smith have asserted their right under the Copyright, Designs and Patents Act, 1988, to be identified as author of this work.

All rights reserved. No part of this publication may be reproduced or transmitted in any form or by any means, electronic or mechanical, including photocopying, recording, or any information storage or retrieval system, without prior permission in writing from the publishers.

No responsibility for loss caused to any individual or organization acting on or refraining from action as a result of the material in this publication can be accepted by Bloomsbury or the author.

British Library Cataloguing-in-Publication Data
A catalogue record for this book is available from the British Library.

ISBN: HB: 978-1-4081-8431-8
PB: 978-1-4081-8439-4
ePDF: 978-1-4081-8599-5
ePub: 978-1-4081-8425-7

Library of Congress Cataloging-in-Publication Data
A catalog record for this book is available from the Library of Congress.

Series: Methuen Drama Engage

Typeset by Newgen Knowledge Works (P) Ltd., Chennai, India
Printed and bound in India

In memoriam
Kenny Ireland (1945–2014)

Contents

List of Photographic Plates	ix
Notes on Contributors	x
Acknowledgements	xvii

Introduction to *Howard Barker's Theatre: Wrestling with Catastrophe*   1
    James Reynolds and Andy W. Smith

Part 1   Howard Barker and The Wrestling School   17

1. A Company and Its Origins   21
    James Reynolds in Conversation with Kenny Ireland
2. From the Actor, to the Actor   37
    Nicholas Le Prevost, Philip Franks, James Clyde, Sean O'Callaghan, Jules Melvin, Victoria Wicks and Suzy Cooper
3. Directing *Slowly*   51
    Hanna Berrigan
4. Amplifying Catastrophe   63
    Ace McCarron
5. On Discipline   79
    James Reynolds in Conversation with Howard Barker

Part 2   Readings/Inversions   89

6. 'To experience a thing as beautiful': The Photographic Practice of Howard Barker   95
    Andy W. Smith
7. Vintage Barker: New Writing in Old Bottles   113
    James Hudson
8. Howard Barker and the Return of Religion   131
    Peter A. Groves

9	Going Underground *James Reynolds*	149
Part 3	Other Barkers	169
10	Acting Barker *Hanna Berrigan in Conversation with Fiona Shaw*	175
11	Staging Barker in America *Andy W. Smith in Conversation with Cheryl Faraone and Richard Romagnoli*	189
12	Barker from a Viewpoint: Staging *Ursula: Fear of the Estuary* *Sarah Crews*	199
13	Staging Barker at Scotland's Conservatoire *Mark Brown in Conversation with Hugh Hodgart*	215
14	'A Gallery of Images': From the Aberystwyth Students *David Ian Rabey*	225
Notes		241
Index		263

List of Photographic Plates

1 *Slowly* in rehearsal; 'like taut pieces of wire'. From left to right: Penelope McGhie, Suzy Cooper, Vanessa Ackerman, Megan Hall. Photographer: Maciek Surowiak
2 Cross lighting in action: Victoria Wicks as Placida in *Ursula* (1998). Photographer: Stephen Vaughan
3 Jan Maxwell and David Barlow in *Victory* (2011). Photographer: PTP/NYC
4 *Mental Institution, Stuttgart, 1945*. Programme cover: *A House of Correction*, 2001. Photographer: Eduardo Houth
5 *Mal de Reine*, Alain Jassy, 1950. Programme cover: *Gertrude – The Cry*, 2002. Photographer: Eduardo Houth
6 *Anti-profiteering Poster, Hungary*, 1943. Programme cover: *13 Objects*, 2003. Photographer: Eduardo Houth
7 Programme cover: *Found in the Ground*, 2009. Photographer: Eduardo Houth
8 Pressure on the body: *Chthonic* space in *The Europeans* (1993). Judith Scott as Katrin. Photographer: Leslie Black

Notes on Contributors

Howard Barker is the Artistic Director of The Wrestling School, for which he writes, directs and designs. His plays have been performed around the world, and in almost every major British theatre. Barker's writing career spans five decades, during which time he has written well over 100 works for theatre, radio, marionettes and opera. He has also published several volumes of poetry, and three critical essays on theatre. Barker's paintings are held in national collections; in England, at the Victoria and Albert Museum in London, and in Europe.

Hanna Berrigan is a theatre director and Wrestling School Associate. She directed the world premiere of *Slowly* in 2010, and worked as Assistant Director to Howard Barker on *I Saw Myself* (2008) and *Found in the Ground* (2009), and as chorus director on *BLOK/EKO* (2011). She has also directed a rehearsed reading of *Dying in the Street* at The Print Room (2013). Other directing credits include: *Public Property* (Trafalgar Studios, WhatsonStage Best New Comedy nomination), *La Musica Deuxième* (Gate), *The Lover* (Gale Theatre, Barbados), *Paradox* (RSC Fringe Festival). Hanna was Associate Director on *The 39 Steps* for four years. Her Edinburgh Fringe production of *Potted Sherlock* transferred to the West End in 2014.

Mark Brown is theatre critic of the Scottish national newspaper the *Sunday Herald*. He also writes on theatre and the arts for the *Daily Telegraph*. In 1999 he was awarded the Edinburgh Fringe Society's *Allen Wright Award* for 'outstanding achievement' by a young arts journalist. He is a member of the executive committee of the International Association of Theatre Critics, for which he is also a director of young critics' seminars. He is a member of the editorial board of the IATC's webjournal *Critical Stages* and editor of the book *Howard Barker Interviews 1980–2010: Conversations in Catastrophe* (Bristol: Intellect, 2011).

James Clyde has performed many times for Howard Barker and The Wrestling School including: Attila in *A Hard Heart* (Almeida Theatre, 1992), Denadir in *Hated Nightfall* (Royal Court & UK/European tour, 1994/5), Emperor in *Wounds To The Face* (Royal Court platform, 1994), Stucley in *The Castle* (Riverside & UK/European tour, 1995), Carpeta in *Scenes from an Execution* (Barbican & UK tour, 1999), and Gex in *The Ecstatic Bible* (Adelaide Festival, 2000). He was also composer for the original production of *Judith* (Leicester Haymarket, 1995).

Suzy Cooper has acted for The Wrestling School regularly since 2009, when she performed as Burgteata in *Found in the Ground*. She has subsequently performed as Feltray in *Hurts Given and Received* (2010), as Calf in *Slowly* (2010), as London in *Smack Me* (2010) and as Quasidoc in *Blok/Eko* (2011).

Sarah Crews is Senior Lecturer in Performing Arts at the University of South Wales. She is currently undertaking a doctoral thesis titled 'Wrestling with the Text: Performance Practices in Staging Howard Barker', which investigates the process of staging Barker's contemporary texts. As a theatre director, her practice has drawn on Barker's writing as a framework for examining scenography, directing and ensemble studies. In addition to Barker studies, her research interests include scenography and Viewpoints training.

Cheryl Faraone has produced all of PTP/NYC's 28 seasons and has directed many shows for the company, including *Pentecost, Serious Money, Territories, Lovesong of the Electric Bear, Crave, Politics of Passion: The Plays of Anthony Minghella, Arcadia, Stanley, Mad Forest* and many more. Previously, she directed and produced for eight seasons with the New York Theatre Studio. Her work at Middlebury College, where she has taught theatre and gender and sexuality studies since 1986, includes the direction of more than 30 productions, most recently *Vampire, Vinegar Tom, As You Like It* and *Serious Money*.

Philip Franks first performed for The Wrestling School as Kent in *Seven Lears* and Agnew in *Golgo* (1989–90). He also played Scrope in

Kenny Ireland's production of *Victory* (1991–2), and Orphuls in *The Europeans* (1993). He has also worked extensively in film and television, is a member of the Royal Shakespeare Company, and regularly directs for the theatre.

Peter A. Groves is Lecturer in Drama and Course Leader on the BA Performing Arts degree at Brooksby Melton College. He has recently completed a Ph.D. thesis at the University of Warwick, entitled *Sacred Tragedy*, exploring religious and spiritual ideas in Howard Barker's plays (2014). Peter has also directed productions of Barker's *Hated Nightfall*, *Wounds to the Face*, *The Last Supper* and *13 Objects*.

Hugh Hodgart, FRSAMD, is Dean of Drama, Dance, Production and Screen at the Royal Conservatoire of Scotland in Glasgow. He began his professional theatre career in 1976, undertaking a wide range of technical and production roles before achieving his ambition to be a theatre director, first with TAG Theatre Company at the Glasgow Citizens Theatre and then as Associate Director of the Royal Lyceum Theatre, Edinburgh. In 1996 he joined the RSAMD as Head of Acting. He has directed a wide range of classical and contemporary material and taught in France, Germany, Poland, Italy, Switzerland, Spain, the USA and the former USSR.

James Hudson is Lecturer in Drama at the University of Lincoln. He completed his Ph.D. at the University of Leeds in 2010, entitled 'Interrogations of Socialist Theatre in Twentieth-Century Britain and France'. James's other research interests include British and French political theatre of the twentieth century, the Theatre of the Absurd, and, particularly, the dramatic work and theatre theory of Edward Bond. He is also the book review editor for the Intellect journal, *Performing Ethos*.

Kenny Ireland worked extensively as an actor and director during a long career in theatre and television, and led the Lyceum Theatre in Edinburgh as Artistic Director between 1993 and 2003. He worked as an actor on several Barker plays for the Royal Shakespeare Company and Royal Court in the 1970s and 1980s, and established a working relationship with Barker that enabled him to launch The Wrestling School in 1986. Ireland directed the company's first production in 1988, *The Last Supper*, and he remained active within the company until 1995, during which time he directed most of their work, including *Seven Lears* (1989), *Victory* (1991, 1992), *Ego in Arcadia* (1991), *The Europeans* (1993) and *The Castle* (1995). Kenny Ireland passed away on 31 July 2014.

Nicholas Le Prevost has worked extensively with Howard Barker and The Wrestling School. Roles in Barker's work include Ponting in *The Hang of the Gaol* (1978), Gregor in *All Bleeding* (1979), Lear in *Seven Lears* (1989), Charles in *Victory* (1991) and Stahremberg in *The Europeans* (1993). He also directed *Golgo* for The Wrestling School (1989), has given premiere readings of many Barker plays, including reading Casanova in *Christ's Dog* (2006), and recorded Barker's drama for radio, including Gradiska in *Albertina*, and Godansk in *A House of Correction* (both 1999).

Ace McCarron is a lighting designer and a Wrestling School Associate. He first encountered the work of the company at The Royal Court in London, and designed their next production *Seven Lears* (1989), going on to light most of their productions. He has worked frequently in the Netherlands and in Belgium, with, among others, Muziektheater Tranzparant and the Operastudio in Ghent. He has had a long career in lighting contemporary opera, particularly with Music Theatre Wales, and also works as a librettist, winning the Flourish Award, with composer Guy Harries, in 2012. He has recently been appointed as a Dramaturg for the National Theatre of Wales.

Jules Melvin has worked extensively with the Royal Shakespeare Company, the National Theatre, and The Globe Theatre, and has acted in three world premieres of Howard Barker plays. She first performed for The Wrestling School as Leonora in *Ursula* (1998), and has also played Vistula in *A House of Correction* (2001), and Ladder in *I Saw Myself* (2008).

Sean O'Callaghan is an Associate Artist of The Wrestling School. He has worked extensively in the theatre, including work with The Royal Shakespeare Company. He has performed in many world premieres of Barker's work for The Wrestling School, playing lead roles in *I Saw Myself* (2008), *(Uncle) Vanya* (1997), *Wounds To The Face* (1997), *Ursula* (1998), *The Ecstatic Bible* (2000), *Gertrude – The Cry* (2002), *13 Objects* (2003), *The Fence in Its Thousandth Year* (2005) and *Animaux en Paradis* (2005).

David Ian Rabey is Professor of Drama and Theatre Studies at Aberystwyth University. He has directed and/or performed in 15 productions of Barker plays. His critical publications include the monographs: *English Drama Since 1940* (2003), *Howard Barker: Politics and Desire* (1989, 2009), *Howard Barker: Ecstasy and Death* (2009), *The Theatre and Films of Jez Butterworth* (2015) and *Theatre and Time* (2016); and co-editorship of the collections *Theatre of Catastrophe* (2006) and *Howard Barker's Art of Theatre* (2013). His plays include two collections, *The Wye Plays* (2004) and *Lovefuries* (2008). He is an Associate of The Wrestling School.

James Reynolds is Senior Lecturer in Drama at Kingston University. Published work explores Howard Barker's direction of his own plays and the challenges of acting the Barker text; Lepage's work with objects, directorial practice and relationship with drugs; the cinematic adaptation of graphic novels, and the National Theatre's stage adaptations of children's literature. He has also co-published with Zoe Zontou on the theatre of Outside Edge, with whom he also co-edited the book *Addiction and Performance* (2014).

Richard Romagnoli's productions for PTP/NYC include *Gertrude – The Cry, Victory, The Castle, A Hard Heart, The Europeans, Scenes from an Execution, No End of Blame, The Possibilities, Gary the Thief* and *Plevna*. Other notable work for PTP/NYC includes plays by Beckett,

Pinter, Albee, Havel and Snoo Wilson. He is a professor of theatre at Middlebury College, where he has directed numerous plays, including David Edgar's *Pentecost* and the American premiere of Peter Barnes's *The Bewitched*, performed at the Kennedy Center as part of the American College Theatre Festival. He is an American Associate of The Wrestling School.

Fiona Shaw CBE performed the lead role of Galactia in *Scenes from an Execution* at London's National Theatre in 2012, that theatre's first production of a Howard Barker play. She has worked extensively with the Royal Shakespeare Company, and at The National Theatre, and is renowned around the world as a classical actress. Equally at home in modern drama, her repertoire also includes several notable collaborations with the director Deborah Warner, many high-profile roles for film and television, and directing for theatre and opera.

Andy W. Smith is the Associate Head of the School of Media at the University of South Wales. As a research practitioner his main interests are in theatre directing, film acting and scenography. He has published numerous journal articles and book chapters on horror cinema, post-war British theatre and the Gothic in popular culture. He has produced and directed over 15 university theatre productions, including Barker's *Victory* and *The Europeans*, as well as plays by William Shakespeare, Sam Shepard, Anton Chekhov, Caryl Churchill and Martin Crimp.

Victoria Wicks is an Associate of The Wrestling School. She first worked with the company in 1996. Roles include Algeria in *The Fence in Its Thousandth Year* (2005), Tenna in *Animaux en Paradis* (2005), Gertrude in *Gertrude – The Cry* (2002), Mrs Gollancz in *The Ecstatic Bible* (2000), Rivera in *Scenes from an Execution* (1999), Placida in *Ursula* (1998) and Helena in *(Uncle) Vanya* (1996–7). She also presented the character of Klatura in Barker's puppet play *The Swing at Night* for the Puppet Barge and has recorded roles for BBC radio, including *The Love of a Good Man*, *A House of Correction*, and *Knowledge and a*

Girl, and given premiere readings of new plays, including *I Saw Myself, Actress With an Unloved Child, Smack Me, Concentration* and *Dying in the Street.*

Acknowledgements

We would like to acknowledge the time and support of Howard Barker, particularly his generosity in allowing access to his photographic collection and for reprinting his poem *To the Aberystwyth Students*. Hanna Berrigan, Chris Corner and Ace McCarron provided considerable advice and practical assistance, for which we are grateful. Thanks are also due to Colin Chambers, for his recollections.

We would like to thank our contributors for all their work and diligence. It has been a privilege to work with such distinctive and inspiring voices. We would also like to thank our colleagues at Kingston University and the University of South Wales for their support, and also the many students who have inspired us on Barker modules and productions through their passion for the work. Personal thanks are due to our families, partners and friends for their support, encouragement and understanding, and in particular Jane Hubbard, Grace Hubbard-Smith and Stella Hubbard-Smith. We are grateful to Mark Dudgeon and Emily Hockley at Bloomsbury Methuen Drama for their assistance and advice, and to series editors Mark Taylor-Batty and Enoch Brater. As the final version of this work was being prepared, we heard the sad news that Kenny Ireland had passed away. In Chapter 1, Kenny tells his story of The Wrestling School in print, for the first time. This book is dedicated to him.

Introduction to *Howard Barker's Theatre: Wrestling with Catastrophe*

James Reynolds and Andy W. Smith

This volume invites us to reconsider both the work of Howard Barker as a dramatist, and that of his theatre company, The Wrestling School. The work collected here brings together conversations with theatre makers from in and outside The Wrestling School, with first-hand accounts of the company's practice, and a selection of critical readings. The book's combining of testimony from key Wrestling School practitioners with alternative practical perspectives, and with analysis by both established and emerging scholars, ensures that a spectrum of understanding emerges that is rich in both breadth and depth. The essays presented here thus provide not only a practice-orientated entry point from which to engage with the theatricality of Howard Barker and The Wrestling School, but also serve to intervene in our understanding of their work, doing so by connecting it to significant conversations taking place in the world of drama and theatre studies today.

This is, in one sense, an eclectic compilation of writing – a feature which certainly reflects, and possibly derives from, the multifaceted nature of Barker and company. In another sense, what this spectrum of perspectives accomplishes is to link different individuals, experiences, and periods, and, in doing so, invite a timely and much-needed re-evaluation of both dramatist and company. The history of The Wrestling School is told here, and told again, with each contrasting perspective adding a layer of nuance to our understanding. For those new to the work of Howard Barker and The Wrestling School, a brief history of the company's genesis and career is contained in this introduction, and provides a useful starting point from which to build such an appreciation. This is not an objective history; rather, it is based on the personal testimony of key individuals in the emergence and development of The Wrestling School. This and other narratives of the company's history – sometimes explicit, sometimes implicit – resonate across this book, not only with each other, but also with the many creative and intellectual questions that rise to the surface when one engages with this unique theatre company, and writer.

Each of the three sections of the book is introduced individually, and in greater detail, at the beginning of each division. Here, we seek to describe what each section of the book accomplishes in more general terms, and the readings they invite in tandem with each other. Part One: 'Howard Barker and The Wrestling School' interrogates the processes and methods through which Barker and The Wrestling School create theatre, examining relationships between theatricality, language, dramatic action and expressive movement. There is a myth around Barker's work, namely that it is *difficult* to do. In gathering accounts of acting, directing, design, and aesthetics from Barker and company, and making it core to our appreciation, this section accomplishes one of the main aims of this book, namely, to unpick and articulate the unique challenges of meeting Barker's work in practice, and thereby dispel the misperception that his work is *difficult*. What is revealed here is not that it is *difficult* to do, but that it is *different* to do, and therefore needs to be met on its own terms. Barker's theatre is fundamentally like any other theatrical form, offering a particular set of problems which require creative solutions of some kind. If there is a difficulty, it occurs when the particularity of 'Barkerian' creative problems is not appreciated: the need to *wrestle* with creative problems is, of course, embedded in the company's philosophy through its name. Many of the essays within will assist in appreciating, and meeting, the specific practical challenges, or *wrestling*, that Barker's writing creates.

The second section of the book, Part Two: 'Readings/Inversions', offers chapters that, somewhat provocatively perhaps, set out to overturn some of the accepted perceptions of Barker's work, and to invite us to think again about how we consider both his writing, and the theatre practice of his company. These essays read against the grain, showing how Barker and The Wrestling School are more pertinent than ever in thinking about not only the questions facing the art form of theatre, but also the commercial industry which ostensibly exists to serve it. This section captures a snapshot of emerging scholarship, and, unsurprisingly perhaps, reveals a range of fresh approaches to a well-established dramatist and company. In this regard, the book accomplishes another of its core aims, specifically, the reinvigoration of discourses around Barker's work through the introduction of new or emerging voices expressing alternative perspectives.

In his writing, Barker does not court or seek contemporary relevance; here, the contemporary vitality of his work is revealed through its intimacy with global cultural processes, such as the return of religion, and more localized, theatrical phenomena, such as that of new writing. Similarly, while The Wrestling School remains dedicated to the production of new texts, other chapters in this section reveal significantly non-literary influences at play in the development of writer and company, through a focus on the aesthetics of photography and theatre space. Barker's artistic trajectory is usually charted through his play texts, and in relation to the institutions which have commissioned, staged or rejected those texts. In one sense, then, there is a gulf in perception between the practice-based perspectives of Part One, and these research-based perspectives. In another sense, however, through complement and contrast, these sections reveal a commonality of purpose in their articulation, and demystification, of Barker's work with The Wrestling School. A perception that Barker's work is marginalized due to practical difficulty, or lack of relationship with contemporary trends, should at least be diminished by these sections of the book.

The final section of the collection, Part Three: 'Other Barkers', explores the expression of Barker's theatricality by other practitioners, articulating contrasts between often very different creative practices, and in correspondence with productions of key plays in different contexts. 'Other Barkers' looks abroad, to Scotland and America: it looks to alternative methodologies such as Viewpoints; and it looks to the experience of both professionals and students in staging Barker's work, harvesting knowledge and appreciation of practice that both complements and contrasts the work of The Wrestling School itself. The inclusion of alternative practical perspectives illustrates firmly that there is no one way with the Barker text; in this, 'Other Barkers' corresponds neatly with the middle section of the book in providing alternative discourses and accounts. Notwithstanding, although these perspectives may stem from widely disparate corners of the theatrical field, again, reading across the different sections of the book reveals their core of shared concerns. That core here lies in the theatrical imperative to establish a coherent, non-naturalistic style of performance through which the Barker text can be mediated to its greatest effect.

Although it should be evident from the complementary-yet-contrasting sections of this book that we are not presuming to offer here a totalizing narrative around the work of Howard Barker and The Wrestling School (and, rather, are seeking to add fresh and diverse perceptions to the conversation around his work), it should be equally evident that we presume Barker to be as significant a theatre practitioner as he is as a playwright and theorist, and that his work with The Wrestling School amply demonstrates this. The elucidation and reality of that presumption is given significant expression in the chapters contained herein; nevertheless, given decades of productions to consider, and a vast number of factors to reflect upon, there will undoubtedly be gaps in the description that this book offers.

For those new to the work of Howard Barker and The Wrestling School, the most urgent of these to address will be a sense of broader context. Therefore, as noted, we offer here a brief history of The Wrestling School based on a blending of three individuals' first-hand experience into an account of why the company was necessary, how it was instituted and maintained and of how it evolved in relation to its context. Colin Chambers, Literary Manager at the Royal Shakespeare Company in the 1980s (which performed Barker's writing most frequently before The

Wrestling School was born); the late Kenny Ireland, who formed the company in 1986, launched it as a business and charity in 1987, and directed productions between 1988 and 1995; and Chris Corner, The Wrestling School's company manager since 1987. Barker himself covers this ground in *A Style and Its Origins* (2007), but adding a diversity of perspectives to existing understanding nevertheless enriches our appreciation. The Wrestling School has had an exceptionally long and active life as a producing and touring theatre company. Furthermore, it has nearly always produced new work, and after 21 years of practice in 2009, was celebrated through an international festival, which saw presentations of Barker's writing in 18 countries, 7 languages and involving hundreds of performers.[1] Its roots, however, reach as far back as relationships formed in the 1970s.

Barker's writing received quite substantial support from the RSC in the 1970s and 1980s. *That Good Between Us* (1977) was the first production at the RSC's home for new plays, The Warehouse Theatre.[2] Chambers notes that they presented seven Barkers in total; furthermore, Barker remains the only living writer to have ever been given an RSC season (*Crimes in Hot Countries, The Castle*, and *Downchild*, 1985). This took place in The Pit at the Barbican Theatre, London; but the company never presented Barker's work in the Barbican's main house. Chambers notes with irony that while Barker played in The Pit, Trevor Nunn's production of *Les Miserables* was sung overhead in the main house, an emblem of schisms then emerging in theatre more broadly. Significantly, the RSC rejected two major Barker plays, *Victory* and *The Europeans*. Both had the potential to succeed dramatically in a large auditorium, but Chambers notes a key difference: the *Europeans* was an RSC commission, and producing it would also have been a public statement accepting Barker as a main stage writer from then on. Barker's writing had been building to that, but with nowhere to go, the relationship came to an end.

The question of where Barker would place his work arose, and was answered by Kenny Ireland. Barker had met Ireland when he worked on the RSC's Warehouse production of *The Loud Boy's Life* (1980). While working at The Royal Court, and due to the cancellation of a project, Ireland and other actors were asked to find alternatives. Ireland visited Barker at his home in Brighton, where the playwright 'opened a drawer, and produced three', including *Victory*.[3] Although Ireland did not direct the Royal Court production of *Victory* (1983), which was directed by Danny Boyle, he performed in it as Ball, and subsequently in *The Power of the Dog* (1984–5). Ireland's style suited Barker's work, and they got on very well also. The break with the RSC which was happening at around the same time was the catalyst that was needed for The Wrestling School to be formed. Ireland describes how he went about forming the company in 1986:

> I decided I had a mission. And the mission was to popularise Howard's work. I felt that what was needed was to develop a very strong style. I knew that I probably couldn't do it with my experience and reputation, and all the rest of it, it wouldn't carry it, but maybe a lot of actors together might. I enrolled Imelda Brown, Catrin Cartledge, Eleanor David, Paul Freeman, Hugh Fraser, Roger Frost, Celia Imrie, Harold Innocent, David Lyon, Tony Matthews, Clive Merison, Bill Paterson, Peter Spruel, Maggie Steed, Nigel Terry, and Joanne Whalley, who wasn't a film star then. That's the list of the people I got in touch with, I wrote to them all to have a meeting, and they all turned up at my flat, and Howard was there.

Swift action followed. Ireland drafted material for the company's first press release, dated 18 December 1986:[4] registered The Wrestling School as a company and a charity in 1987; appointed Chris Corner as company manager in November of the same year; and, early in 1988, directed The Wrestling School at the Royal Court in its inaugural production, *The Last Supper*.

In a timely parallel with Ireland's 1988 production of *The Last Supper* was Ian McDiarmid's launching of a new theatre in London, the Almeida, with his own direction of Barker's *The Possibilities*. McDiarmid directed *Scenes from an Execution* there (1990), with Glenda Jackson in the lead, and also *A Hard Heart* (1992). Given McDiarmid's concrete relationship with the Almeida, and what Corner notes as the willingness of the

Court to host *Hated Nightfall* (1994) with McDiarmid in the cast, it is reasonable to speculate that, had he been prominent in The Wrestling School, the company might have gained a stronger, or at least a more regular, foothold in London. This, in combination with the national network of connections that Ireland brought to the company, would probably have been the most advantageous position achievable going forward. Of course, this is a speculative point made with the benefit of hindsight. Ireland and McDiarmid were the leading exponents of Barker's work at that time; but there was little necessity for them to combine efforts, when both were able to mount major productions of his plays. However, the history of the company may well have unwound quite differently had these two actor-directors been able to join forces in what might be thought of as peak years of interest.

There are a number of ways that the history of the company might be approached from that point onwards. One might treat Barker's new plays consecutively: however, although The Wrestling School is fundamentally committed to staging new plays by Barker, it does not always stage them in the order in which they are written. Indeed, there are a number of plays by Barker which await a premiere. Or one might read the work of the company as a straightforward development of style which Ireland initiated as director, and which Barker subsequently redefined on his own terms when he began to direct Wrestling School productions in 1994. However, beyond the directing role, a broad range and number of practitioners contributed to the initiation of a company style and others joined and assisted in its evolution; some are represented here, but others, such as composer Matthew Scott and sound designer Paul Bull, are not. Alternatively, one might read the development of the company through its relationships with organizations, institutions and theatre buildings such as the Arts Council, RSC and the Royal Court. But this would be to define and understand The Wrestling School less in terms of its work, and more on the terms of the generic tensions which play out in the landscape of British theatre, and which affect independent theatre makers on a daily basis.

In navigating these pitfalls, the perspective of company manager, Chris Corner, is particularly useful. This is due, in part, to Corner's unchanged role in The Wrestling School since its inception. With the exception of Barker as 'writer-in-residence', Corner is the only member of the company who has held the same post throughout its history, and worked on every production in the same role. Corner's involvement with The Wrestling School began with a chance introduction to Kenny Ireland in the bar of the Royal Court, in November 1987, and continues to the present day. Introduced by the then manager of the Court, Graham Cowley, Corner was appointed as company manager. Experienced in production management, Corner adopted the role of general manager as well, when it became apparent that there was nobody to undertake those duties. It was, he says, 'a steep learning curve for both of us really' as he and Ireland grew into their new roles.[5]

The Last Supper was staged with financial support from the Leicester Haymarket, and 'a lot of help from the Royal Court'. Practically, this was a formal co-production between three theatre partners, assisted by a grant from the Arts Council – a form of support that, although it gradually diminished, remained unbroken until 2007. The support of the Leicester Haymarket, however, 'was more significant and more essential' than that of the Royal Court in terms of mounting this first production, and thus launching The Wrestling School. It was, nevertheless, similarly vital in launching the company that its first production was mounted at a key London theatre such as the Court. The artistic director at the Haymarket, Peter Lichtenfels, was 'incredibly supportive', helping to draw up the initial co-production contract between the institutions involved, and the Haymarket supported the production by putting in finance, and building and production managing the set. 'Effectively', Corner says,

> the production was mounted at Leicester Haymarket and then taken on tour. That's what made it physically possible, was the fact that they effectively produced it, took the play on, and then Kenny and I and a couple of stage managers effectively transferred it to the Royal Court and also to the Gulbenkian in Canterbury.

Corner dispels any sense that The Wrestling School was bedding in at the Court; the Court was, subsequently, much less supportive. There was a feeling there that 'the work was too specialized', and the audience for Barker 'was too narrow'. Perhaps consequently, 'they were not interested at all in co-producing *Seven Lears*' (1989), the company's next piece. Rather, this became a co-production between Leicester Haymarket and the Sheffield Crucible, with a small tour, but no clear plans for London performances. Nevertheless, because *Seven Lears* (and its companion piece, *Golgo*) was 'seen as being a very good production and well-received, it was basically put into storage and then remounted for the Royal Court' the following year. There was a level of disgruntlement at Leicester that 'the show went to the Court, when the Court didn't make any financial contribution', but Ireland and the actors were keen to have the work seen in London, and they prevailed.

There was at that time, Corner remarks, 'a great deal of willingness and team-ness' from the technical staff of the different theatres involved, including the Court, in surmounting the practical challenges of transferring Wrestling School designs between very different venues. Thus, although the financial and practical support that these venues offered was dispersed, these early shows 'came together remarkably well' due to a network of skilled practitioners committed to the work. There was a sense that a national network was opening up for The Wrestling School, but the situation in London was different. The company had presented *Seven Lears* in a kind of mini-rep with a shorter piece, *Golgo*, but the Court was uninterested in it. Ireland insisted, however, 'and they very reluctantly gave it two or three performances'. Such tensions undoubtedly contributed to a long break in the relationship with the Court, but Corner also has a more direct explanation. London theatres were 'less well funded than some of the regional theatres', often relying directly on ticket sales; as *Seven Lears* and *Golgo* 'didn't do terribly well, box office-wise', the Court 'could no longer afford to take the company on', and 'consequently that meant the end of the relationship'.

The Greenwich Theatre at that time was committed to 'radical ground-breaking work', and the venue emerged as a new partner in London, for a while becoming the company's base. The company presented *Victory* there in 1991. This, however, 'was all too much for conservative Greenwich', and the relationship was short-lived. But Corner is quick to dispel the notion of repeated homelessness for the company being a defining motif. The Wrestling School, he says, 'never had a home' per se; the closest it came to one 'in those early years was the Leicester Haymarket', where the company was thought of and treated 'as a company in residence', at least until the departure of Lichtenfels. Similarly, Corner disagrees with any neat periodization in terms of the company's relationship with London theatres which would have it strictly divided and thus understood in phases, that is Royal Court-Greenwich-Riverside. Indeed he points out that *The Europeans* was presented at Greenwich in 1993, *Hated Nightfall* was staged at the Court in 1994 and *The Castle* was produced at the Riverside Studios in Hammersmith in 1995. Nor is there a particularly neat division between the years when Ireland was director, and when Barker himself took the reins. Barker's first direction was *Hated Nightfall* in 1994, but Ireland returned from his appointment as the artistic director of the Lyceum in Edinburgh to direct *The Castle* in 1995, and the 1997 production of *Wounds to the Face* was directed by Stephen Wrentmore. Spread across years, these transitions highlight the slow development of the company through its circumstances. Corner does, however, identify *Hated Nightfall* as a key moment of a much more rapid transition in the company, not simply because it was the moment when Barker first directed his own work, but because a unique set of circumstances presented the opportunity to forge ahead in terms of theatrical style. Indeed, the piece won Best New Play in the TMA Regional Theatre Awards, and Ian McDiarmid, as Dancer, won Best Actor in the Manchester Evening News Awards. These were the first awards the company were to win, and it is important to explore the success of this piece in some depth.

Barker came to direct *Hated Nightfall* partly out of 'sheer practicality'; Ireland simply wasn't available. But Corner also notes that Barker had reached a moment of skill and confidence in terms of his capacity to take the company in a particular artistic direction, which would be different to Ireland's. The Court felt that the presence of McDiarmid in the cast would support the box office, and 'they were willing to take a Wrestling School show' for the first time in five years, but, importantly, the venue also felt that 'with Howard directing there would be an interesting story to be told', and this did indeed 'generate a lot of press'. Additionally, while Barker and Ireland had never had 'any major artistic disagreement', it was clear that Barker's approach would be different. As an actor-turned-director, Ireland characteristically directed 'very accessible productions', which sought to make 'every moment in the show very clear, and very understandable for the audience'. Corner attributes this to Ireland's training as an actor, which foregrounded the need to understand what a 'character was doing and why they were doing it at any one particular moment'. Barker, however, is 'much happier with ambiguity and obscurity', and characteristically directs without placing an interpretation upon the text for the audience.

Furthermore, *Hated Nightfall* 'was a very different play', one which clearly 'marked the moving on in Howard's writing'. Like *Victory*, the play is based on historical characters, but they are notably further removed from actual history. Corner knew from the outset that the production would be 'significantly different', simply from the way that Barker talked about it. It was, he says, an important aspect of his role at that time to make sure that the production team around Barker were aware of the relatively 'limited experience he had as a director' compared to Ireland. Although steeped in theatre through many years in the rehearsal rooms of leading directors, Barker had much less direct experience 'of the practicalities', so Corner put in place and briefed a team prepared to work closely and conscientiously with the new director. Corner observed them working very hard to find out what Barker 'wanted to happen on the stage, what he wanted it to look like, and sound like and feel like'. A key feature of this was that the designers in particular were not able to fall back on industry slang, 'tried and tested methods', or 'references to other productions', and this 'liberated, perhaps forced, them to think in new ways, in order to really try to understand what Howard wanted to see on stage'. This, Corner believes, is another reason why *Hated Nightfall* was 'such a jump stylistically': the collaborators 'were being encouraged by the dialogue with Howard to find completely new ways of doing things'. Johan Engels designed the costumes for the production, as well as the set, which 'was not like anything [Corner had] ever seen or worked with', and Ace McCarron's cross-lighting of the production was 'beautifully used', and became one of the company's signatures. *Hated Nightfall* ultimately represented 'a radical departure' for The Wrestling School from its previous work, not only in terms of direction, but also in terms of acting, lighting, sound and design, and therefore overall style.

Another important development which Corner identifies, and that occurred around this time, was the formation of a relationship with Neil Wallace, then the artistic director of the Tramway in Glasgow. Wallace had been behind the Paris revival of *Victory* in 1992, and *The Europeans* had opened at the Tramway in 1993. Wallace joined The Wrestling School as executive producer. Crucially, through his role at the Tramway, he had developed co-production partnerships with several European theatres, and he was thus able to expand the network of The Wrestling School beyond the British context. *The Castle* (1995) was the first of these co-productions, and in the same year *Hated Nightfall* was presented in Paris and Berlin. Following a similar pattern, *(Uncle) Vanya* (directed by Barker) and *Judith* (UK premiere directed by Ace McCarron, Leicester Haymarket, 1995; European premiere directed by Howard Barker, 1996) were premiered in Britain in 1995, and revived to tour Europe. In 1996, *Judith* went to Edinburgh, Amsterdam and Gothenberg, with *Vanya* touring to Copenhagen, Limoges and Riga. Ten years had passed since Ireland had conceived of the company, and in that time it had become an undeniable success on all terms. Although the middle of the 1990s represents a peak in the company's touring – Corner refers to it as the company's 'Grand Tour*ing*' – the company's reach continued to develop, perhaps most notably through the co-production of Barker's seven-hour piece *The Ecstatic Bible* with Brink Productions and the Adelaide Festival in 2000.

As with all theatre companies however, there were tensions at play. Barker sought only to present new work through the company, but there was 'constant pressure' from venues, and indeed from Wallace, to present better known pieces 'from the past'. Corner describes how this pressure led to the 1999 revival of *Scenes from an Execution*; Wallace persuaded Kathryn Hunter to take the lead role, and the play was performed at The Pit in the Barbican, with Barker directing. The strategy was instrumental; presenting a well-known piece at a high-profile venue would 'get large audiences, put the company firmly on the artistic map, enable it to do more radical stuff in the future while still drawing audiences, and get venues to open their doors'. The production was excellent and very successful, with Barker and Hunter respectively nominated for TMA Regional Theatre Awards for Best Director and Best Actor. Barker even 'rewrote it quite substantially in order to get down the number of characters so that we could actually afford to do it'. Shortly afterwards, however, Wallace departed from his role as Ireland had, to take up an artistic directorship at a distance that made further collaboration impractical – this time in Amsterdam.

The Wrestling School continued to work internationally in the 2000s, notably collaborating in 2005 with the French company Mala Nocha in staging *Animals in Paradise* in translation (*Animaux en Paradis*), but with far less of the density of touring which had characterized activity in the 1990s. At home, it became 'increasingly difficult' to get British venues to support the production of new work, and the company's touring network reduced accordingly. Corner identifies the main problem that the company faced in the early 2000s; despite open recognition of The Wrestling School's artistic successes, London theatres have had no programming money to assist with co-production for many years, and would not offer box office deals to the company. Corner puts it simply: 'Radical work is never going to attract large audiences'. This leaves the option of hiring a venue, but the cost of that is such that it rapidly eats up small production budgets, leaving no other option than putting on cost-effective work, usually with small casts, creating what

Corner describes as 'an ever decreasing spiral' in terms of attracting wider financial support.

Nevertheless, and again in 2005, Corner and Barker approached a number of regional theatres and secured a co-presentation of a new play, *The Fence in Its Thousandth Year*, with Birmingham Rep, Oxford Playhouse, Colchester Mercury and York Theatre Royal. As with *Seven Lears*, there was no London venue arranged, but the piece was also performed at RADA's Jerwood Vanbrugh Theatre, where it was very well received. Importantly, this also established a relationship with RADA, which has subsequently hosted a number of Wrestling School performances, including *I Saw Myself* (2008) and *Blok/Eko* (2011; first performed at Exeter's Northcott Theatre).

Possibly the most significant alteration in the production history of the company was the loss in 2007 of Arts Council funding, which was due largely to a change in the assessment criteria by which grant applications were evaluated. Corner notes that

> A key criteria had always been 'Developing the Artform'; incredibly, this was removed from the list of the criteria for project funding. ACE no longer seem to care about the development of art for its own sake, only how it could be 'applied' to make a difference to society. Hence an artist-led, cutting-edge company like The Wrestling School could be refused funding.

The Wrestling School had demonstrated artistic excellence and development continuously for 19 years, and still met those criteria resoundingly, but the introduction of requirements to ensure wider social engagement with the arts meant that a Wrestling School application for project funding was rejected for the first time. The loss of venues as touring partners meant that the company's reach in terms of creating wider engagement with the arts had diminished, and Corner notes that this was a factor in the decision. It was a potentially crippling blow; the Arts Council is, effectively, the only source of funding in the United Kingdom for companies such as The Wrestling School. Fortunately, an anonymous, privately funded benefactor emerged to support the company's work over four years, enabling them to present five new pieces from 2008 to 2010, during which time the aforementioned international festival of Barker's work also took place. Corner is not slow to point out the cultural irony of a private American donor funding the work of a major British playwright.

Where next? In 2013, a new London venue, The Print Room, hosted a weekend of readings of four new works by Barker, one of which, *In the Depths of Dead Love*, was broadcast on Radio Three in December 2013. Also, in 2012, the National Theatre presented its inaugural Barker production, with Fiona Shaw leading in *Scenes from an Execution*. There is cause for optimism, therefore. The Wrestling School continues to seek funding for its own productions, and a new Howard Barker play presented by the company is surely just a matter of time. However, the fact that The Wrestling School still has to push hard to produce its work is a damning indictment of the residual cultural conservatism in much of the UK theatre industry. What Corner's discussion of the company's history reveals is that, over the course of its existence, the theatre industry has become increasingly risk averse, and unwilling to support innovative work unless it is simultaneously commercial. We should reflect coldly upon how rare it is that real theatrical innovation and commercial appeal are found as bedfellows. The over-dominance of commercial imperatives more often than not narrows the parameters of artistic activity in negative ways, and given that this is implicitly coercive, it is a testament to The Wrestling School that it has consistently produced world-leading theatre across four decades, without sacrificing its artistic integrity.

Part One

Howard Barker and The Wrestling School

Introduction

In his autobiographical work *A Style and Its Origins* (2007), Howard Barker offers his own narrative of the history of The Wrestling School, and, crucially, of the development of its particular style of performance. Here, several key practitioners articulate features of their own theatre making with The Wrestling School, elaborating on the company's style and techniques in the areas of dramaturgy, acting, directing, design and aesthetics. The chapters that follow in the first part of this collection, therefore, provide additional, alternative or contrasting perspectives on the evolution of The Wrestling School, adding nuance while simultaneously introducing new voices to the existing conversation around Howard Barker's theatre – several of which are heard here for the first time. While supplementing our contextual understanding of Barker and The Wrestling School, therefore, Part One also offers a collection of testimonies that are quite unique in their focus on Barkerian theatre practice. We noted in the introduction that such first-hand articulations of practice are core to the approach of this book. Barker's plays are sometimes perceived as *difficult*, but our position is that they are not difficult, but, rather, that they are *different*. The misperception of difficulty arises, largely, by applying ineffective methodologies which are not capable of yielding performance from the Barker text. If the particularity of the Barker text is appreciated, and the possibly unique challenges it presents are thus identified, the work presents little or no more difficulty than the staging of a classic text.

Nevertheless, in order to meet the Barker text and appreciate it as the template for performance that it is – rather than being halted, perhaps, at its literary qualities – it is extremely useful to read and reflect upon the accounts of those who have ventured into this territory, often repeatedly. Although The Wrestling School is not a permanent ensemble, many of the contributors here have worked with the company on a regular basis, and the dissemination of practice that compromises this section thus offers a significant account of the demands of the Barker text in performance. Unsurprisingly, perhaps, given the depth of experience presented, the company's writing here provides us not only with lucid insights into how Barker's writing for theatre works practically, but also produces a history of the company's evolution.

In our introduction, we drew on Chris Corner's perspective regarding the evolution of The Wrestling School. Having worked as company manager since 1987, Corner's account of this trajectory is unique, and as we have seen, is particularly revealing in regard to the relationship of the company to broader trends within the theatre industry itself. Chapter 1, 'A Company and Its Origins', furnishes us with a telling of the company's history and its development in the words of the late Kenny Ireland – actor, director, and the driving force behind the formation of The Wrestling School in the 1980s. In conversation with James Reynolds, Ireland accounts for the forces which led him to create The Wrestling School. Ireland provides a unique insight into key moments in the company's early history and, crucially, defines what he saw as the theatrical imperatives which led to the dramaturgical principles underpinning the style of The Wrestling School – perhaps even to the present day. The differences in approach and principle between Ireland and Barker are given full expression here, particularly in relation to Ireland's approach to acting style and audience. These perspectives add new angles and nuance to existing understanding, and to the discourse around Barker's work. In Chapter 2, 'From the Actor, to the Actor' a subtle perspective on stylistic development with regards to acting accompanies the specifically practical focus of seven Wrestling School actors, as they reflect upon performing Barker's work. These actors – Nicholas Le Prevost, Philip Franks, James Clyde, Sean O'Callaghan, Jules Melvin, Victoria Wicks and Suzy Cooper – collectively span several decades of Barker's writing, and represent a cross-section from each key phase of The Wrestling School's work. Although other voices are missing – and several Wrestling School performers have written about the challenge of acting Barker elsewhere – this chapter reveals the evolution of a unique acting practice, brings several new voices into the conversation, and highlights both continuities and changes in approach, while simultaneously offering a subtly refracted history of Barker's evolution as a theatre writer. In Chapter 3, 'Directing *Slowly*', Hanna Berrigan focuses on a specific production, analysing in detail the discipline of directing Barker, through an account of her direction of *Slowly* for the company in 2010. *Slowly*, effectively a chamber piece for four women, is one of Barker's most challenging texts for the performer because it involves the most considerable restriction of movement. In this context, Berrigan illuminates sharply both the company ethos, and her work as a director for The Wrestling School, while at the same time expressing the artistic freedom that company collaborators enjoy in meeting the creative challenges set by the Barker text. This chapter demonstrates unequivocally that, in the context of an accurate appreciation of the Barkerian text, the discovery and implementation of an individual approach to directing – as opposed to imagining that there is a 'right' way to 'do Barker' – is fruitful, and even essential. Ace McCarron reflects upon his considerable history of work as a lighting designer for the company in Chapter 4, 'Amplifying Catastrophe'. Taking in the often pressurized working conditions, the design imperatives produced by Barker's texts, the challenges of creating the exordium, and key production moments in the stylistic development of The Wrestling School's distinctive use of side-lighting, McCarron's account further describes a theatrical practice in constant evolution, and, as elsewhere, creates in parallel another subtle account of the company's history. McCarron here provides us with not only an account of how theatre technology is deployed in delivering the Barker text in performance, but also, and importantly, how technical elements serve to amplify the text to the catastrophic. The final chapter of Part One, 'On Discipline', records a conversation between James Reynolds and Barker that is based around the many references the writer makes to the notion of discipline in his critical writings. The dominant themes of Barker's critical writings on drama and theatre are, first, a rallying cry to reject the implicit censorship of Naturalism, and its inevitable imposition of reality as a ring-fencing of imagination – and secondly, a call to reinvent forms of tragedy capable of restoring imagination to drama, and the primal powers of performance to theatre itself. The conversation presented here reveals the demands placed upon the performer not only by Barker's rejection of Naturalism, but also by the Barkerian text itself. What is revealed here in particular, is a crucial dynamic between the moral speculation and dramatic invention of Barker's playwriting, and the demand this places upon the company for theatrical innovation and skill in presenting such work. Although clearly informed by a critical reading of the contemporary theatre landscape, this conversation reveals considerations of practice to be at the heart of Barker's thinking.

In summary, then, Part One offers a dissemination of Howard Barker and The Wrestling School's work from the inside, bringing many new voices into the conversation, while generating a multifaceted account of the evolution of a unique theatre practice. The detailed understanding of theatricality, company, and history this produces reveals the particular problems of staging Barker, and by revealing these differences, facilitates their solution in creative work.

1

A Company and Its Origins

James Reynolds in Conversation with Kenny Ireland

JR: What was your earliest involvement with working on Barker's drama?

KI: In the early 1980s I worked with the Royal Shakespeare Company at the Warehouse Theatre (now the Donmar Theatre). We did three plays, one of which was *The Loud Boy's Life* (1980), Howard's play about Enoch Powell, thinly disguised. And I loved it. It was first time I had come across Howard. And he and I got on really well. I don't know why, but we just did. And I loved the work, the poetry of the plays. Then I went to work with Joint Stock, and we did the *Ragged Trousered Philanthropist*. Joint Stock was a co-operative; at the time we would interview directors and writers on their projects. What they would do is workshop the ideas, and writers would go away and write the play, and then they would come back, and rehearse it. One project that Max Stafford-Clark wanted to do, he did the workshop, but he came back and he said, 'We haven't got a play, the workshop hasn't worked'. So we were told, and we sat around to discuss this. We never voted, it was always consensus, and long, long discussions. We had the options, Bill Gaskell said, either we give the money back to the Arts Council, or we find a scripted play. So we were all sent out to see, and I thought of Howard. So I went down to Brighton, and said look, 'Do you have any plays?'. And he had been kind of out in the wilderness for a couple of years, so he opened a drawer, and produced three. Like he does. And it was *Victory*, *Downchild*, and *Crimes in Hot Countries*. So I took all three.

JR: You were the finder, but didn't direct the Royal Court production of *Victory*?

KI: Danny Boyle, who was the Assistant Director at the Royal Court, and had been the stage manager on *Ragged Trouser*, he brought back a play of Nick Darke's called *The Body*. Everybody read all the plays and they preferred *Victory*. Bill Gaskell said to me 'You've directed stuff up in Scotland, do you want to direct it?' And being Scottish, I had that kind of thing inside where you go 'Yes!', but outside you go 'Well, I don't know . . .' And Danny said 'I'll do it'. And that's how Danny directed *Victory*. And to give him his due he gave me the best part in it, Ball, the cavalier. We did that at the Royal Court, with Julie Covington (1983). I ended up directing *Victory* later, for The Wrestling School (1991), and up at The Lyceum in Edinburgh (2002) when I was Artistic Director there (1993–2003). I had said to Howard before, when we'd been at the RSC, 'Would you be interested in doing a project for a workshop?', and he'd said 'No, I don't do workshops, but if you want me to write something, then okay'. The next year another Joint Stock workshop failed, and I had a play of Howard's called *The Power of the Dog*. Joint Stock produced it, and we opened in Hampstead and we toured it around (1984).

JR: How did these experiences lead to the formation of The Wrestling School?

KI: So I had this connection with Howard, and I knew a lot of actors. What I felt was that, because Michael Boyd had discovered him at Sheffield, Nick Kent had discovered him at The Tricycle, and he had been done at the Royal Court – they had all done plays, but kind of dropped him. He hadn't found any place *to do*. I'd realized there were a lot of people interested – you talk to other actors and they say 'Oh Howard, I just love him'. But I read a report that Nicholas Wright did on Howard for the Royal Court, and one of the phrases that leapt out at me was 'I don't think Howard will be satisfied until he plays to an empty theatre'. So I was fascinated by all this, and I decided I had a mission. And the mission was to popularize Howard's work. I felt that what was needed was to develop a very strong style. I knew that I probably couldn't do it with my experience and reputation, and all the rest of it, it wouldn't carry it, but maybe a lot of actors together might. I enrolled Imelda Brown, Catrin Cartledge, Eleanor David, Paul Freeman, Hugh Fraser, Roger Frost, Celia Imrie, Harold Innocent, David Lyon, Tony Matthews, Clive Merison, Bill Paterson, Peter Spruel, Maggie Steed, Nigel Terry, and Joanne Whalley, who wasn't a film star then. That's the list of the people I got in touch with, I wrote to them all to have a meeting, and they all turned up at my flat, and Howard was there. There was never any question of it being a permanent company. We only could ever afford to do one production a year. Sometimes we did more because we got invited to festivals. I saw it very much as that we were on a quest to develop the style. And Howard and I had discussed it. I wanted the company to explore formal ideas, very much, because I thought his writing was of an epic, heightened quality, and he hadn't at that time, but he could write for choruses, and also verse was something that I thought. Part of the original application to the Arts Council was to say that we wanted to explore formality of presentation, choral speaking, and Howard wanted (and this is something which interestingly I think was an experiment, rather than something that we achieved) to explore non-continuity of character. What Howard wanted was to play scenes for absolute extremes, which meant the characters tended to be mad.

JR: Following different rules?

KI: Yes. Which I think was a really interesting intellectual idea, and we did try it. Funny enough the people who were in the original productions were Nick Le Prevost and Roger Frost, who were both trained at Drama Studio. Their whole training was they had to find the real person that said these lines. Which they did. And they kept playing the extremes, but it just meant both of them were incredibly mad. All these people were, Jane Bertish another, they were all actors who appreciated the language. My contribution to it was very much that I wanted the audience to be thrilled by the production.

JR: Why did Barker's work need its own theatre company at that time?

KI: Something I realized when I was working with Howard on The Wrestling School was that lots of directors try to do the same thing with a play of Howard's as they do with a normal play. They go 'Right I understand that, that's premise A, and I understand that, that's premise B, and I understand that, and I can see where we're going...' And then he withdrew it.

JR: Withdrew...?

KI: He withdrew comprehension. By having a scene where you just go 'What?' Now if your approach is like the one I described, at that point you have two choices. You either go with it, or you disengage. And an awful lot of people disengage. I would put forward that the directors that I'm talking about – people like Richard Eyre and Nick Hytner – disengage because they view their job as being in control of the meaning. I didn't, really. I think at the time I just wanted to direct Barker's plays, but later I realized that what I wanted was to find a new way of audiences appreciating theatre. Howard to me was between text-based and physical theatre, he represented something in the middle, so basically I said to people what I want the audience to do is to sit there and go 'I don't know what it means but it's fucking amazing'. That was the premise I wanted the audience to see. And it worked, because the work got reviews like a 'rollercoaster of the soul'. Coming from a background of no experience in theatre, not being a University person, and just loving the theatre, and wanting other people to love it, I wanted people like me to love it, I want people to be able to sit there. If there's 200 people in a room watching one of his plays, Howard wants 200 different reactions. And he allows for that, by withdrawing comprehension. It's a complexity that cannot really be grasped in one viewing, which is what theatre is about. Our production of *Victory* at the Lyceum was a success, and it got rave reviews, and packed out, and I thought 'Great, that's just what I wanted'; Howard came up, and he was very pleased. But *Victory* has a thing which we call the 'Nine Cunt Flourish'. In the first scene. So I thought there might be some trouble. After one matinee performance, and this woman came striding up to me across the foyer, and she was I reckon in her eighties, nineties, an ex-schoolteacher with a voice that would make grown mens' backs straighten, steel grey hair, tied back, and she said 'So you'll be Kenny Ireland, aye?' Because of course it was in the programme. And I thought here we go. And she said 'Absolutely thrilling. Bit shocking. But I didn't mind that. And some of it I didn't understand. But I got the impression that the playwright didn't really mind that. So I let it all wash over me. And it was absolutely thrilling'. And I thought . . . You've got it. And that's why I formed The Wrestling School. Because I wanted people to have that kind of an experience. And I think it's really important to do that, it's important politically to do that. Because you're saying to an audience, this is a new way of experiencing theatre. You don't need to understand everything I'm putting in this box before you move on to the next bit. Because you'll experience this play, you'll go away thrilled, and the bits in it that come back to you are because you were thrilled, and then you'll sort out in your own head – 'Oh, that's what it's all about!' So every time I knew it was going to become difficult for the audience I didn't go 'Suck it up, tough if you don't understand it', I gave them something theatrical or visual or musical. That's why the composer Matthew Scott was involved; we called the opening piece of music 'The Grabber'. So it was always this using Howard's text, understanding it, working with him on it, and presenting it, but knowing there would be moments where the audience . . .

JR: Where comprehension falls away, there's the compensation of something beautiful, theatrical?

KI: That was what The Wrestling School was about. That was why we wanted to develop a style like this. And I think that's what worked, initially.

JR: In my experience of Wrestling School performances, the style that you're describing – of intense text performance punctuated by moments of striking theatricality – seems to still be very much in evidence, although probably with an even greater synthesis of acting and theatricality. Having set a course for the company, why did you then step away?

KI: What happened was I got offered the job that I had always wanted, which was Artistic Director of the Lyceum. I had trained as a director at the Lyceum, and also had run the Studio Company there. And I thought that The Wrestling School had to move on a bit . . . So I left. And I felt slightly like I was abandoning it . . . I think maybe Howard felt the same but I don't know . . . When I left he became the director but he also became the designer of The Wrestling School, under a pseudonym, so it was a complete work of art of his. But like any work of art, when he came to direct it, he adapted it again. So this would be an adaptation of complexity, combining the whole thing into something that was a work of high art. He has gone on record as saying that I didn't understand his later plays; he's also gone on record as saying I did the best production of *Victory* ever, so I'm happy with that.

JR: Has the company's style changed?

KI: I think he's gone on to make work that is beautiful but removed from the audience even further. Now I don't disapprove of that, and I love it and I go and see all his plays, but it did mean that the idea of creating a mass audience . . .

JR: Fell away?

KI: I think any kind of working to make it happen fell away . . . Which is probably how it should be. Because everybody before me wanted to mould Howard – 'Why doesn't he write plays like this again?' – Nick Kent, the guy who ran the Tricycle, would say to me 'Why doesn't he write plays . . .'

JR: Like he used to?

KI: I never said that to Howard, I don't believe it, I don't think he could stand still in that way. I didn't have a vision about how the writing would go, that was Howard's job. But I feel that in directing his own work he creates something which is further removed from the audience. I meet so many people who say 'I lived in Leicester and I saw *The Europeans* [1993], and I thought it was utterly wonderful, that's why I wanted to become an actor'. It did have an impact on a lot of people, but the idea of it being something that the ordinary punter could watch and be thrilled by kind of went away. And the work became a victim of this debate about what 'elitism' means. I don't think it's essential to bring everything down . . .

JR: To the lowest common denominator?

KI: But you can also err on the other side, which is saying . . . 'Well, it doesn't matter'. *It does.* Howard will still be creating stuff, and it will still be beautiful, and it will be lovely till the day he dies, but he's not really supported by the Arts Council or the big theatres, and he should be, he should have residences and just be asked to write. Howard knows the impact of a moment of great beauty. Unfortunately he never has had the money to do anything on a large scale, which is why I was so pleased to see *Scenes from an Execution* (National Theatre, 2012), which by its nature is much more accessible and linear, but the images – that's what Howard needs. Matthew Scott used to say that when he composed music for plays he worried about dwarfing the text, because music is much more powerful than the spoken word. But he never had to worry about that with Howard's work, because of the epic quality of the writing. It's Greek in its content, so it's got that kind of statement. Basically I wanted to facilitate Howard. I didn't go into it thinking I would mould Howard, I never did that, we got together because we wanted to work with him, and that's how it has to be. I felt very strongly that I could act as a bridge to the audience somehow. And that's what I wanted to do. Because I politically felt that the theatre at that time was excluding a lot of people at that time simply because it was being used as a weapon, an intellectual weapon.

JR: What sustained The Wrestling School in terms of the funding it attracted?

KI: Chris Corner has a lot to do with it. He came in in January 1988 for the first Wrestling School production, *The Last Supper*. I brought Chris in, but I can't remember where I knew him from. I did all of the original work, registering the company, setting up the charity and all that. Chris would do all the budgeting, all the ticking of the boxes. Chris and I did the administration together, but when I left and Howard carried on, Howard was very much the artist, and Chris then did all the forms. So I basically ruined Chris Corner's life.

JR: As a writer, Barker already had important relationships with the RSC, and venues like the Royal Court, when The Wrestling School was formed. How did you try and expand the audience with his work?

KI: I went into the National Theatre and spent a good half an hour talking to Jenny McIntosh, and I did a really good job, but Richard Eyre didn't see me, and I know that he just didn't like the work. As far as Leicester, Sheffield – it was people that I knew who ran the theatres. Those places had studio theatres, we very seldom got into the main houses. But they could afford a guarantee for a week. And that was how you could put the budget together, by playing in London, and in playing in all these venues. Most of them lost money. We did *Victory* at Greenwich. Matthew Francis brought us in, and that's one of the reasons why he ended up getting the sack. They lost a lot of money on it because some of the Greenwich audience just went 'No'. Nick Le Prevost was filming and he had one night shoot, so it meant there was one performance he couldn't do. So it looked like I was going to have to cast somebody else, but 'I said, no, you do it, I'll go on for you'. So the Stuart King suddenly became Hanoverian. I learned it and I had it all blocked, but that was the night that the 'Friends' of the theatre organized a walkout. And of course you have the first scene with the 'Nine Cunt Flourish', and then you have the scene with Bradshaw in the house – they hadn't got it organized to go at that. But then you have the entrance of Charles. The big entrance of the King. I come on, and 32 people walked out. So that was what it was like.

JR: The company tend to stage their work in a front-facing configuration, but there are some exceptions to that. What do you think works best spatially?

KI: I don't think that there's a way of doing it, it just so happened that the studio theatres we were in, it would reduce the audience dramatically if we tried to play in the other configurations – we had to play in so many different venues, that's probably why we ended up doing them like that. Although the images – if you have the picture frame – it does help to create those images. The style obviously evolved, and came from two sources, originally. The text, and then the images that the designer created. I think followed then by the images that I then created in my head. So what you come down to, I've never written this down or thought about it very much, is a series of images which would create excitement in the audience. I never wanted to bore the audience. I've always tended to move quicker than I should, there's always been a pace about my work. And that's why we called the opening music 'The Grabber'. So you would have lights coming down, with a piece of music that make the audience go 'Oh!' Then in the first image the doors flying open . . . There was always a strong connection between the excitement that the audience felt, and the music, and the image. And then you would allow the text to happen. So that created productions where the text overtook these elements of the production.

JR: Howard's approach to directing is quite similar, he sets up a series of images and uses sound in a similar kind of way. What would you say the differences are in your approaches? Is there a difference in the relationship you try to create with audiences?

KI: I don't think I was led by the audience, because I knew what we were doing had to be led by Howard. Definitely. I wouldn't ever try and – what's the word – dumb down Howard Barker. I only felt I had a responsibility to pinpoint the moments when it would be difficult. And the work has got more and more difficult. And that's probably why it has become more and more isolated. Except for those who love it, or are addicted to it like I am. But I have a feeling that Howard adds another dimension when he directs. I felt it was my duty to understand the plays – and make the actors have *an* understanding. I've never really worried that it was my job to have one single meaning – which a lot of directors think is their job.

JR: To create closure?

KI: I think this is a form of theatre which liberates the audience from that.

JR: I would like to ask you about acting Barker's work. Ian McDiarmid has a particular habitation of the text, which Howard very much approves of in his writing. One of the things that interests me of course is that McDiarmid was so involved in the 1980s, but he's not on the list of actors who formed The Wrestling School, and I wonder if he was invited to be part of the company? Or was it that you had your own vision about the style of acting which worked for Barker's plays, and didn't want to go in that direction? I suppose it might just be that he wasn't available.

KI: I certainly never said I didn't want Ian involved, he was doing his own thing at that time, that would be why. You'll find it later in Howard's own productions, especially with Victoria Wicks. I'm not sure it's a good thing, I think that might be where I disagree with Howard, it's possible, and again it's about a bridge to the audience. What Howard is afraid of is fussy naturalistic detail that gets in the way of the text.

JR: There wasn't a schism in conversations about how it should be played, there wasn't a drama about the acting?

KI: There was never a drama, we only ever had one row ever, which was on the opening night of *The Last Supper*. I cut a bit of Tony Matthews' speech after the preview, and Howard got hold me in the stalls, and he was a bit upset, and said you can't do that, you can't cut that. But the cut was for length, as I was thinking we would lose the audience at this point. And at that moment the only thing I could do . . . was cut. I never did it again. He said you can't do it. He said the classic words, 'I'm the writer'. My reply was 'Okay. Fucking sue me then'. We never talked about it again. We never fell out about style. I think Howard was interested in having various styles. It was called The Wrestling School in so far as it was a school of like-minded people, it was also somewhere where we learned, but it was more like a school of painters. And I think yes there is a schism, now, because he gets Victoria Wicks, or Melanie Jessop before that, to speak in a way that alienates.

JR: The language quality is foregrounded, rather than the emotional quality?

KI: It just doesn't have the right emotional quality for me. I understand what he's doing, he's focusing on the text. As an actor, I've always had a large style. And I think Howard liked that. And he always said that I could speak his text. I give all the words, but I find the person that can say these words. Howard doesn't trust everybody to do that, so he prefers you not to. Which I think is again this thing of trying to separate from the naturalistic. At a certain point, probably not long after I left, I think The Wrestling School moved into the area of performance art. It's almost a masochistic act to go and see some of Howard's plays. Which I'm all for, but I'm not sure everybody is.

JR: Because of the element of repetition?

KI: Repetition, and the lack of naturalistic and emotional hoops that you can hang onto – 'I like that character, I like this character, this character speaks to me, I know where I am with this character' – do you know what I mean? I don't think you can deny it. I've seen things at the Baltic in Newcastle, a series of screens, and people repeating stuff over and over, and you walk through it and the cumulative effect is what you come out with . . . You are moved by it. And that's what artists do, they create the whole environment to create something. And the line is blurred now.

JR: When he directs, Barker seeks to limit sympathy in acting, the actor's sympathy for the character, so that the language is spoken without pity, or self-pity, in relation to the situation. Is that something you recognize in the earlier work?

KI: I was very interested in *Seven Lears* (1989), which is one of my favourites. Because Nick Le Prevost, who played Lear, and Roger Frost, who played the fool, were both trained in Naturalism. And they found it very difficult, so they just worked very hard, without reducing this thing – which I think is the basis of Howard's antipathy towards Naturalism – which is that he writes a scene for the sake of a scene, or sometimes each line for the sake of the line. So when actors are trying to find a way through his plays, unless they're not told not to, they do tend to lower one scene a little bit, and raise another scene little bit, to make it easier for themselves, or just to create a wonderful character that the audience identify with. But what I think is necessary is that the actor just works harder to find the character, and if that means that the character is psychotic in some way then that to me is okay, that manages to play. But I think to just not, for the actor to not bother, is well, you're actually missing a bridge to the audience. I think that's probably where I disagree. If you are looking at this for a methodology of acting, it can't be there. I don't think it is there. Because this is a method of acting that the playwright would like you to do. But the primary thing that I think is the power of Howard Barker's work is that he is advocating, or I presumed he was advocating, that audiences should view his work as you would a piece of music, or a painting, as a whole. And therefore all the little performance styles are almost unimportant, because it all builds up to create something that you take away with you, that is questioning things in society that don't often get questioned. Like pity, forgiveness.

JR: The thing that takes priority is the overall scene, the fact that whatever method you've got in terms of your acting, is all part of the greater artwork?

KI: Yes.

JR: Everything has to work towards that moment of meeting the audience – it's a total artwork?

KI: Yes.

JR: How did you arrange your work with Howard?

KI: I would have a phone call with him, and I would say we should be doing this, and this is the latest news about it. And then Howard would sit down and write me a long letter going back on everything we'd said. Which was fine by me.

JR: One of the features of the company's early press releases is a commitment to a lecture workshop programme [JR reads from press release, undated]:

> The company feels that some understanding of the theory and methods behind the work will be of interest to audiences, thus in conjunction with appropriate productions, a short programme of lectures, seminars and discussions will be available. These will explore aspects of the background of the work, the creation of *Seven Lears*, presentation methods of the company, and its wider implications for the development of new directions in the theatre. [This] is intended to encourage deeper involvement of the audience in the work; to cause a suffusion of a method by which the audience can come to terms with the sensuality and complexity of this type of production. This innovative scheme will be an important step in the development of the methods of the company, and of a greater receptiveness in the audience.

JR: Engaging with audiences was a genuine emphasis of the company from the beginning?

KI: Yes it was, because I felt that my agenda was to popularize Howard's work, and therefore I felt that if audiences understood all of this . . . I did it in workshops. My job was to seduce the audience. We used to do, you know, 'meet the audience', and talk about Howard's work. We always used to do pieces – like the prologues to *The Bite of the Night* – in workshops, because I think they explain a lot. [KI reads from letter, undated.] 'Here is a piece I wrote today, it's really a song. Capitalized bits are for the entire group to speak in unison. It needs to go very fast'. I remember this. That was something I asked Howard to do for a workshop so that the company could have something that was illustrative.

JR: Barker went so far as to write you a piece specifically for experiment in public workshops?

KI: Yes, so that when we were presenting the theory I would talk about choral work and say how theatrical it could become, and we didn't need to work on the play itself. It's wonderful if you do it with a group of actors.

JR: *Blok/Eko* (2010) uses a large chorus at points, but I think *Ursula* (1998) was the last time chorus was used throughout.

KI: Neil Wallace was the executive producer. Yes, I think the chorus was my idea, I wanted to move . . . and I've used it since, the last three productions I've done have been adaptations of Scottish novels, up in Aberdeen, and touring around Scotland. I find the chorus is just a wonderful . . . If you're adapting a novel you can create the atmosphere, and create the landscape, with the chorus.

JR: So your use of the chorus in *Seven Lears* was a continuation of practice?

KI: I'd done some formal chorus work on a fourteenth-century Scottish piece with a huge male chorus, but it wasn't from that that I wanted to use the chorus. I think it was because we were looking at things that would lift us away from Naturalism. Because we identified that the norms of theatre primarily involved Naturalism. I'd done Peter Hall's *Animal Farm* (1984) at the National Theatre down here, before The Wrestling School, and that had a chorus. And I had been in the *Oresteia*. Which was big Greek chorus work, and mask work. So I was quite interested in doing that, and I'd worked with some very good people, such as Harrison Birtwistle. So I was kind of into it, I was really interested in the power of it theatrically, rather than what the text had to say, do you know what I mean? I always felt that it had to be one voice, or overlapping voices that created an element, but that the narrative had to be in the text and carried on in the text, and that they were observers and couldn't be there. The power of the chorus became obvious straightaway, I felt, because it allowed Howard to be able to represent large things that weren't being personified, large ideas, visually and musically.

JR: How might the roots of The Wrestling School style be traced back to the idea of the chorus? In seed form it contains the shift away from naturalistic movement and language, the movement away from naturalistic style, the bringing together of acting and music and movement. How important is that in terms of being a lever away from Naturalism? As you indicate, chorus creates an emphasis on form.

KI: I'm loathe to say anything like that, simply because I kind of think Howard is going to say it's not. But I think it is, I think it was, a big lever away. But, also, we wanted to use designers who weren't going to design naturalistically, and also the text, again it comes from the text. Howard doesn't set scenes in a room. He doesn't write in a room. I had quite a thing about seeing large-scale work in studio theatres, where a huge play is being contained in a small area, and I was really excited about the energy of that.

JR: Did you think that the 1985 RSC Barker 'season' in The Pit worked, on that principle?

KI: I didn't think they actually exploited that. I was interested in the power of Howard's writing, which should be done on a large scale, with big budgets, the kind of scenery that Hildegard Bechtler did for *Scenes from an Execution* at the National. It did set the play even though it didn't work a lot of the time. I like the idea of just the ideas and the chorus. None of which would people think of putting in a studio theatre at all, but I liked the power of that, and I think to a certain extent that was what gave the company its style, that it was too big for its boots. In a way. That kind of made it, the audience kind of went 'Wow!' But that doesn't mean to say that that's how Howard Barker's work should be done, it just means that at that point, establishing The Wrestling School, and getting all these amazing reviews for The Wrestling School, that's what I felt we should do. Which was to overpower the audience. That also brings up the subject which you haven't asked me, which is, 'Is it possible to say that The Wrestling School was bad for Howard Barker?' Because I know there was a feeling because of our success that other people didn't touch him, because they thought 'Oh well, The Wrestling School does Howard Barker plays', which I think is probably true that it happened with some people, so I don't know . . . his work has spread to other theatres abroad.

JR: Colin Chambers, the literary manager of the RSC in the 1980s, pointed out to me recently that unlike other Warehouse Writers jettisoned by that company at the same time, Howard didn't go under as a writer, but was actually able to develop artistically, and on his own terms, because of the timely formation of The Wrestling School.

KI: Obviously if The Wrestling School had failed, it wouldn't have done Howard any good. Maybe its success damages him in some way, but I hope not. *The Castle* is running off-Broadway . . .

2

From the Actor, to the Actor

Nicholas Le Prevost, Philip Franks,
James Clyde, Sean O'Callaghan, Jules Melvin,
Victoria Wicks and Suzy Cooper

Nicholas Le Prevost

It's more than half my life ago now, but working on Howard Barker's play *The Hang of the Gaol* was, it still seems to me, a turning point in the way I would view the business of being an 'actor'. The RSC opened the Warehouse Theatre in Covent Garden in 1978 as a venue for new writing; it still smelt of bananas. We started rehearsal for *The Hang of the Gaol* in November, with a wonderful director, Bill Alexander, and a strong company. It was difficult because it seemed over weighted when we tried to stand it up. Gradually we understood that we had to put much more specific energy into it, more clarity, more pace, but most importantly always keep it very firmly on the ground.

There's nothing like being in the first production of a new play, and when the rehearsals started to move we knew it was a powerful play, very funny at times too, sardonic, angry and inspiring. As my understanding of what actually I was being asked to do increased, and as I watched the others fill their roles, brilliantly, I experienced a sense of real liberty; in a complex, very grown-up job, these people were serious, clever, dedicated, I didn't feel out of my depth, it was all right. We had a very successful run, not long of course, we were rehearsing the Christmas Show soon after, I think we might have extended a week, perhaps not, but interestingly a lot of people came back to see it two three times. Theatre tickets were cheaper then, there was generous subsidy of the arts, actors were better paid too, it was a more equal society.

Finding myself in this play, one profoundly in opposition to the status quo (which suited me), a play which didn't employ Naturalism, which rang with wit and intelligence, where ideas and images poured on your head, I realized there is no need to 'pretend'. Your duty was to fulfil, with everything you could muster, the text. That, as a consequence, you become a character, and a character 'larger than life', was a product of your pursuit of the text and no 'pretence'. I was part of something, a play, a complex device to exchange ideas, which excited and amused in doing so, and now I was performing my part in it. It felt terrific. And I've come to prefer the verb 'to perform'. I know what a good performer is, not so sure about good acting. Howard Barker's writing is very empowering stuff to perform but there are some dangerous pits in which to fall. God save us from The HOLY! The POETIC! The MISSIONARY! The HUMOURLESS!

Howard came to rehearsals every day from Brighton. It was just great having him there, it added to the excitement of new minting the play. In fact Howard always attended rehearsals whenever I've worked with him, and always added an authorial voice, while not treading on the director's toes, although it has to be said that he would, sometimes, when asked for advice directly by a confused actor, insouciantly offer an explanation that inadvertently upended the last half hour's work, causing Kenny Ireland to draw in breath like some baited bull and mutter a violent 'Thank you Howard'; to which Howard would blithely say 'Of course I've no idea how you show that.' Rehearsals were always exciting, it was difficult stuff, but there was a lot of laughter; they were, in retrospect, a real experience of ensemble work.

My great experiences of performing in Howard Barker's plays, with The Wrestling School, with directors like Bill Alexander, with Howard himself, but especially with the marvellous and dangerous Kenny Ireland, have been the most exciting work I've ever done.

Philip Franks

The early days of The Wrestling School were defined by one relationship – that of its writer, Howard Barker, with its director,

Kenny Ireland. It was the contrast between the two men that provided the aesthetic and distinctive tone of the work. Like a classic comedy double-act, Kenny and Howard complemented each other to a ridiculous degree. Kenny was passionate, practical, loud, argumentative populist, and secretly deeply emotional, even sentimental; Howard was courteous, wry, cool, elitist, and secretly scabrous and unflinching. They even looked like a double-act – Howard, slim and elegant with his slightly haughty oval face, Kenny burly, circular and scarlet.

I joined the company to play Kent in *Seven Lears* (1989). At the time, I was treading water as an actor. I had recently played Hamlet, and nothing seemed very interesting after that. I was surprised to be asked to do one of Howard's plays. I had been turned down for a part in *Women Beware Women* (1986) at the Royal Court some years before, and had resigned myself to thinking that maybe I wasn't 'that kind of actor'. I'd admired the plays, especially *The Castle* (1985) with its dazzling central performance by Harriet Walter. Sitting in a cafe reading *Seven Lears* made me want to act again, not just for bread and butter, still less for fame and fortune, but because it seemed genuinely important. The ambition of the piece – responding face to face as it were to the greatest tragedy in English, the language, Jacobean in its mix of humour anguish and poetry, and the content, using the prequel structure to investigate the impossible demands of moral certainty and the inevitable atrophying of the human spirit, all combined to make my mouth go dry.

I stayed for three years, on and off, appearing in *Golgo* (1990), *Victory* (1991) and *The Europeans* (1993). I was proud of the work we did and surprised by the way that tensions could prove to be properly creative. I don't like confrontation and hadn't believed that it could produce really good work. I was, I think, wrong. Theatre is the most collaborative of art forms, but the collaboration doesn't have to be based on mutual congratulation – indeed it's better if it isn't. Kenny was determined that Howard's plays reach as many people as possible, as viscerally as possible. To this end, he worked with designers, Chris Dyer, Johan Engels and Rae Smith, who provided him with hot debate, not pretty presents. Similarly, he cast actors who brought a lot to the table and were not content to be pliant puppets. There was a lot of argument – the company was aptly named.

The results were exciting and full of memorable images: the vast, studio-filling flying machine in *Seven Lears*, the lonely jetty in *Victory* ('like a landscape by Mr Van Oots') and the towering moving walls, pierced by shafts of light, in *The Europeans*. We upset some people, thrilled many and bored few. The texts were thorny, difficult, provocative and painful. Kenny's humanity made sure they were also funny, moving and (although Howard would loathe the word), accessible.

James Clyde

I first came across Howard Barker's work at drama school in the mid-1980s. Our acting teacher, Susan Todd, asked us to choose a play that we considered a radical piece of theatre: I chose *Amadeus*. Somewhat annoyed by her picking apart my argument as to what constituted 'radical', I challenged her to name a play that lived up to her definition of the term. She began to talk about *The Castle,* Barker's play set in an English village during the Middle Ages; Crusaders return from the Holy Land after seven years to find that the women have turned the village into a commune. The Crusaders bring with them an Arab mathematician to design and build them an immense, impregnable castle. Even in the telling, the play seemed to transcend both its initial concerns with gender politics and its apparent use of the castle as a metaphor for the nuclear arms race. The final stage direction, '*Fighter jets streak low overhead*', sent me straight to the library to take out a copy.

Reading it, I found myself responding in a way that was oddly visceral. The play's themes were laid out and duly wrestled with – war, desire and transgression, science, Christianity, old magic, humanity's place in the landscape – but it was the characters in the shadow of the castle that enthralled, the extremity of their desires, the conflicts within. Of course, the language itself was where the play's power lay: as well as being densely poetic it was muscular, irreverent, the noise of a spade being thrust into hard ground. And it was incredibly funny.

Shortly afterwards I went to see Barker's adaptation of Thomas Middleton's *Women Beware Women* at the Royal Court (1986). To see the work performed onstage was revelatory; my initial intuition when reading the plays was confirmed – Barker is not concerned with subtext. Characters' motives are often complex, but there are no hidden agendas. It was also apparent that a particular type of actor seemed best suited to the work. The facility to meet the work's verbal and emotional demands was a given, but lyrical, quick-minded performers, like Maggie Steed and Simon Russell Beale, who were able to convincingly portray the characters' complex and contradictory inner states brought the play's poetry to riotous, compelling life.

The audience response was another revelation; to be sitting in a theatre I'd been to many times and to see members of an audience turning to acknowledge each other – whether astonished, angry or amused – was edifying for me. Several discussions seemed to be going on in the stalls, while at one point a woman across the aisle was on her feet shouting at the stage, 'That's blasphemous! You're not allowed to say that!' At the same time, she was laughing so hard she could barely get the words out. It seemed that the catastrophic events of the play were forcing its audience to manifest their own inner struggle. I knew then that this was the kind of theatre I wanted to be involved with. It wasn't morally or politically instructive, there was no fixed agenda, no adherence to social realism, no descent into satire. It wasn't concerned with providing comfort in the form of easy answers, it wanted you to leave the theatre in an agitated yet heightened state, awash with ideas and questions, your perception of the world sharpened, transformed. For me, whether as audience member or performer, Howard Barker's plays have always had at their spiritual core a message that could mean our redemption if only we had the guts to accept it: *Die. Die to yourself. See what's left.*

Throughout the 1990s I performed in several of Howard's plays, most of which he directed himself. I found him to be erudite and charming, sometimes cold but, especially in the company of actors, gregarious and – dare I say – fun. But it has often been a depressing experience to see his work being marginalized. Talking to artistic directors around the country about his work during the last 25 years I discovered that many would sing Barker's praises but would never consider putting on any of his plays, and many would be actively hostile. For me, part of The Wrestling School's agenda was about strengthening the writer-actor axis, something a director-led theatre can find threatening. Over time I got to hear the usual lazy watchwords being flung around – 'polemical', 'patrician', 'misogynist'; it was astonishing how *angry* they would get.

In 1995 I appeared as Stucley in The Wrestling School's production of *The Castle* directed by Kenny Ireland, something of a dream come true. After a show in Plymouth, we came out of stage door to be confronted by a young squaddie who had seen the play. He was in a highly agitated state, his girlfriend and his mates trying to calm him down: 'What the fuck was that? Eh? What have you fucking done to me?' He was angry. He was laughing. He was changed. 'That's the first play I've ever seen. Are they all like that?'

Sadly not.

Sean O'Callaghan

There was a talkback after a performance of *I Saw Myself* (2008) at the Vanbrugh Theatre. A member of the audience asked what was the 'process' in rehearsal when working on Howard's work; Howard passed the question on to me, and I said that simply we sat around reading and trying as best as we could to understand the play, and then got on our feet and tried to discover more by actually performing the scenes. Ten minutes after my answer the same question was asked by the same audience member. Howard looked at me and I said that with my previous answer I had not been dismissive, that was our process, and that in approaching a difficult text you do not need a difficult 'process' to makes things harder. I am sure the questioner was dissatisfied with my answer, but simplicity of approach to plays that are far from simple is crucial to approaching Howard's work.

Before working with Howard I believed in the idea that an actor's job was to interpret and inform an audience, some kind of cipher, in retrospect a rather grand way of seeing the role of an actor. With Howard this changed, it was about simplicity, allowing the play to reveal itself without the self-aggrandizing actor placing himself between play and audience. This is not to demean the role of the actor, but instead places a responsibility on the actor not to be loved or liked in a piece, but to be accurate, to present enough character so the audience can see the play, but not to watch the actor's tricks. In an age where actors seem more celebrated than writers it is important for the actor to know when to stop, not to put himself in some way above the piece. The best example of this is the actor's use of irony, it is too easy with Howard's work to ironize, the cheap laugh with the raised eyebrow. This renders the lines as disingenuous and takes the audience away from the centre of the tragedy. This is best demonstrated by comparing two leading roles, Lucas in *Ursula*, and Claudius in *Gertrude – The Cry*. Lucas is a character who spends his time observing and commenting on Placida, who is discovering huge unfathomed depths about herself; he doesn't really grasp this, and without asking for favour the audience can understand and to a degree sympathize with Lucas. Claudius and Gertrude are central to the tragedy; their desire and search for perfection – 'The Cry' – regardless of its consequences can arouse an audience's antipathy. These characters are at opposites, but in playing it is crucial that, for example in *Gertrude – The Cry,* characters like Hamlet and Cascan do not ironize or else Gertrude and Claudius will look ridiculous; they are dangerous characters and any attempt to lighten or ironize by other characters undermines the play. The Wrestling School is aptly named; the actor's role is to wrestle with the text, and to try and understand, not to teach or feel for an audience, and not to entertain.

Jules Melvin

I first worked with Howard early on in my career when I was a young actor. The minute I got the script for my audition for *Ursula* (1998) I was obsessed and in love with it. I didn't know why apart from loving to say the words, the words made me feel and fed me. I had no idea who Howard was and had never seen one of his plays. When I eventually did I was gobsmacked. I had no idea, as a bog-standard Comprehensive school leaver, that people wrote like that. I am not an intellectual person and often felt (and sometimes still do) not academically capable as many of my fellow company members. I am dyslexic and find a special connection with words. So for me Howard's rehearsal room was a delight. No more sitting round a table talking about history, or endless humiliating improvisation sessions to 'find' the character. The words are the working kit.

Often during *Ursula*, I must admit, I would not be rock solid as to what was going on at a particular moment, but that can be the best state to play from. You play the immediate truth, speak the words, lean on them and that's all you need to do. Easy, as Howard Barker has done it all for you. The truth is housed in the words, their rhythm and formation. Howard's written work has a beautiful format on the page as well. Lovely patterns that quite naturally form like an emotion on the page. In *A House of Correction* (2001) I remember a section of words that strode with enormous purpose, jarring occasionally with frustration down the page. I knew just from looking at it how Howard intended it to sound. I think he can hear exactly how he wants it to sound long before he casts the actor.

I find working with Howard stress-free, and a liberation from most rehearsal rooms I have been in. He respects and trusts his actors, he doesn't over-rehearse, starts and finishes on time. Those things mean a lot to me. They show consideration, value and respect. I also find him funny, caring and deeply humane. He expects you to know your craft and responds by fine-tuning the detail when directing. He's not very good at dealing with an actor who cannot grasp his way of working.

If they try to over-complicate his very clean, clear way of doing things he just doesn't understand or know how to help. Frustratingly perhaps for that actor the answer should often simply be . . . just say it.

Victoria Wicks

Rehearsing

When I first worked for the company I was struck by the simplicity of the rehearsal process, and that there was something very 'clean' about the way we were working. Most of the other actors had worked for HB before, so I was very fortunate to be able to watch the way they worked together. Two things were evident: that HB worked quite quickly, and that we were completely safe to try things out; if he didn't like what you did he would just say so, very simply, and ask us to try something different. He was very clear about everyone's intentions and about telling the story, and that gave us the freedom and the confidence to drive our characters on through dense text or actions, in which you might have felt exposed had the intention and purpose they served not been clear. No games were played and there was no sense at all that HB actually had a 'way' with actors, a 'technique', or that he wished to manipulate the actors; he was just very polite and quiet and friendly. The result of this was that the actors were asked to work in a very simple manner, with no artifice, which was very refreshing. If a character was shocked then you were to play that shock, if hurt to play the depth of that hurt.

HB has a very good eye for space and positioning, what is often referred to as his 'painter's eye', and he would sometimes ask us to make specific moves to create a visual image. He was also very interested in the power of gesture to communicate a thought or a feeling, and encouraged this sparingly. This placing of the actors, the use of gesture, the design, and his sound and lighting requirements were used to the most beautiful effect. It was very unusual and exciting to watch and to be part of. Far from feeling as though we were puppets, it felt as though he had great respect and trust in the skills we brought to the piece so we were all working together: a true symbiosis of component parts.

Acting 'style'

I think we have to be careful about whether the attributes we attach to acting for HB are not simply the same ones we might attach to any playwright. I could just write: say the words, say the words, and the rest will follow, and while that's almost true, for me the difference is not in how much an actor commits to the text, but in their willingness to go further, to *submit* to it. By that I mean that they need to relinquish the usual routes which an actor, either by instinct or by training usually relies on in rehearsal: the need to look for subtext, the urge to interpret the text, to look for a character, to find a walk or a voice, and crucially, to place themselves in the production and try to produce an effect on an audience.

Submitting to the text also means trusting, absolutely, that it will give you all you need to perform it. It means resisting the temptation to take an attitude to it, to comment on it, and crucially it means losing the notion of yourself: the actor's ego. Actors have subtle ways of sliding themselves in-between the text and the audience; they do it through their body language with a gesture perhaps, a look, a tone in their voice perhaps, the chew or swallow of a word. The effect is the same: it corrupts the purpose of the dialogue. Certainly the characters in Barker's plays are trying to force their opinions on the other characters, but not on the audience. This takes great courage from the actors; you have to hold your nerve because if you don't you can very quickly slide into irony, and ironizing is a far more comfortable place to be, it's easy, it feels safe and the audience loves it.

Very often the things people do and say in Barker's plays are shocking and if the director takes the line that it is simply too difficult to believe that the character really means what is on the page they will opt for the sub-text: 'You're not going to believe what I'm going to say now', and the result is comedy. I saw a reading of an extract from one of his plays that had the audience laughing from one line to the next; they adored it, but they heard nothing, and probably thought nothing either, except how wonderfully clever it was. The audience was laughing at the audacity of it all, but because the actors weren't asking you to believe what they were saying, the result was that at best the characters seemed to be merely arch observers of their own situation, and at worst, they appeared sadistic. I have also seen productions where there seems sometimes to be a fear of playing the emotions in HB's work, and I'm not sure why this is. The emotions of the characters are just as exposed as their thoughts are exposed. What characters think they say, and what they feel they show, and this applies as equally to tenderness as it does to violence.

For me this leads to the most crucial element of playing Barker's work: the willingness of the actors to play the very high stakes that the texts demand of them. In the plays no one speaks without seeking an effect on another, or even on themselves. Everything is said for a purpose: to provoke, to coerce, to challenge, to acquire power over others. This produces great clashes of will and danger, and the stakes they are playing for are always very high. If you do not play these stakes, then you are not being truthful to the text; it is intensely demanding and it requires an absolute faith in the text and a very high level of concentration. Often the stakes are high right from the very beginning of the play, and will go on and on and on being raised to the very end of it. They may be conveyed in delicate nuances or they may be banging collisions, and there may be seemingly irrational about-turns, but always the tension of the challenge must be held, right to the very end. Of course you may be able to use a lightness of touch in your playing, but you cannot relax, you cannot lose sight of the intent of your actions or words. You are always in a state of tension.

I think there is and should be a correlation between the tension an actor experiences and the tension the audience feels. Naturally the audience is tense, it is listening to language that seems to be their own, but somehow isn't; it is more complex, and very quickly they realize the moral order of the play doesn't tally with the religious or social order in which they are living. The audience and the actor both experience disturbance, strain and tension, dislocation, and the sense of being alone. The audience is alone in its response to what it is seeing on stage, and the actor is alone; the texts do not offer characters a lasting refuge in one another. For both actor and audience the anxiety can be freeing; it feels dangerous and daring and ultimately liberating.

In performance

I often used to experience anxiety before going on stage, even during my preparation: warming up, dressing, making up. When I performed I always had a discipline of silence and listening, I mean I was always on the side of the stage listening, so I was always present in the action of the play even if I wasn't on stage; for me it was actually necessary. Sometimes I felt I didn't want to go on, that I didn't want to 'go there'. I once saw a very highly regarded concert pianist sit at his piano at the start of a recital, his hands held over the keys, and I felt, suddenly, exactly the same anxiety, apprehension and tension as I felt at the beginning of a play. For me it was such a *physical* act. You begin on the first day of rehearsals with nothing but the script and you submit yourself to it. You have to *bind* your heart, your courage to the text, and if you really do that you will find the voice to speak the words and the movements of your body will follow; they will always follow the spoken word. I submitted myself physically to the work almost I think without thought – it followed. Sometimes, yes, it frightened me. These plays are often very shocking, they cross boundaries, and actors are not immune to the things they have to say, but you must be true to the piece; if it's an ordeal, it's an ordeal, so be it.

Suzy Cooper

I met Howard in the summer of 2009. It was a meeting that had been set up via the usual scenario through my agent and I had been sent the script the night before. I had not been exposed to Howard's writing, so I suppose one could say that I had an uneducated approach to it having neither seen, studied or read any of his work. On reading it for the first time I was completely overwhelmed by the power in the language and the atmosphere that it created. I met Howard the following day and read with an unusual confidence, as I felt quite sure that there was only one way to read it. Luckily for me Howard enjoyed my interpretation, and we discussed briefly the context of the piece, the character and the lack of conscious narrative. This I was very excited by. I got the job.

The first day of rehearsals was in a church hall in Pimlico. It comprised of a 'meet and greet' where tea and coffee is drunk and actors nervously mill around introducing themselves to each other, followed by a read-through. To hear the play read aloud was fantastic. Howard told us that this was the first time he had heard it too, and that we could ask him questions that referred to what happens in the play, but that we could not ask him what any of it meant as he didn't know. For an actor working with a writer this could have been terrifying, but with Howard one felt exhilarated by this utterly honest admission. I knew from here on that the rehearsal process was going to be unorthodox.

Quite simply Howard has a vision of his work that I can only translate or understand by way of considering it as a landscape. A great piece of art work that is informed by powerful and provoking language, which in turn informs an immense physicality and imagery. The actor in Howard's work is the vessel, the brush stroke that makes up a picture that is the author's. Howard is not interested in an actor's motivation, only in the big picture. Of course, to perform authentically one must find a truth to whatever one does, but for Howard that is an actor's duty, and he is not involved with that process. So it really is no good saying 'I don't feel that my character would do or say this here' . . . you must find a way of making it work. To understand how to play Barker you must listen to the rhythms of the language, and don't mess about with them. They are vital, punctuation and the language holds all the character indicators. A physical freedom is essential as the work errs on the side of abstraction.

That being said, Howard is hugely supportive and intensely inspirational on the rehearsal floor, and as you trust his choices the experience is very uplifting and freeing. I would like to add however, that due to the content of Howard's work being mostly very dark, one is required to access emotions and feelings that are both draining and painful. It is usual for most of us to become ill at the end of the run, this I think becomes a sort of badge of honour.

Working with Howard has been a privilege and an education far beyond any other 'process' that I have experienced. To really understand how to play Barker you have to unleash a part of you not required in much other work. In short, I have become a stronger actor as a result, and see art and life with a different perspective.

3

Directing *Slowly*

Hanna Berrigan

I first met Howard Barker in 2008, when he was interviewing for an assistant on *I Saw Myself*. We met in a crowded café near Green Park. Howard took the only remaining stool, leaving me to stand for the interview. I was amused at this apparent discourtesy, but also felt strangely reassured; I knew from this that he was not a person who felt the need to stand on ceremony. His interview technique was unconventional, too. He started with something along these lines: 'I'm not interested in your ideas. I don't want to hear your opinion. And I don't want you to sit there looking out of the window, bored out of your mind, thinking you could do it better, wishing you were somewhere else.' Not only was he refreshingly honest, this was perceptive of him – assistants do get bored. They're often the only person in the room not *doing* anything, and they want the director's job. And perhaps, without meaning to, he'd also expressed some vulnerability, which I connected to: I'd just been directing in Australia where I'd had an assistant who was older than me, who definitely thought she should have my job, and it had created a destructive atmosphere. He asked me why someone with my experience would want to do a job with so little input, and for so little money. I replied honestly: I was fascinated – how could I not be? I got the job.

Working as Howard's assistant was hugely valuable. He doesn't have a 'method' as a director, but I think that methods are sometimes used to mythologize or complicate what is often very simple. Howard is clear, straightforward and totally respectful; he treats actors as if they were intelligent people with imaginations, whom he happens to like. He ran into difficulty when he was not met with respect in return. I was angry that such a *good* director was being treated as if he weren't, and consequently not getting the results he wanted. What a director truly wants in an assistant is someone who is supportive – not unconditionally – but at base. It turned out he *did* want my opinion – I was unguardedly supportive.

When Howard asked me to be assistant director on *Found in the Ground* in 2009, I said yes, despite the fact that it meant turning down directing *The 39 Steps* in Moscow. It was a strange decision in some ways, given that *The 39 Steps* job offered better money, more responsibility and that I love Russia. But I had found a sort of unique artistic home with The Wrestling School. I felt a tremendous sense of excitement and connection in the work. I took a particular interest in directing the chorus of four nurses (two of whom were actresses I'd found for the company), without knowing that Howard had written a play with a cast of four women for me to direct. That play was *Slowly*. I was so happy when I was told that I was to direct a Howard Barker play for The Wrestling School, I could scarcely let myself believe it was true. I thought about it very little, therefore, until the venue, Riverside Studios in London, was hired and the dates, in May 2010, were set. Then, suddenly, they were, and I had to believe it.

Howard spoke to me about casting *Slowly*, long before anything else, because he, like me, gets excited by actors. Several of Howard's plays have been inspired by actors, in fact. Some people say that directing is 70 per cent casting. If this is the case normally, it is even more so in a Howard Barker play. Not every actor can do 'Barker', and it's often the actors you would least expect. It's not about being intellectual; it's about a love of language, about having confidence in it, the ability to be *in* it, and knowing how to manipulate it. If an actor tries to act *around* the language (as many have learnt to do while working on badly written TV scripts) s/he will fail; it is a waste of the text, shifts attention from the words (which are expressing quite complicated ideas much of the time), and makes the text difficult to understand.

The simplest way to express what it takes to act Barker perhaps, is that with Barker, as with Shakespeare, the thought is in the word. It is the word, in fact. Conversely, and awkwardly, the thought might be the opposite of the word, but, nevertheless, the thought and the word are inextricably connected. Some actors think that playing the intention is the thing. Giving an intention to a line, however, simplifies and generalizes, neither of which Howard ever sets out to do. His characters are using specific words, in specific combinations, to explain a thought or an idea, or even an emotion, which can only be expressed in that particular way. The actor should not paraphrase Barker, any more than you would a poem. Playing an intention *umbrellas* meaning for actor and audience: Howard is more interested in exposing the individual drops of rain, because through them, and only through them, is the meaning precise. Hence – *The Wrestling School*. Howard's characters are wrestling with language, wrestling to articulate their thoughts and feelings, in the moment. This is what makes the experience of watching and playing Barker so intimate and dramatic. It is also what makes it so addictive. Actors who have played Barker subsequently have difficulty in finding value and pleasure in acting other writing – unless it's Shakespeare or Beckett.

The casting of *Slowly* was complicated by the fact that Gerrard McArthur and I would be sharing two performers. The play was to be staged as part of a mini-festival of Howard's work at the Riverside Studios, and my cast, therefore, was partly to be shared with Gerrard's cast for *Hurts Given and Received*. This presented quite a challenge, as *Hurts* demanded a performer over 40, who would be naked on stage, whom I wanted to cast in *Slowly*. It was essential that Howard, Gerrard and I agreed on someone who was best for both plays. I cast my mind back to a period when I'd been a staff director at the National, five years earlier. I'd spent a lot of time then talking to an actress called Penelope McGhie who had a small part in the play I was working on, but did what she did brilliantly. We got to know each other well because she had a large understudy role, which I directed, and because I enjoyed listening to her talk about the various directors she had worked with at the National (she's extremely experienced), and what actors want out of a director. I remembered how good she was with text, what a powerful voice she had, and I asked her to audition. I didn't know that she loved Howard's work, nor that acting for The Wrestling School had been a career-long ambition of hers. She read brilliantly. Gerrard and Howard were delighted, and I cast her as SIGN, the apparent leader in the group of *Slowly*'s four women. Gerrard cast Suzy Cooper in *Hurts*, which meant she would be in *Slowly*, and I was thrilled. Of the two larger roles in *Slowly*, I knew Suzy must be CALF, as her power is subversive. It was right that she slide under SIGN to reveal herself as the strongest by the end of the play.

Howard was set on my casting Megan Hall, who had been in the chorus of nurses in *Found in the Ground* (given that I had recruited her from *The 39 Steps* myself, this was no hardship either). Howard felt that everything she did, she did exquisitely. The role gave her a firm future in The Wrestling School – Howard has cast her in everything he has done since. I'm immensely proud. Howard did not know whether she should play PAPER or BELL, but I was sure she should be PAPER. Megan is someone to whom speedy delivery and agile changes in thought come easily. I've come to take a great deal of notice of the names in Howard's plays, as they are often onomatopoeic. Without knowing anything about PAPER, one might imagine that she is light and fluttery like a piece of paper in the wind, and like the sound of the word. She is. BELL's voice, on the other hand, is true to the simile her name is used in – it's as clear as a bell. It rings out against other voices with simplicity and extraordinary purity. I'd met an actress with this quality, Vanessa Ackerman, again, five years earlier, when I was working as an assistant director – this time at the RSC. She'd played the lead in *Two Gentlemen of Verona*, where I noticed she had a very particular ability to make Shakespeare's text sound totally unaffected, as if the words were absolutely her own, and absolutely modern. Her lack of affectation in speaking Shakespeare left audiences at the RSC divided – some thought she was the best thing in the production, others, the older generation perhaps, found her normality and truthfulness unsettling. Perhaps they prefer Shakespeare distant. For me, however, she was one of the easiest people to listen to, as there was so little *acting* going on in her performance – just words. I was sure that she was right for BELL as soon as I read the play, and Howard agreed when she auditioned.

Howard and I spoke very little about *Slowly* before or during rehearsals, but I noted two very important pieces of direction embedded in the text. One is that each character is described as 'A Woman of Profound Conformity'. The other is that these women 'ARE IMPERIAL IN GESTURE, WHICH IS TO SAY, SPARE'. From this, we understand that the culture the women inhabit demands that they remain very still. They conform to this culture absolutely. The profundity of the conformity suggests that conformity itself is cultural, so what we are looking at are four women who are effectively slaves to their culture, and who believe in it and its superiority over other cultures very deeply.

It struck me that a piece about people who are accustomed to being extremely still should be approached in relation to movement. The culture they live in dictates that they remain still, and so movement is constantly repressed. This means that they are, in fact, in a constant state of tension. To draw an analogy; the English, more than any other culture perhaps, believe in the importance of being nice and polite. Beneath the surface, therefore, one finds cynicism and insult, and if you listen carefully, you can hear aggression behind the charm when decorum is put under pressure. If a person were to open up the collective mind of the English and peer inside, she would find a vitriolic list of the things they would have liked to say. (Incidentally, I myself am almost entirely English, and don't intend to distance myself from the situation.) In the same way for my actors in *Slowly*, I decided that movement should be constantly bubbling beneath the surface. Rather than being still like sacks of potatoes, they are still like taut pieces of wire. The *potential* for movement is immense (see Figure 1). As pressure builds, so does the conflict between the need to unleash the rising pent-up energy and the necessity of staying still.

For PAPER, this pressure bubbles over, and in an act of rebellion which belongs to her emotion, *against* and because of her culture, she gets up from her chair several times and then, preposterously, moves around the room. The reason why Megan was able to do this so well was that her mind had convinced her body that getting up from her chair and running around the room was a transgression. We could see the struggle between mental and physical energy being played out in front of us. Observing her was compelling, because what she was doing looked thrilling and frightening to her at the same time. She was able to portray what transgression feels like just by standing up and running around because she had done such detailed work in preparation. The link between the mental and the physical in this action is very important (as was BELL's snorting laughter – another thrilling loss of control) because an *entirely* physical approach to a play is empty. My approach in rehearsal was to ensure that the physical and the mental were linked.

In David Mamet's film, *House of Games* (USA, 1987), Mike points out to Margaret that she has a 'tell'. He is able to guess which of her closed fists contains a coin because her nose points, ever so slightly, towards the fist which holds it. He says: 'The things we want, we can do them or not do them, but we can't hide them.' The actors and I worked on the same principle – that nothing is completely hidden, that somehow, even involuntarily, the body and the face are legible in tiny ways – that they are in fact maps containing information about the person inside.

We always started rehearsal with physical warm ups, so that the actors woke up their bodies and felt that they truly were inside them. After the basic warm up I used an exercise I learnt in a Helena Kaut-Howson workshop, where one actor finds a physical position which is both firm and flexible, and is then pushed, body part by body part, by another actor. The idea is that the actor being pushed does not collapse or wobble, but accommodates the push by letting it ripple through her body as far as it travels, and returns to the equilibrium of stillness. It's a good way of making sure an actor is loose physically, yet not so loose that she can't stand their ground. It's also a good way to make sure that actors are reacting proportionately to what they're given. If an actor can do this physically, they're more inclined to be able to do so mentally.

Theatre is dull or just plain bad when one feels that characters are over or under-reacting to what is happening on stage, because one feels that their reaction is prepared rather than spontaneous. Most importantly, for my purposes, the exercise got my actors in tune with one another physically, so that they became able to read the 'maps' laid out for each other.

Soon after we started doing these exercises, it became clear that the actors were highly sensitive to and perceptive to one another's movements, and therefore their thoughts. The detail with which they were able to observe and reflect one another was so extraordinary (we also did a great deal of mirroring) that they all seemed to develop a sixth sense. They were as surprised as I was about how connected they were able to be with one another. They started observation exercises looking at one other, but soon were able to pick things up just sitting next to each other. The reason I wanted to develop this heightened sensitivity was because I wanted the characters in the play to be connected while not looking at each other. In the world of *Slowly*, it is a transgression to look directly at another person. I wanted all the movements, because of the stillness imposed by the culture, to be very slight. The inhabitants of the culture, therefore, needed to develop a collective hypersensitivity. It was essential to develop a clear physical unity between them (they breathed, they fluttered, they blinked together) in order to feel the force of the collapse in unity later in the play. Even the tiniest of movements has power when done in unison. What the actors achieved in terms of performing miniscule movements as one, gave them an almost unearthly quality which was extraordinary to witness.

I did not do any research to prepare for rehearsals. Research is not something I avoid as a rule – I have enjoyed it in the past – but it would have not been useful in my preparation of *Slowly*. The physicality in the writing of *Slowly* had been inspired by ancient Chinese culture, where stillness played a great importance and subtle movement contained great power (as in Qigong and Tai Chi for example). My stage manager told me that if her favourite director had been doing *Slowly*, she would have researched ancient Chinese gestures, and drawn upon them in rehearsal. While research into that culture may have been very interesting, it would not have been useful. Howard had started by choosing two Caucasian actors (Megan and Suzy) for *Slowly*, so it's clear that the ancient Chinese culture was merely a starting point. If I, as a director, had imposed gestures from Chinese culture on the piece, not only would the actors have been taking on something foreign to them (as it was, the gestures came entirely from them), but also, the play would have been about Chinese history, which it is not. If it were, I would have cast Chinese actors. As it was, the play became universal – as Andrew Haydon so deftly expresses:

> At the outset, you're pretty much prepared to take the severe early-modern costumes on trust – believing the women to be perhaps the ladies in waiting to say Mary Queen of Scots, or, with the addition of 'barbarians' perhaps some Mittel-European countesses. But then there's this brilliant moment where one of the women says, 'We will undo our costumes at the throat / when we have exposed our throats we will call him . . .' What's brilliant about it is the fact that in these particular costumes the throats of the four women are already exposed. Suddenly, you get this sense that the costumes can be regarded as entirely symbolic. Instead of this coming across like a period drama, the viewer is freed to imagine these women anywhere in the world.[1]

The idea that these women could be anywhere is entirely the point. Like the gestures, the costumes were specific to the production. The style was invented, not borrowed, and therefore uniquely non-specific.

Although it would have been pointless to bring specific research to a production which is beautifully universal and non-journalistic, I did however bring one piece of text to with me as a reference point. It was this:

> Are we going to have a population of 1,000,000 blacks in the Commonwealth, or are we going to merge them into our white community and eventually forget that there were any Aborigines in Australia?[2]

These are the words of A. O. Neville, Chief Protector of the Aborigines (1915–26), in support of the policy of *absorption* or *assimilation* in

Australia, which was meant to ensure that mixed race aborigines would produce children only with white people, so that over the next few generations white Australians could eventually, as Neville put it, 'breed out the colour', or (as it was put colloquially) 'fuck them white'. At the beginning of *Slowly*, Howard quotes a few words – 'The Process of Disappearing' – from Strabo's *Geography*. In Strabo, the tribes of the ancient world disappeared by mixing with other tribes, so they brought Neville's words immediately to my mind (I used to be a television researcher and had wanted to make a programme about the Stolen Generations).

When CALF says to SIGN: 'You are disappearing', she not only refers to her diminishing decorum and strength (which are arguably one and in the same in this culture), but also the beginning of the disappearance of the race itself. BELL and PAPER's instinct for survival means that they will breed with the incoming 'barbarians'. It is asserted that their babies will not look like them, and so it is likely that the encroaching army is racially distinct. I used the thinking behind the policy of assimilation in Australia because I wanted to encourage the actors to think on a tribal/racial level – something which I do not imagine one normally does, but which the characters in the play certainly do. Such is the racial and cultural pride of the older generation represented by CALF and SIGN, that they uphold racial purity above all else – even if that means that their race dies out.

It is assumed without question that the encroaching army will be violent rapists. They are called barbarians. It is interesting to observe that the word barbarian comes from the Greek, meaning simply 'not Greek'. The true meaning of the word resonates in *Slowly* because such is the extremity of the decorum imposed by the culture they adhere to, that one can imagine any other tribe must be looked upon as uncivilized. For example, CALF recalls searching for her mother in a garden and passing her three times without seeing her, so impeccable was her stillness. When Vanessa said the line 'Imagine them fucking you' about the approaching barbarians, I told her to imagine being fucked by a dog, because I really wanted her disgust at breeding with an outsider to be extreme (I could always tell whether she was imagining this or not!). The fact that her instinct for survival is stronger than her extreme disgust is one of the things which make her journey in *Slowly* so compelling.

I had a great production team. Ace McCarron, who usually lights Wrestling School productions, was unavailable, and so suggested I ask his assistant Sally Ferguson. She did everything I asked for, and more. She gave the actors' faces and hands an extraordinary other-worldly quality and worked with fantastic care and detail. The piece looked better than I could possibly have imagined. The usual sound designer for The Wrestling School was unavailable, and so I brought in one of my contacts, Edward Lewis. He was just as keen as I was to find just the right tones for the background, and we worked together on the almost imperceptible shifts these tones would make. His attention to detail, patience and understanding are extraordinary. If there was a departure from The Wrestling School style at all in my production, it would probably be in my treatment of sound. I like to use sound more subtly than Howard does, so it alters the mood without being noticed. Howard kept asking me whether I didn't feel I wanted to add more sound, but I resisted his influence in this respect, and I don't think he minded. 'Tomas Leipzig' was on board as set designer and came up with a brilliant, economical and beautiful design as he always does.

While I'm immensely proud to be the first female director to work for The Wrestling School, I don't see it as a milestone, because I don't think of The Wrestling School as being a sexist institution. I see myself as a director who happens to be female, and I think this is how Howard sees me too. Whatever one thinks of the work (it has been labelled misogynist – I dispute that, but would need another chapter to explain why), I state simply that my personal experience of working with Howard is that he is among the kindest, most respectful and least condescending men I have come across, which must stand for something. In her review of *Slowly*, Mary Mazilli wrote: 'Berrigan's directing is shrewd and sensitive, giving a "genuine" feminine touch to what is in the end, a male artificious depiction of women as victims and as incapable of rational decisions'.³ It's interesting to me that I didn't think that the play depicted women as victims, and I don't think it portrays them as being incapable of irrational decisions. The key to my giving the play a feminine touch is perhaps not seeing women as women, but as people. I think a lot of people still don't see women as being people – even sometimes women themselves. It never occurred to me that the women were portrayed as victims. It is, of course, a point of fact that women *are* raped by incoming armies (sometimes men are raped too), but what each of the women in *Slowly* do is deny the barbarian aggressors the possibility of a simple violation.

Despite my picking apart of the praise in Mazilli's review, I'm immensely proud of it, just as I am of Andrew Haydon's review. Mazilli called *Slowly* a 'sublime theatrical experience': it was certainly sublime to direct.

4

Amplifying Catastrophe

Ace McCarron

I first encountered The Wrestling School in 1988, when they toured into the Royal Court Theatre with their first production, *The Last Supper*. I was not personally acquainted with Howard Barker at that point, but I had both seen and worked on a few of his plays. I had met Kenny Ireland, the director of that show, in Scotland, and I knew Chris Corner, the administrator and producer of the company. The lighting designer of this show was the late Andy Phillips; aggressive, passionate and hugely talented at plotting lights during technical rehearsals.

The Last Supper has two prologues which entreat the audience to seek no information from the play, to judge it on its originality and to view it from a particular metaphysical viewpoint: that God exists, but residing within the mass of humanity. I watched the process of the technical rehearsal setting out to make these ideas manifest. I was most impressed at the ambitiousness, the unashamedness of the actors and the reliance on technical elements which were arrayed at the disposal of the moment. After a theatrical tour-de-force, involving original music by Matthew Scott, strong and purposeful lighting from Andy Phillips and bold but painstaking cueing by Andy Cooper, the company's stage manager, an entirely different world appeared on stage. This world, by a mixture of sudden and deliberate choreography and attuned and purposeful lighting, facilitated an extremely enhanced contact with the ideas unleashed by the text. In effect, stage conventions were shattered, the work ploughing relentlessly through to the essence of an idea being articulated. This was a powerful element in the act of detaching the viewer from the possibility of assessing the play through traditional wisdom, social norms or religious knowledge. Stagecraft had been deployed in a surgical way to permit only an immediate audience response, based on innate human values. Lighting had been used, in effect, like a microphone for the visual elements of the play. For their next production, *Seven Lears* (1989), Andy Phillips was committed elsewhere. Kenny Ireland had seen my work for Théâtre de Complicité, which demonstrated a similar service to the amplification of the moment, and I was approached at an early stage in the conception of this piece.

Certainly, with The Wrestling School, I believed I had found a company which was very keen to use the skills I had developed with other companies, and I was encouraged to take them further. In the United Kingdom, it is not unusual for someone to become a lighting designer because they have merely a well-developed knowledge of the technology usually deployed in this field. In London, where upwards of 25 productions open every week, many designs will be carried out by people falling into this category. My own fascination with the art of drama, fueled by attendance at the productions of, and later by work with, The Glasgow Citizens Theatre, pressed me more towards being concerned with the choices made in the execution of a play's rehearsal. For conventional, non-automated lighting, the technological and procedural aspects of the job of lighting designer are not really very complicated. I frequently admit that anyone capable of artistic judgement can design lighting as well as I can, but that I can do it quickly. The real specialist knowledge that I have acquired is to understand the artistic ambitions of talented directors, and without wasting time with options they would clearly not be interested in, produce at speed lighting that usefully serves their purpose. It is difficult to create highly specific lighting for a play when resources are limited and without clogging up the technical rehearsal process with repeated refocusing of lights. My experience working in opera forced me to prepare designs to a degree whereby lots of effective lighting can be available for rehearsal very quickly. Indeed,

I would always rig several options into my designs, and sometimes these would be lights, conceived often as an afterthought, that would be used very frequently in a show. It is possible to trace a change in the rationale of set design over the history of The Wrestling School, but the canons of how the performances utilize lighting remains quite even. The scheme of work I carried out under Kenny Ireland's direction remained in place when Howard took over, and it remains in place, with enhancement from several techniques I have subsequently developed. Lighting, as I shall explain, can provide an extra dramaturgical dimension to a show about to leave the rehearsal room. A lighting designer who is curious about plays and the conventions developed in the course of rehearsals has always something to learn, and, consequently, some new risks to take.

Considerations of form

Theatre companies who programme the plays of living writers in their season are very suspicious of the idea of a playwright acting as director for their productions. It takes a certain skill to invent a style of production which can be convincing in the resolutely non-cinematic world of live drama. The majority of new playwrights conceive of situations and characters which work in an entirely cinematic way, and are frequently unaware of the non-naturalistic factors which will ensure effective communication of the text. Primarily, I think of the hypnotic, poetic and the frequently non-realistic power of voice, and, as so often is the case, Elizabethan drama represents a kind of ideal. Shakespeare and his contemporaries knew that they were writing text which, basically, had to be vocalized to the point of shouting. This rules out certain registers and forms of speech, but also invites the capacity of others. In a parallel way, because Howard's work does not require the building of a stage world which is plausibly a representation of a contemporary or historic situation, there exists the scope for the building of extra dimensions to the production through irony, dislocation and a surreal sense of beauty which may serve the production well, but in a tangential way. Designers of set, costume, lighting and sound are always excited by the opportunity to create something very original and which can serve a production in a fundamental way. Most designers talk of getting a special kind of excitement when only a few pages into reading a new and engaging text. With every Wrestling School production, there were always designers eager to advance original ideas and also to work very hard to realize them. In advancing this creative instinct, and bringing it to the work of the company, Howard himself demonstrated the detachment of an aesthetically ambitious director, relinquishing the preciousness one may detect with a playwright determined to see the pictures in his or her head brought to reality on the stage.

Howard had witnessed his plays being produced for years by a variety of directors. In the early days of The Wrestling School, he witnessed Kenny Ireland and a company of very experienced, and vocally gifted actors deliver complicated readings of his work. When Kenny accepted the full-time job as Artistic Director of the Royal Lyceum Theatre in Edinburgh, Howard felt entirely equipped to become The Wrestling School's primary Director; his first production, as director, being *Hated Nightfall* (1994). The momentum of the company bequeathed him the habit of trusting in the necessity for elaborate design, and the resources to realize and transport on tour, sets of reasonable scale. There had not been much continuity in the practice of appointing designers, but successful designs were brought to the stage by talented people, such as Dermot Hayes, who worked on the early shows, *The Last Supper* and *Seven Lears*; Rae Smith, with whom I had worked at Théâtre de Complicité, and who designed the architectural, but highly flexible set for *The Europeans* (1993); Johan Engel, who bridged the eras between Kenny Ireland and Howard with designs for *Victory* (1991) and *Hated Nightfall*; Robin Don designed *(Uncle) Vanya* (1996); and Robert Innes Hopkins who designed a very simple, but strikingly effective set for Howard's production of *Judith* (1995). Frequently, these were successful designers who had growing commitments with companies planning productions far in the future, which made them unavailable for further work with the company.

Pakhuis 17 – A new aesthetic emerges

Robin Don's design for Howard's 1996 production of *(Uncle) Vanya* comprised of quite a large set, despite its creation for performance in the modestly proportioned Almeida Theatre, whose stage it entirely filled. Robin had worked there frequently, and like myself, knew the space very well. I had worked there as the Chief Electrician before I started working as a freelance designer. Robin's set comprised a ground floor and two slanted balconies of a building which was contrived to split in two, revealing a beach. Due to the success of this production, Neil Wallace, the company's producer in the early 1990s, was able to secure extra performance dates in Copenhagen, where the company enjoyed a relationship with the Kanonenhalle. As the proposed dates for *(Uncle) Vanya* were during a busy festival, another venue was proposed; Pakhuis 17, a former storage warehouse in the docks area. The budget did not extend to transportation of the set, and I was approached for advice as to whether the lighting resources would be sufficient and flexible enough to permit a radical re-staging of the work in the short time available to us for technical rehearsal. After an exceedingly exciting rehearsal period, utilizing only a chair and two suspended mirrors, but with full lighting resources, we delivered a reconceived staging of the show which was in many aspects stronger. In marshalling fewer resources, but with increased opportunity to solve problems of articulation in a creative and co-operative way, the company strode into new territory.

In providing a general area cover for the show, I took more risks than I had ever taken. In fact, I have never repeated this level of risk because I have not worked with a company of actors who displayed the necessary willingness, skill and trust to use such lighting well. There were two components to the general cover. One cover was located far upstage on the floor. At each side, I used three lanterns which were focused, most unusually, to point above the audience. The second cover was provided from lighting support bars, rigged by the local crew, at about 2 metres from the floor, and running up and down each wing. Sharp profile lights were focused into stripes running slightly downstage from stage right, and slightly upstage from stage left. The stripes only hit the floor on the opposite side of the stage, but on the nearside, because of the shallow angle of the beam from a low-mounted lantern, a decent amount of coverage was available to light an actor, say, from the torso upwards. Because the beams were all separate stripes, there was an inbuilt, almost kinetic effect on an actor as they walked downstage, alternately in a strong shaft of light and in complete darkness. The shafts of light were contrived to come from alternate sides of the stage. As such, actors had to find their light, either by standing on a shaft of light on the floor, or by sensing out a beam which was shining above it. I started out by focusing the beams at a width of only about 800mm, but, arriving with the cast and seeing the beams, Howard asked if the beam width could be reduced to 300mm. For me, this more than doubled the risk I was taking, and as I took a chair and narrowed the beams I giggled at the thought of how much of a problem I was generating for the actors, but, in this type of case, it is better to start out with small areas before finding out that they require to be expanded rather than try to confine actors into smaller areas than they have rehearsed with. 'Why are you laughing?' asked the actors. 'Because this is your general cover', I replied. Amid bemusement rather than protest, we commenced.

With many of the regular performers, I had previously worked hard to make it easy for them to find small beams on dark corners of stages. The newcomers also launched themselves into a game of finding spots on the stage where they could appear incredibly strong amid the darkness. In fact, so much did they enter the game that Georgie Sowerby, playing Sonja, managed to find an area of total darkness in which to stand before stretching her hands up into a very strong beam of light to roll up her sleeves, before striding downstage to strangle Sorin, the doctor. This struck me in that I was probably going to be awarded the credit for the strength of this moment, unless I managed to persuade people otherwise. A strong lighting moment on a stage is usually achieved by judicious use of darkness, and this always involves a deal done with a performer and a director regarding where it is possible that they can stand. It is always a pleasure to work with actors who are willing and also have the technique to do this, and it has been the norm in The Wrestling School that they will work hard for such effects.

Bespoke subversion

Howard's plays seek to discourage audiences from bringing their specific historical knowledge to bear on the interpretation of a scene which they are watching. His plays are clinical in their absence of direct historical context. Rather than utilize design as a way of building plausibility, they invite design to assist in subverting contextualization. There is a sequence in the first prologue to *The Last Supper* where there is a litany of popular subjects for the kind of outraged political drama that was the stock-in trade of the subsidized new writing companies of the 1980s. The response of the chorus to each is 'I already knew that!'[1] This might be a mission statement for The Wrestling School. Drama that sets out to convert and reshape the opinions of its audience fails when the liberalization of the press and the increasing speed of its news cycles bring issues to a population with great urgency. Drama is a very slow medium for original comment, and, nowadays, audiences consist of people who are generally well-versed in current argument. Although Howard started off in an era when political theatre could voice opinions and political perspectives not routinely aired in the mass media, this situation has now changed. Radical theatre had to seek for another reason to be in front of an audience and its emphasis shifted to the inner self and began to portray and investigate the dreamscapes of the mind. The political project, in most cases, was dropped, but Howard continued to address the way in which the perspective of the individual could flourish amid a society which was becoming more materialist, traditionalist and was promoting a distaste for a theoretical thinking.

Howard's texts offer little opportunity for self-congratulation in pre-empting a conclusion based on background knowledge. In parallel with the overall project of a text, the design can, therefore, be formed around the ambition to underline the experience and revelatory transformation of the characters, frequently in a way that is shamelessly overt, and, in the eyes of the audience, indelible and memorable. Rather than presenting an initial image of a location which complements our knowledge and sensibilities of a specific period, The Wrestling School's productions offer plain, blank, elemental spaces which are only contrived to service sequences of recurring moments or single moments of great strength. They are also contrived to discourage the audience from formulating constructs of context which might assist in a superficial interpretation of the text. The overall effect is to encourage an audience to listen and watch.

Lighting techniques for enhanced presence

This is my main project in devising a scheme of lighting for each Wrestling School production. Among the techniques I bring to bear is a reliance on the systems of lighting from positions at the side of the stage. Most theatres generally provide lighting positions in the auditorium areas which allow lighting directly from the front or from a high circle position. If you imagine that the direction towards the back of the stage is the north point on a compass, conventional lighting theory accepts that lighting from a high angle from South-East and South-West will provide exemplary illumination for the face. By use of such techniques, however, modelling of the face has fewer options when those lights are chosen for a scene. Side lighting theory places the key lights coming from something close to head height from due East and due West. In practical terms, this can be difficult or indeed, impossible, to achieve depending on the extent to which the set configuration will permit this deployment. If it is possible to rig and use lighting directly from both sides, there are already parts of the face which are rendered in shadow. The helpful effect of this is to accentuate the shape of the face and the way it moves expressively, and this can be sustained even if the lighting levels are extremely high. The other advantage of side lighting appears when the focusing of the lighting on the actors can be shepherded away from whatever scenography sits upstage of the actor. If that scenography is lit by entirely separate lights, then the lighting designer can be in complete control of the contrast between the actor and their background. This may seem trivial, but variations in these levels can produce subtle, but powerful, effects during a scene. Choosing the correct position and speed for such a change requires experimentation, and an industrious stage manager, attentatively calling cues from the book. A good lighting designer will gauge positions where something crucial to the development of a scene is being said by an actor, thus diverting an audience from noticing that the lighting has changed. But this change, if it is something they do not consciously notice, is something that they can certainly feel. As well as controlling this contrast, colours and the distribution of lights on a face are two other things that might be usefully manipulated in such a way to strong but subtle effect.

With their plethora of scenes and their need for propulsive stagecraft, *Seven Lears*, *Victory*, *The Europeans* and *The Ecstatic Bible* (2000) represent the most complicated designs I have yet undertaken for the company. I toured with the first three, ensuring that the rather complicated focusing was carried out well. Sometimes the crews of the theatres to which we toured had not seen work which was so reliant on sidelighting and consequently were puzzled by my priorities. Creating hanging positions for lights in the wings is not often very easy, and an added complication is that the cast must have an unblocked avenue through which to enter and exit, occasionally at great speed. For *Victory*, Kenny Ireland and I devised a scheme for rapid scene changes. I had voiced the opinion that the Joint Stock production of *Victory* (1983) suffered from excessively fussy scene changes. Because a rifle has to be buried in the course of the play, a system of decking was used for the whole stage, and these decks were re-arranged by the cast during scene changes. I suggested that the disruptive effect of this was to render each scene as a little play in itself. Textually, the scenes are contrived to alternate between narratives and locations, and I felt that the flow of the play suffered by this plan. We worked hard to eradicate all the gaps in the scene changes, and I managed to pick out the single characters who might appear in both scenes and isolate them in a spot as actors simultaneously marched on and off. Matthew Scott provided brief snatches of bold music for the very few seconds this took. Isolating these characters was done from tightly focused sidelighting, thus minimizing the image of a spotlight beam on the stage floor. Thus the number of lights in the wings was very high, but a rapid fluidity was guaranteed.

With willing performers and despite dwindling state support, the company has always been able to launch into the most ambitious work with faith that the actors' performances could always be matched by staging that was, perhaps, equally alive, and malleable enough to underscore moments whose power and significance would emerge at any stage of rehearsal. I have always found working in this kind of way difficult and stressful, but hugely rewarding. With Wrestling School rehearsals, I can begin this work in the rehearsal room, getting out of my chair to demonstrate changes to the blocking which can facilitate simplification and, usually, strengthening of transitional moments. If these moments require revision on stage, when the lighting has been prepared, I still make my way to the stage to demonstrate options. When light is contrived to come from unusual angles, an actor sometimes does not feel that they are illuminated, at which point I stand in the position myself and invite the actor to form a judgement and perhaps display the limits of head angle where a shadow would begin to occlude their expressive action.

Production rehearsal with The Wrestling School

A play's technical rehearsal has aspects of both the shooting and editing phases of film production, and because of the pressures of time, a lot of work on this has to be done quickly. The making of a film might be considered to have three separate writing processes. A film project begins with a typed script, which must be consistent and complete, in terms of its plot and style. During the process of shooting, certain aspects of its text and style may be revised as a new visual and gestural life is breathed into the project. In the more relaxed atmosphere of an editing suite, a film is re-created once more, where more consideration is given to the shape of the story's trajectory, and frequently, immense changes are made. Aside from the more obvious tasks of illumination, representation of weather and changes of scene, a lighting designer can have a similarly crucial part in augmenting the unfolding dramaturgy of a play. Productions may be easily assessed in terms of this contribution by considering how sophisticated the process of technical rehearsal has been in service of that production. The style with which this has been executed is very apparent. There is a certain traditional craft in organizing transitions in the course of a play. Gone are the days when a composer was engaged to provide music as a curtain fell and stage-hands worked feverishly to effect a scene change. Emphasis is now placed on the continuity of experience as a play runs its course. Given that an entirely unexperienced world is created for The Wrestling School's productions this continuity is of extreme value. All elements in the experience of the show serve this continuum to a very high degree. If a text depends, like in *The Ecstatic Bible*, on the creation of a system of morality alien to the post-Christian world, then it serves the audience well for there to be an embodiment of an alternative system, be it architectural, aesthetic, sartorial or acoustic. These elements must be policed with great attention and imagination, requiring to be neither too rigidly consistent nor confusingly loose. It can be a difficult process to imagine and propose how these elements might work for each production, and frequently, a lot of experimentation is undergone as the show is developed in the technical rehearsals. For the production of *Ursula* (1998), Howard, through his long-time sound designer associate Paul Bull, used snatches of violent music as a kind of parenthesis in speeches, and this was developed over the first performances of the first run in Birmingham. It was also a complicated process for me to decide which music could remain uncomplemented by a response in the lighting and which demanded it. In cultivating such practice, and the language where such options might be assessed and valued, the company began to work with an identifiable style. Sets incorporated the capacity to have lots of dark space. Lighting produced widely varied distributions of area with the greatest use of contrast which the facilities would permit (see Figure 2). Sound and music was loud, short and dramatic. Props and scenic elements would descend rapidly on ropes. In general, this aesthetic was well-placed to survive diminishing subsidy, utilising the kind of equipment which most theatres would already have, but was still able to ensure that the texts were receiving a rare level of support. In the pursuit of this, the technical elements of the performances were placed almost entirely in the service of radical dramaturgy.

While this may appear to adopt trends prevalent in theatre and opera production over the same period since the inception of The Wrestling School, there are important differences. First, such practice came into being with re-interpretation of classic texts. Particularly in opera, audiences, who return to see many different productions of the same piece, were felt to require brave and frequently outlandish stage interpretations of the work. Opera audiences are frequently quite vocal when these interpretations depart from the intention of the composer and librettist, and only assume the indulgences of the director. Productions of plays may fare better because, even with Shakespeare, there is never quite the same assumption that the audience has a template of the play in their minds, whereby they could see an interpretation as a variation on something that sits within a collective consciousness. Classic plays may be skilfully produced in this way, but the process by which a new play can encompass strong and rigorously conceived staging is a more difficult undertaking, usually because a writer either does not have the imagination to create such opportunities in their texts; the technique to handle them in a way which invites creative responses from others; or faith in the idea that a sceptical literary manager will be sufficiently excited by non-verbal elements through which the staging is permitted to provide crucial articulation of the drama.

The exordium

The Wrestling School's production of *(Uncle) Vanya* was also the start of a company tradition in formulating the continuum of dislocation specific to each show. In his text for *The Gaoler's Ache for the Nearly Dead*, Howard wrote what he called an exordium.[2] This is fundamentally a scene without words. In this particular example, Little Louis, the heir to the French throne, is revealed. Heads appear from hatches, crowds surge past and the boy decapitates one of the heads. What Howard has written here is a sequence of paintings, and as such, they may not be interpreted in the same way as the subsequent text. However, they declare something of the nature of the catastrophe in which the plot will sit, demonstrate the theatrical language, and the material limits of it, which the performance will utilize, and also leave unanswered questions hanging in the air. Ironically, when Howard, along with co-director Gerrard McArthur came to direct this piece (in 2014), the imaginative gusto with which the company would create an exordium produced something quite different. The *(Uncle) Vanya* exordium was rather elaborate. Two servants, inching across the inclined balcony of the set to loud and repetitive contemporary chamber music, carrying large trays of mild steel crockery, would meet in the middle. They would freeze, the music would stop and then they would tip the contents of the tray, each holding some half-a-dozen cups and saucers, over the balcony, to land on the stage. Sorin, the doctor, who had been dosing downstage in a chair would then wake up, say 'What's that?' and fall again to slumber. The music would recommence and the servants would then continue to the sides of the balcony to reappear with another load of metal crockery. In total, about six loads of crockery would form a small heap in front of the set. As the exordium music faded away, the cups were left on stage as an enduring obstacle for the performers. The visual resonances from this were numerous, but not specific. The image of Sorin, drowsing, perhaps indicates a dream of unwitting decay; the metal of the cups shows a tradition which ought to shatter, but doesn't; the detritus displays a malaise somehow not sufficiently urgent to provoke remedy. From the moment the audience enter the auditorium they have an experience which is sufficiently loud to counter the chatter of other spectators and they are already immersed in the performance. Technically, the exordia are always extremely complicated; the manipulation of such strong elements requires particular care and there is always the question of deciding and communicating when the audience is judged to have arrived and when the house lights can be lowered. We play very safe with this, and always let an exordium run its course. They are too complicated to interrupt. They have involved video, as in the erotic thrall of Shardlo witnessing the recurring footage of a giant explosion in *A House of Correction* (2001); the recurrent dusting of a series of ill-formed life-cast heads in *Judith*; the sound of passage of low-flying jets over cowering refugees in *The Ecstatic Bible*, which could be heard 100 metres from the front door of the theatre. They demand a large part of the technical rehearsal time, because they are difficult to prepare in a rehearsal room, where not all the elements can be assembled. Nonetheless, they include elements which will resurface in the course of the play so experience gained in staging the exordium will tend to speed up the rehearsal of later sequences. It could be argued that the practice of including an exordium has influenced Howard's dramaturgical thinking as it is expressed in his texts. The stage directions and minimal language which make up the vignettes of *The Forty* (2014), for instance, can be seen as a logical extension of the exordium practice.

The ambition of most of Howard's plays is immense. I even know this from friends and colleagues who have just seen one of The Wrestling School's performances. They talk of experiencing things that the arts and the media never ventured to do before, or of ideas with which they felt conversant, but expressed with a dramatic power which really precipitated an unexpected emotional engagement. As such, I feel that the excitement I experience, working in such a detailed way with the company, really does result in adding to the audience's experience.

5

On Discipline

James Reynolds in Conversation with Howard Barker

JR: In *Arguments for a Theatre*, you write that the Theatre of Catastrophe rejects the disciplines of humanist theatre, particularly the imperative to 'be lucid'.[1] But the idea of discipline is one that you tackle in your writings on theatre repeatedly, and variously. Indeed, you describe Catastrophe as 'a theatre of powerful disciplines'.[2] However, and in apparent contrast, you also speak of the potential for theatre to be 'a de-civilising experience, a series of permissions to transgress, an act of indiscipline or a mutiny'.[3] These two points of emphasis, I think, show that you use the idea of discipline in contrasting ways. Your theatre prioritizes 'emotion, irrationality and beauty',[4] and therefore artistic discipline is a pre-requisite in practical execution. But there is also a rejection of discipline, in terms of making your plays conform to the orthodoxies imposed by 'order, discipline [and] the collective will as shaped by the contemporary conscience'.[5] In *A Style and Its Origins*, you describe a dynamic between discipline and the development of The Wrestling School style, a dynamic informed by a concept of discipline with many layers and incongruities. Indeed, you write that *Judith* led you to the fiercest discipline – that of a 'total aesthetic'.[6]

My first question, then, is whether or not there is a tension within a theatre that requires stringent artistic discipline, but which unflinchingly explores moral transgression in front of its audience? And my second is whether or not meeting this tension has produced a development of skill? I mean this in the sense that staging wrong actions might require greater levels of artistic discipline in order to carry them off in performance. Thirdly, if it is the case that two principles feed from each other, to what extent has this been one of the drivers in the evolution of Wrestling School practice in terms of writing, staging, style?

HB: What I have always been conscious of is the low level of connection between the audience and the art of the stage. Let us take the accident as the best example of this. 'Dog on Stage' might be relevant here.[7] The distraction is always more fascinating than the play, dying actors, tripping, etc. Why is this, when we ostensibly go to a theatre to be 'in another place', that is, immune to banality? For me this is particularly pertinent, because the style of the work is unfamiliar, and its demands vastly greater than 'popular' theatre, conscience-led entertainment etc. The connection is weak, because there is an element of unwillingness in all encounters with art, as with sex ('too much trouble to seduce', as I wrote). Thus, to take in order, the audience experiences i) no familiar territory, that's to say, imaginative, ii) no moral consensus, and iii) a peculiar discourse, poetry. Catastrophe, then, has nearly everything against it except i) a certain type of audience that has curiosity, and ii) the susceptibility of a certain type of audience to beauty, probably not many individuals in all. The onus on The Wrestling School therefore is to guarantee that even its worst enemies haven't the excuse to diminish the Theatre of Catastrophe by declaring it inept, its actors unskilled, its production values poor. On the contrary, to enable the spectacle to escape the pitfalls of bathos even in the most extreme excess of language and action, we require higher disciplines.

A process of reactions has enabled my distinctive manner to develop. But I have always, at a deeper stratum, disliked The Theatre's way with a corrosive text. At every point I have felt the obligation to separate imagination from decency, kindness and civility. In doing so, I liberated it, for imagination hates constraint. I've said often, nausea compels me to shift my ground. I smell The Theatre as a bad odour, but it is hard to be immune. In my own productions I wanted not to be in Theatre at all . . . This recoiling from the odour of The Theatre is perhaps even more reason for hostility to my work, than the substance of it. Even my allies rarely eliminate it. I find it hard to describe. To be a master of theatre you must loathe The Theatre, loathe how it thinks of itself, its dedication to pleasure, gratification and so on. The artistic discipline I am talking of all the time is actually anathema to The Theatre, even if it thinks itself disciplined in that its actors are trained and so on. Its odour is really in the absence of a real vocation in its practitioners, who ache for celebrity and status, and in their hearts are compelled to delight their audiences, and cannot help themselves. I have rarely encountered an actor who did not in his psychology, want to delight his public, and live in dread of alienating them. This is the bad odour of The Theatre. Many of my allies are susceptible. Only Victoria Wicks and Melanie Jessop resist it, and they are 'eccentrics'.

JR: You are drawing here on your distinction between the art of theatre, and The Theatre itself, the distinction between art form, artistic practice and the institutional-commercial centres which largely dominate them. This, I think, is a central plank in your analysis of where theatre is, currently. Elsewhere, though, you write that 'If a serious theory of dramatic practice is to exist it can only do so on the basis of an analysis of social formation'.[8] One aspect of your reading of society is that it is 'disciplined by moral imperatives' that are simplistic, and therefore that complexity and ambiguity in theatre can be 'a political posture of profound strength'.[9] In your theatre, resistance to simplicity is produced largely through your own discipline in terms of writing poetic tragedies. But you argue that the dominant 'discipline of political theatre eliminates complexity and contradiction' from theatre, preferring 'clarity and realism' which have 'effectively abolished poetry from the stage'.[10] Furthermore, our convention for poetry in theatre remains dominated by the Elizabethan and Jacobean verse drama, making the acceptance and establishment of new poetic conventions more difficult still. What do you think the contemporary condition of poetic drama is, given these double limits?

HB: The fact is, for me, theatre is other-life, so to imitate the footsteps of common experience wouldn't contribute, and when an actor enters, or moves, or initiates an action, she must establish the non-realistic at every turn. Naturalism will disintegrate, and is doing so, but not to the advantage of the tragic text. But the irritation of theatre directors with old forms only produces gimmickry and technological innovations. Language is difficult because it is i), still regarded as antique, or ii), the performers can't do it, and so try to devalue it. The issue is this – to think complexly. If thought is complex, expression must be. Therefore, the poetic is the tool, and the only tool. Think of a poem by Céline. But who thinks complexly? The Theatre, after all, hates complex thought, it belittles itself always, always it lacks ambition.

Theatre is never ambitious enough. Where it is ambitious, it requires more substantial structures. These might be concrete, such as designs which serve to concentrate and not dissipate attention, or vocal qualities which communicate emotion and poetry. If the themes are tragic (and therefore, stressful, anxiety-creating) this applies more still, since the public is nearly always in flight and must be kept by a certain rigour in production. Inaudibility would be fatal if the characters are in complex relations, and frequently altering their postures vis-a-vis one another. Now, to heighten speech assures the public it is in a different place, that *this* theatre at least, is not part of the street, with its humiliating efforts at mimesis. My experience tells me that indiscipline in practice could not support these texts, but would break the hypnotic regard which binds the public to the stage (i.e. 'I can't hear', 'the metrical tune of the sentence has been broken', and so on). I would dare to say cacophony would not serve, nor a chaotic approach to staging ('I'll stand where I like . . .').

JR: Naturalism, as the prevailing 'discipline[s] of the stage',[11] might be said to epitomize that lack of ambition, being coterminous with 'social discipline', 'defined obligations' and 'governing laws'.[12] Indeed, you argue that it has 'contributed to a new style of social conformism', resulting in a 'theatre of morals as rigid as the mediaeval stage'.[13] You also write that the demand to make work accessible imposes 'hatred for abstraction' on artists and art forms,[14] but that it is only 'by infringing the rules of playwrighting' that theatre is able to realize its most profound effects. How would you describe the relationship between your sense of discipline, and that imposed by the context or contexts you have worked in?

HB: I am over-the-horizon now. Instead of coming in to a public, I am further from one. Certain elements of a young audience are not upset by ruptures, narrative leaps and so on. But they can't be held by performance, the seductive processes can't work on them, beauty is unaffective, and 'strange' ideas are viewed as crazy eccentricities. This is the triumph of populism and its media. You don't need to shoot your enemies anymore. But I always return to the same point – we aren't here to convert the masses. We have no *function*. Those who wish to believe lies must be left to believe them. We talk only to the restless, for whom life is not enough, in other words, the tragic personality.

Looking historically at drama, it's hard to discern whether repressive, conformist societies generate imaginative artistic gestures or the opposite. I am aware of the deepening of a moral consensus in European culture in my time which – because it requires so little repression – is more pernicious than say, Soviet communism, with its brutal apparatus. And we must acknowledge Soviet communism provoked, and even financed, works of genius far more extensive than we ever achieve here. I am thinking of Tarkovsky, supremely. The cheerful, ever-laughing, ever more accessible world of modern democracy, with its perpetual pseudo-collaborations, inter-active stuff, its dread of death, and its actual misery, has to be fought with complexity, not another barrage of 'alternative' populist slogans.

You may have read that my writing of *Victory* followed the sordid experience of popular theatre in a Community Play I was dubiously entailed in. For romantic reasons, I committed myself to a thing I already sensed to be repellent to my aesthetics. I was in love with a woman involved in it. This lurching away always pushes me to a place I want to enter, but am timid to enter. And it seems my timidity is correct, for *Victory* was ignored by Max Stafford-Clark and the 'radical' gang of Brechtians at the Royal Court for three or more years, and was staged by accident, coming about as the result of a planning disaster in Joint Stock, and not staged by the Royal Court itself. The humanists are utterly proscriptive. *The Castle* was tossed out by the Oxford Playhouse who commissioned it, and by the RSC. An accident, again, allowed it to happen years after. For many, many years I believed I was a failed writer. But I had only failed to be ideological.

JR: You write that 'the deepest power of theatre' is its resistance to coercion, and that it is 'fundamentally disobedient'.[15] Nevertheless, you do write of some aesthetic laws – art must serve its maker before it can serve others, for example, actors must 'obey the musical law of the text',[16] for another – but in other places you are against creating laws for practice. How important is the idea of discipline *creatively*?

HB: Yes, certainly the disciplines have been creative, and not in the least restrictive. For example, if I am certain an actor familiar and gifted in these methods can utter complexity, contradiction and so on, I am then able to further deepen the storm in the character's consciousness. This in itself makes for a musicality, which again enhances the production's refusal of the known, its sense of the uncanny in the human mouth.

JR: You write of the panic that audiences experience when their 'trained obeisance' is overturned by ruptures such as the unknown, the uncanny or 'the breaking of the narrative thread'.[17] The audience, too, can have its discipline: as you write, there are 'rules of witnessing,[18] conventions, which can be broken. Indeed, in the darkness of the theatre, you create work that seeks to licence imaginative freedom, making a space where there are 'No disciplines, no recall to conscience', and where the rules inside are 'different from the rules outside'.[19] How important is your use of a stylized pre-performance, what you call the 'Exordium', as a way of breaking through the discipline the audience brings with it, before the actors begin to deliver the text?

HB: Very important, and you are correct about the value of the Exordium. The odd thing is, while they might comprehend its purpose, no directors of my work have initiated them, therefore presenting the public with a conundrum almost at once, without preparation. This may be a reflection of their anxiety at inventing such a thing, which doesn't come naturally to directors, they think of it as an art-installation, which it resembles. You write of this as if it were a vortex, and I think it is, but the moral speculation I talk about isn't simply the product of a private practice – it's the life of the street, not the enclosed theatre that creates the struggle between the conscience and the artist. I've no interest in what actors think, nor do I try to engage them in my own thought. We neither argue nor debate the play – its so-called 'issues'– they are there, of course. The dramatist lives in the world and suffers it. That's the origin of the play's crisis, in effect. My intense concern is that the experience of the play is not diluted by weak practices.

JR: In your work with actors, it seems that you set out to intensify practice rather. You state that physical discipline imposed upon the actor, such as stillness for example, creates a situation where every movement that is then allowed has, as a result, greater significance as an exception. Similarly, the 'fastidious' costuming[20] which you describe imposes its disciplines upon the body, but implies and invites greater revelation. How difficult is it to achieve this intensification?

HB: It is nearly impossible to make an actor move in the way I describe. More and more they are taught to assume their own decisions are better, even if they haven't the least idea of how this appears from the public point of view. This is training, which asserts the right to 'feel' above the requirements of the production. Only a brilliantly physical actor will understand why the strict positioning, and the imposition of a gesture, creates a new style, and that inhabiting the gesture, and not struggling against it, is actually the actor's role (not just 'playing the role . . .'). We cannot move out of Stanislavskian theatre so long as teachers repudiate these aesthetic obligations and insist on the performer's autonomy. 'I am not a puppet' whines an always-second-rate actor. They should look more closely at puppets, who, with a single tilt of their heads, say more than these self-expressive performers, 'feeling' their ways.

JR: You write that 'projection and articulation' have been minimized as a result of Naturalism's dominance, and as a result of its project, that these disciplines of voice have become 'politically suspect',[21] probably because of the association between Received Pronunciation, social class and elitism. But your work requires often profound vocal athleticism, and thus a rigourous technical discipline from the actor?

HB: Social realism – a politics, I need scarcely say – finds all contrivance suspicious, all developed skills, elitist. This might be said to apply to the idea of beauty itself, which might be the property of a class, another social distinction, as human beauty is. The persistent identification of the 'artful' with privilege and anti-democratic instincts is annihilating. 'It's not the real world' is a similar complaint. 'She doesn't look like us' and so on, 'so how can I be involved?' Who is to blame for this? It is the outcome of a sustained attack on the imagination in Western democracy.

JR: You characterize your rejection of social realism as the result of 'rigourous contemplation'[22] of theatre, morality and politics – a rejection that led to 'an aesthetic programme'.[23] Indeed, you write that The Wrestling School style developed in sharp contradiction to social realism, avoiding its suffocating effects on artistic practice because of 'a profound discipline',[24] and rejecting its ethics. The Wrestling School style, therefore, is 'the outcome of discipline both moral and practical',[25] and stands as 'the moral element in an imaginative world that stresse[s] its own immorality'.[26] I think you put this most concisely in *Arguments for a Theatre*, when you write that 'The compulsion of this spectacle is its own morality'.[27] Although you value imagination far beyond relevance, it is probably fair to say that your work is as rigourously considered as it could be in terms of a relationship to the world. Is there a sense in which your idea of discipline is almost military in its scope of resourcing and preparedness?

HB: The moral aspect of the staging is precisely its recoiling from spontaneity, its repudiation of the familiar, the quotidian, in a world which privileges the ordinary as an ethic. But before asserting that this might be a military formulation, recollect that the military form of discipline is designed to create absolute command, so the individual soldier is essentially a machine. This doesn't happen here. Each actor is employed for her specific gift. I talk of the ensemble as an *orchestra*. The strictness of the staging, the use of chiaroscuro lighting to enhance the unreality, and so on, nevertheless requires the individual – and licenses her – a higher degree of self-expression than 'Naturalism' can, for Naturalism is an 'ism', a law, a service to the observed. Here we eradicate all such responsibility to the tyranny of the familiar. This is a release of the actor's soul, and in full-flight it's visible, and an inspiration to herself and the overwhelmed public.

JR: In the medium of theatre you work as writer, director and designer – but you also work in the medium of oil paint – not to mention photography or poetry. An equally various number of artistic touchstones are cited in *A Style and Its Origins* – Grien, Dürer, Altdorfer, Bartok, Rilke, Apollinaire, Céline, Stockhausen, Bach, Berio, Ligeti, Cristou – along with artworks and places which initiated pieces such as *Ursula, Scenes from an Execution, The Castle* and *Victory*. Given that your 'theatrical imagination operate[s] in the visual as well as the literary sphere',[28] how would you respond to the suggestion that your description of yourself as not only director and writer but as 'visualiser'[29] indicates that your discipline is, to at least some degree, *interdisciplinary*?

HB: All the forms I employ are connected if not ostensibly, certainly at a profound level. For example my pictures are figurative, narrative to an extent, and even take the level of the circle in the theatre as the perspective (I prefer to watch plays from there). Are the figures in them somehow 'actors'? They might be. They make seductive propositions. I don't think the consequence of this is that I direct in an 'interdisciplinary' way, simply because any half-decent director employs the stage space with certain principles in mind (simply, this actor is obscuring that one . . .) and after all, the poetic discourse of my work is where theatre started out. Enslaved by a political agenda, it's the misery of realism – 'the workers are too stupid for poetry' – that has abolished its beauty.

Part Two

Readings/Inversions

Introduction

While the previous section was made up of writing on practice from inside The Wrestling School, Part Two: 'Readings/Inversions', presents research-based perspectives from outside the company. The reason for this sudden shift in gear goes beyond the desire to create a bold contrast; here, rather, having considered how Barker and company tell their own story, we have collected chapters from outside the company that, perhaps provocatively, offer different narratives – ones that are grounded in the broader context of culture and society, or which read the artistry of the company on different terms. As we noted in our introduction, this is a multifaceted theatre practice, and a broad spectrum of interpretation is required in order to capture as many angles of significance as possible. Barker has, in his theoretical writings, developed a position through which to explore his work; *Arguments for a Theatre*, first published in 1989, is his initial attempt at theorizing the Catastrophic theatre and to account for its ontology. The articles and essays in *Arguments for a Theatre* stem from a variety of sources over a period of time, and are often derived from newspaper articles and papers presented at academic conferences and symposia. These early essays reveal a break with socialist theatre, an attempt to account for a range of complex dialectical impulses that formed the tension of Barker's artistic desires in the early 1980s. The transformation in Barker's theatre writing since this period has seen him develop his theoretical principles around radical changes to the notion of theatrical character, a debate on the value of dramatic language and an enquiry into the tragic condition that asks serious questions about the relevance and purpose of theatre as we reached the millennial age and beyond. As Barker writes in the preface to the third edition of *Arguments for a Theatre*:

> These essays, poems, manifestos, take as their starting point not only the agony of artistic production but also the agony of artistic experience, the pain not only of the creator but the pain of the witnesses. It is tragedy, therefore, that is being uttered here, as one might speak a secret curse in the confines of an alien religion.[1]

Each chapter in this section competes to draw our attention to somewhat neglected areas of Barker scholarship, and perhaps necessarily, therefore, reads against the grain by inviting us to reconsider his theoretical writings, his drama, and Wrestling School theatre practice. Each chapter thus offers a reading of Barker's drama or theatre which seeks to invert some of the established assumptions surrounding this work. This selection of perspectives is more provocative than pugilistic; rather than seeking to replace existing understanding, these chapters seek to add to it, by complicating accepted ideas and offering new interpretations. By presenting fresh approaches to Barker and company, this section of the book also aims towards a reinvigoration of the conversation around their work. The readings offered here also reveal that Barker and The Wrestling School are intimate not only with the vital questions affecting theatre as an art form, but also with the dominance of commercial imperatives – imperatives which increasingly determine the behaviour and choices of a theatre industry which is still widely, but inaccurately, presumed to remain in service to the development of the theatrical art form. In *Death, The One, and the Art of Theatre* (2005), Barker presented a poetic critique of the relationship between the art of theatre and Theatre-as-Industry. These chapters effectively extend that debate, connecting Barker's drama and theatre with greater specificity to elements of culture and aesthetics that impact upon both art and industry. This widening out of the existing conversation also extends the demystification of practice that was initiated in the first part of the book.

The first chapter in this section, '"To experience a thing as beautiful": The Photographic Practice of Howard Barker', sees Andy W. Smith exploring Barker's work as a photographer and his use of alter-egos to screen his work as a designer for The Wrestling School, and accounting for their contribution to the construction of the company's aesthetic. By the same token, these are features of Barker's work that have become aesthetic constructions in themselves, ultimately coming to act as visual and auditory keys to understanding his drama and theatre. Smith shows how Barker's deeply personal memoir *A Style and Its Origins*, by his photographer alter-ego Eduardo Houth, informs Barker's photographic practice, leading to an accumulation of images – primarily used in Wrestling School publicity and programmes – which (perhaps unconsciously) appropriate and recontextualize the modernist and surrealist traditions of European photography. Such images contribute sharply to perceptions of theatrical style, and create a narrative around The Wrestling School by connecting it to the broader frameworks of visual culture. Smith thus offers a fresh way of reading the aesthetics of stage imagery as they have developed in this practice, images that are more often presumed to derive solely from the language of Barker's playtexts. At the same time, this chapter complicates the historical narrative of the company by revealing how these images have sought to shape perception through the physical materials exchanged with, or seen by, audiences attending Wrestling School performances. In Chapter 7, 'Vintage Barker: New Writing in Old Bottles', James Hudson also offers a re-reading of Barker's work, re-positioning it in relation to debates regarding the status and value of 'new writing'. Hudson's analysis reveals the extent to which Barker's writing not only provides an antithesis to the dominance of naturalistic theatre forms in much new work, but also, simultaneously, how Barker's writing has influenced key individuals across key phases of the new writing phenomenon. Hudson shows clearly how the dominant characteristics of new writing are, frequently, precisely those rejected – often vehemently – by Barker. What emerges from this chapter, therefore, is a clear picture as to why Barker's writing remains *new*, despite the longevity of his career, and also largely cut off from the various forms of support that are available for much that comes under the aegis of new writing. Both the historical and conceptual narrative which Hudson offers, therefore, reveal how the work of Barker and The Wrestling School is intricately related to one of the most influential trends and concerns of contemporary British theatre. Hudson's reading invites us to reposition Barker and company in the centre of current debates regarding the state of playwriting in Britain. Furthermore, by illustrating the cultural forces that shape the phenomenon of new writing, Hudson shows that, while Barker himself separates the art form of theatre from the theatre industry, neither he nor The Wrestling School are entirely insulated, or separate from, those forces. A similar intimacy is accounted for in Chapter 8, where Peter A. Groves examines Barker's work in relation to what has been perceived as a broad shift in culture towards de-secularization. Thus in 'Howard Barker and the Return of Religion', Groves examines the key role that religion plays in Barker's drama, and, in particular, his encounters with the Abrahamic religions of Judaism, Christianity and Islam. Groves reflects in depth upon Barker's radical, theatrical excavation of moments in Europe's spiritual heritage, and shows that a deconstruction of monotheistic ideas and narratives informs the tragic and atheistic spirituality that Barker offers in its place – a feature which Groves argues connects Barker strongly to the prominent Christian mystic, Meister Eckhart. As first revealed in *Arguments for a Theatre*, Barker has continuously rejected any demand to create a theatre based on the principles of accessibility and relevance. And yet Groves's reading reminds us how often it is that in seeking their own registers for meaning, artists of all sorts often achieve the kind of relevance which cannot be accomplished in frantic attempts to be contemporary. Barker's work is, perhaps, at its most prescient in its focus upon the enduring difficulties of religion, and Groves here connects – and shows the relevance of – that work to our global, and contemporary, backdrop. In Chapter 9, James Reynolds pursues a similar focus, but with a different object. 'Going Underground' also seeks to characterize spirituality in Barker's work, doing so through an account of different features of theatre space as they relate to his drama and theatre. Where Groves reads the treatment of monotheism in Barker's work, Reynolds tackles the more pagan element of the *chthonic*, and its influence upon Barker's spatial aesthetics. Tracing the institutional partnerships formed by Barker and The Wrestling School, this chapter invites us to consider a parallel between the material circumstances of production, and Barker's evolving deployment of theatrical space. Indeed, Reynolds argues that Barker's theatre has moved ever closer to the ancient roots of performance in its use and philosophy of space, in an aesthetic process parallel to the material issues that have faced The Wrestling School in terms of accessing theatrical spaces. As elsewhere, this chapter provides us with an alternative history with which to enrich our understanding. However, Barker's trajectory of development is most often charted through his play texts; this chapter, therefore, also creates an alternative reading which describes how both writer and company have instead evolved through their relationship with theatrical space.

In short, Part Two offers alternative readings and new propositions regarding Barker's theatre with The Wrestling School. By collecting together research and perspectives from outside The Wrestling School, this section broadens our focus and further extends our understanding of practice. In tandem with Part One, therefore, this section helps to clarify further the nature of Barker's theatre, while adding to the critical conversation on that work by connecting writer and company to important features of aesthetics and culture.

6

'To experience a thing as beautiful':
The Photographic Practice of Howard Barker

Andy W. Smith

To experience a thing as beautiful means: to experience it necessarily wrongly.

Friedrich Nietzsche[1]

Everything is a subject for photography including your own fantasies, your own truth, your own desires, your own fears. That's where you live. You don't live on the streets looking at people's faces or looking at sunsets. You live in your mind. And you know your fears more intimately. What I want from you is your secrets. That's the only thing you can give me: your secrets.

Duane Michals[2]

I am a lost filmmaker . . .

Howard Barker[3]

Although well known as a director and designer of his own plays with The Wrestling School,[4] Howard Barker is also acknowledged as a poet (with seven publications over the last thirty years) and a painter with a number of international exhibitions to his name. Michel Morel has explored the relationship between Barker's painting, poetry and drama, arguing how 'the paintings and poems may allow one to read the plays more effectively'.[5] Charles Lamb has also written about how Barker's painting practice informs his other work as a designer and writer: 'It would not be going too far to suggest that these vistas with their yellow miasmata foster an authentically catastrophic feeling such as one might expect from the originator of the Theatre of Catastrophe.'[6] In the introduction to his painting catalogue *Landscape with Cries* (2006), Barker writes that

> It is perhaps unusual for a single individual to work creatively in more than one medium . . . I was inevitably drawn towards the body and its gestures and the vocabulary of the gesture, of how the body 'speaks' its pain, even when, as in the picture plane, words are absent. My pictures therefore, are something between a theatre situated in a landscape, a landscape almost featureless, and a film still and it is possible film might have been the integration of all those aspects of the drama that preoccupy me . . .[7]

Barker has commented that 'I am a lost filmmaker . . .' and has written a number of film scripts that remain unproduced. Barker's aggregation of gesture, object and composition of space and time can be seen in his work as a photographer, an austere, stripped down aesthetic that logically extends his painting and design processes into the eye of the camera.

This chapter therefore proposes a fourth, vital element of Barker's artistic practice to go alongside theatre, poetry and painting: his photographic output work for TWS publicity and programmes, an increasingly significant practice as it defines a visual aesthetic which the company has become increasingly well known for, as well as creating an *oeuvre* to rival his other work as a visual artist. Barker's photography practice is in keeping with his work as a painter in that he has refined a method and style over a period of time: Barker works primarily using monochromatic (B & W) film; he develops and prints his own photographs from his basement darkroom, and still shoots on film with a camera dating from the 1960s. He remains resolutely analogue in his practice; the process of developing photographs using chemicals and enlargers, of manipulating and developing the image by hand, is a crucial part of his method. The development of Barker's photographic practice is further complicated by the creation of an alter-ego through which the later work is constructed: Eduardo Houth, the identity through whom Barker has also written his deeply personal memoir in the third person, *A Style and Its Origins* (2007).⁸ Barker addresses the intricacies of self-authored biographical narrative through the voice of Eduardo Houth; as Lynda Haverty Rugg writes,

> Autobiography, like photography, refers to something beyond itself; namely the autobiographical or photographed subject. But both autobiography and photography participate in a series of signs that we have learned to read – at one level – as highly indeterminate and unreliable.⁹

Barker's use of Houth as his authorial voice allows for a certain distancing effect in *ASIO*, and the development of Houth as the 'photographer' for TWS creates a further level of indeterminacy in how the later photographic work of the company can be viewed.¹⁰

However, Houth is not an exception here, as he follows Barker's use of 'fictional identities assumed by him to screen a range of his activities'.¹¹ These secret identities or *nom de guerres* were originally conceived by Barker as a way of creating a 'total aesthetic for which he alone assumed responsibility',¹² and acted as a defence mechanism against what Barker saw as the 'English prejudice against writers directing their own works . . . he did not wish to compound his offence by admitting he was entirely responsible for every visual and audial element as well . . .'¹³ Barker's work as a *metteur-en-scène* necessitated the creation of these 'fictional friends': Billie Kaiser, who is responsible for the costume design; Tomas Leipzig, who has designed the sets for all Wrestling School productions from *Ursula* (1998) onwards with the exception of Caroline Shentang (also another Barker alias), who designed the set for the iconic production of *Gertrude – The Cry* (2002); and Paula Sezno, responsible for the sound design for the 2009 production of *Found in the Ground*. As Houth notes in *ASIO*:

> His imagination expressed itself in many and contradictory forms: in his painting, in his set and costume designs, a severe, monochromatic discipline imposed itself. The sets of Tomas Leipzig for the Wrestling School are distinguished by their economy and beauty, Billy (sic) Kaiser's costumes by their stylish regime of haute couture.¹⁴

These 'designers' are now well established in the history and contexts of TWS, and serve their function of allowing Barker to develop his highly refined production style without attracting the opprobrium of the theatre critics, already suspicious of Barker directing his own plays. *The Guardian* theatre reviewer Lyn Gardner has written 'I just wish he would get himself a director and dramaturg'[15] and also talks about 'the frustrating Barker obscurity that comes when a writer directs too much of his own work and doesn't have to justify and test his writing enough'.[16] Ian Shuttleworth writes: 'It's as if he were not so much a playwright as a genre unto himself.'[17]

Quite often, theatre critics such as Gardner and Shuttleworth would routinely praise the set and costume design of TWS productions while criticizing the writing and directing,[18] a contradiction not lost on Barker:

> The whole notion of heteronymity in the W/S was a feint against the English prejudice which derides any individual who can or tries to be competent at more than one thing. If I had allowed my own name to be put against author, director, set designer, costume designer, and more, the howl of contempt would have been deafening. I nimbly dodged that, and at the same time, created the illusion that the W/S was a big organisation, when in fact it is scarcely populated at all.[19]

Barker's careful construction of fictional biographical details in TWS programme notes 'populates' the company with award-winning artistic designers, further creating the outward impression of a company that is resolutely cosmopolitan and eclectic in its aesthetic sensitivities:

> *Designer – Tomas Leipzig*
> Youngest ever winner of the Berne Prize. Credits include Strasser's *Wozzeck* and the controversial blood and glass set for Plotinski's *Spring Awakening*. Recently completed his first film based on Isaho Agaki's *Subway Murders*. Future projects include Shostakovich's *Lady Macbeth* in Grenoble and a film based on the death of Friedrich Nietzsche.[20]

Costume Designer – Billie Kaiser
Fell in love with the Wrestling School during its visit to Berlin with *(Uncle) Vanya* in 1997. She designed clothing under her own cult label Honneker in the early 1990s before turning to stage and film. Her most recent work includes Christian Gille's opera *Mother Courage At The Court Of The Hapsburgs* (Lubeck and Madrid) and Hudaconceva's short film *A Medical Dictionary* ... Billie now lives in Trieste.[21]

As the 'careers' of Tomas Leipzig and Billie Kaiser become more entrenched within the history of TWS so the accumulation of biographical notes becomes more incongruous:

> A stage designer and film-maker, Tomas's collaboration with Howard Barker extends to his first award winning design for the German premiere of *Seven Lears* in 1990, a controversial set design incorporating over 100 animal carcasses. Tomas's short film about the birth of Hitler, *Christ's Dog*, won the special prize at the Dresden Film Festival in 2004. He is currently filming *The History of a Hole* in his native Bohemia.[22]

As Barker notes, '... the career of Leipzig and Kaiser has been so preposterous, that you have to be a little gullible not to sense this (and of course you were meant to ...) however the fact is some of these designs have worked brilliantly, and solved theatre problems in a way strictly theatrical.'[23] This stratagem also applies to the use of images in TWS programmes, and Barker's photographic images for TWS exposes a haunting, clandestine *knowledge* that is profoundly disconcerting and transgressive in its representation of bodies and objects.

Bodies

All photographs are memento mori. *To take a photograph is to participate in another person's (or thing's) mortality, vulnerability, mutability.*[24]

Susan Sontag

The early programmes of TWS used a variety of images and found sources for promotional material, along with production photographs whose main purpose was to document the practice. Following the departure of Kenny Ireland in 1995, Barker's subsequent takeover of the directing of the work also saw a shift in the overall design aesthetic for the company. The first TWS programme photographic image that Barker made was for *(Uncle) Vanya* (1996). Although the photograph is unaccredited in the programme, Barker did not take the photograph himself; rather, he set up the image and had a professional photographer take the picture. The B & W photograph is stark and *chiaroscuro* in its impression: lit by two shafts of light, a hand reaches up inside a wardrobe, where a gun is hanging alongside a dressing gown and a shirt, referencing Chekhov's maxim 'If in Act I you have a pistol hanging on the wall, then it must fire in the last act.'[25] As I have written elsewhere, 'Barker's *Vanya* changes the relationship dynamic between the characters by doing something Chekhov actively rejected – he allows Vanya the chance to act on his urges by shooting at *and* killing Serebryakov, thus fulfilling and abstracting the will to live that Chekhov's characters are constantly deferring.'[26] Barker describes the image for *(Uncle) Vanya* as 'a transitional picture, nether lifted from an original "classic". . . nor fully a Houth'.[27] The photograph for the programme of *(Uncle) Vanya* continued the previous process of TWS programmes, where the carefully chosen visual imagery speaks back and into the thematic contexts of each production. This initial image conceived by Barker is an early example of the style of photography that would come to be associated with TWS publicity: high contrast B & W photos of mysterious figures placed against incongruous settings, sometimes naked, faces always obscured or absent, and usually posed by actors associated with the company.

Following on from *(Uncle) Vanya*, the production programme for *Ursula* (1998) takes the same thematic style: B & W, an enigmatic figure, dressed in a nun's habit, caught at the moment of leaping over a puddle of water with her image reflected in the water and reversed so that the mirrored reflection with its attendant blurred outline is the dominant point of the photograph. This image is reminiscent in its graphic matching in form and style to Richard Avedon's striking photograph *Homage to Munkasci*. This photograph, published in the September 1957 issue of *Harper's Bazaar*, sees model Carmel deftly leaping over a puddle on a Parisian sidewalk. Avedon's photograph is itself a knowing reference to Hungarian photographer Martin Munkasci's *Puddle Jumper*, published in *Harper's Bazaar* in 1934.

The following year saw *Und* (1999), Barker's one woman play written for Melanie Jessop, a Wrestling School regular and one of Barker's self-confessed 'muses'.[28] The front cover of the programme for *Und* depicts an image of a naked female body, cropped from the neck to the hips, in a medium close-up, and superimposed just underneath the pubic hair of the model is a fine china tea cup and saucer. The cup and saucer, important reoccurring motifs in Barker's drama, becomes the focal point for the set design of *Und*:

> To those who saw *Und*, few can forget the disturbing spectacle of the unoccupied set, the steel tray flying on long rods of steel with the rhythm of an industrial machine, its tea service awesomely still while a trickle of sand, wavering, dropped from on high to create a mound on the pierced floor, uncanny signs of absences . . .[29]

As Eléonore Obis has written of Barker's use of the body in his drama, 'When the naked body appears, it becomes the driving force of the *agon*, a main dynamic in the underlying conflict that defines the relationship between characters and presides over the way they communicate: nakedness implies both the vulnerability of the naked character as well as its power on others.'[30] The naked body then is a powerful signifier in Barker's work, 'nakedness is the great secret of the stage, and the stage an art of secrecy . . .'[31] and Houth elucidates how this is intimately tied up with the status and movement of the female characters in Barker's drama:

> . . . his fastidious clothing of the body, above all the female body, implied, invited, even demanded, the revelation of the nakedness that lay beneath it . . . it was embedded in the spectacle, a calculation that

was inevitably an impatience . . . Barker saw nakedness both as pity and power . . .³²

The power of the body in relation to photography has been well documented since the invention of the daguerreotype in the mid-nineteenth century; John Pultz writes that

> . . . during the period 1910–1940, both male and female photographers fashioned their careers, and Modernism itself, around the power of their pictures to give form to heterosexuality. Modernist photographers produced an erotic female body that was exclusively heterosexual . . .³³

Barker's framing of the naked body in *Und* bears relation to Pultz's analysis; the 'erotic female body', through sign and language, exists in Barker's work as palimpsests of desire, writing over centuries of visual culture depicting the female as 'nude'. Obis quotes Berger: 'a naked body has to be seen as an object in order to become a nude [. . .] Nakedness reveals itself. Nudity is placed on display.'³⁴ Barker's image for *Und* is reminiscent in style and tone of Alfred Stieglitz's portraits of his wife Georgia O'Keefe, constructing a visual similarity through the use of cropping 'to produce sexually charged, unnatural, decontextualised body fragments'.³⁵ The use of high contrast, tightly cropped, sometimes abstracted figures to emphasize sexuality and therefore the gender of the model was a constant trope in Modernist photography, prevalent in both male and female photographers.³⁶

These stylistic themes are developed further in the production programme for *A House of Correction* (2001). There are two main photographic images for this programme. The front cover has a B & W image of a naked woman, except for male boots and a cap hiding her face, hunched over on a wooden 'flip up' chair. The photograph is taken with the camera poised at a low angle with a narrow depth of field, such that with the angle of perspective the eye is drawn to the naked figure at the top right of the photograph, exactly where the room meets in a corner – the corner symbolizing a point of punishment, a 'house of correction'. The photo is foregrounded by a floor that during developing has been gradually overexposed;[37] as the eye moves further up the page the floor begins to come into focus, imbuing the photograph with an unsettling atmosphere of vulnerability (the naked body juxtaposed against the whiteness of the walls and floor, aided by natural light flooding in through a window to the left of the figure), with the isolation of the naked figure adding to the incongruity of the male attire on the female body. The model is in a position of kinetic movement, perched perilously on the edge of the chair, adding to the overall uncanny effect of the image. The logo of TWS is the only form of writing on the front cover, a break from previous TWS productions that also had the title of the play on the cover of the programme. On the inside of the programme the photograph is titled 'Mental Institution, Stuttgart, 1945' (see Figure 4). For those audience members not familiar with the design aesthetic of TWS, it could be assumed that this is indeed a 'found photograph' sourced from an archive like earlier programme images and not an original creation by Barker. However, with Eduardo Houth yet to be credited at this point in the company's history, Barker's deliberate obfuscation of the photograph's derivation follows his previous strategy of constructing fictional identities in order to screen his work outside of directing/writing.

The back cover image for *A House of Correction* programme opens up a further interesting debate about the provenance of photography and its ontological meanings: titled 'Staircase, Sopron, Hungary, 1911', the photograph is a blown-up image of a staircase in medium close-up, with worn wooden stairs and an ornate steel banister. In fact, this photograph is one of the most famous in the history of the medium – taken by an early French pioneer of photography, Eugène Atget, in Paris in 1911, and subsequently appropriated by the Surrealist movement in the 1920s. Published in the Surrealist magazine *La Révolution surréaliste* in December 1926, Atget's image has been eulogized by Julien Levy as 'its pregnant emptiness and serpentine movement toward a hidden place achieved a subtle mystery'.[38] Ian Walker notes that 'What we might now call an "Atgetian" aesthetic – the everyday recorded with such understated directness that it comes to seem haunting, somehow inexplicable – can be found throughout early Surrealist practice, and was allied to the impulse that gave *La Révolution surréaliste* its air of ascetic formality'.[39]

Walker's connecting of early documentary photography with the later movement of Surrealism is encapsulated by his close readings of Atget's images as reproduced in *La Révolution surréaliste,* quoting Walter Benjamin writing of Breton: 'He was the first to perceive the revolutionary energies that appear in the "outmoded", in the first iron constructions, the first factory buildings, the earliest photos, the objects that have begun to be extinct, grand pianos, the dresses of five years ago, fashionable restaurants when the vogue has begun to ebb from them.'[40] Walker elucidates this by referencing Dan Graham: 'Benjamin wished to demonstrate that for his generation slightly out-of-date – just past – objects of mass culture possessed a latent revolutionary power, a notion he developed from surrealism . . . For Benjamin, this was one way the "commodity dream" might be broken. This process would reveal "an actual though hidden past, mostly eradicated from consciousness but briefly available in moments of dreams, hallucinations, stoppages etc."'[41]

The emphasis on 'objects of mass culture' is explored in Barker's next stage of photography, as Eduardo Houth begins to take shape as an alter-ego. Houth writes in *ASIO* that 'Barker thought the material detritus of society was imbued with suffering or loss',[42] and this analysis can equally be applied to the front image of *A House of Correction* programme: the juxtaposition of the photograph's fictional title – 'Mental Institution, Stuttgart, 1945' – against the formal composition of the image creates a disassociation between what is read as being 'real' and what is self-evidently a construct. As Houth notes, 'the play (*A House of Correction*) was situated precisely where the world ceased to be represented'.[43] In an interview with Mark Brown, Barker notes that his design intentions for TWS lie in a certain simplicity in the use of colour but achieved in such a way as to de-naturalize the audience's perception of the 'real' world: 'I'd want to announce, in costume, this isn't the world as you know it'.[44] This logic follows through in the presentation of invented worlds through the medium of photography, refined over a number of years to the point where the aesthetic signature of the company is mediated across not only theatre but in the publicity and promotional materials of TWS. This is further emphasized by the significance of the programme cover for *Gertrude – The Cry* (2002).

Barker has previously described *Gertrude – The Cry* as his 'greatest work on love'[45] and 'in this climate, revolutionary work'.[46] Barker's re-writing of Shakespeare's *Hamlet* lies in his criminalization of Gertrude and her attendant refusal to suffer shame through desire that T. S Eliot recognizes as the origin of Hamlet's psychosis in his 1922 essay 'Hamlet and His Problems': 'Hamlet is up against the difficulty that his disgust is occasioned by his mother, but that his mother is not an adequate equivalent for it; his disgust envelops and exceeds her.'[47]

Barker's re-fashioning of Gertrude as an agent of her own desire is reflected in the choice of photography for the programme. The front cover of the programme is an image of a naked woman, lying face down in what appears to be woods or forest in an autumnal setting.[48] Her body is partially covered by small branches and leaves, while the only item she is wearing is a pair of black high heels. The face is partially obscured by the angled position in relation to the camera, and by the woman's hair. The photograph is B & W and marginally over exposed such that the skin of the naked woman glows with a luminescent quality, with a loss of focus towards the outer edges of the photograph.

In this powerful and disturbing image, Barker enters the dense forest of Shakespeare and creates a metonym for female sexuality through the figure of Gertrude, reified in the photograph through the naked body of the female as victim. In its intimations of sexual violence and death it corresponds to what Barker defines as the tragic experience in theatre, as Shakespeare's Gertrude (her sexuality moribund in the autumn of her years) is resuscitated by Barker's insistence on her refusal to bend to moral codes. David Ian Rabey writes that 'Gertrude depicts the mature woman as a sexual existential heroine',[49] and the programme photograph foreshadows the 'exquisite crime'[50] of passion that begins the play – the copulation by Gertrude and Claudius over the dying body of the King.

The photograph can be read either as a documented crime scene or a film still;[51] the question of authenticity is further complicated by the credit on the inside of the programme: *Mal de Reine*, Alain Jassy, 1950 (see Figure 5). Translated interpretively as 'the sick queen', the invention of fictional photographer/filmmaker Alain Jassy historicizes the context of the photograph, imbuing it with an artistic legitimacy associated with the film and photography movements that saw France as the centre of the visual *avant-garde* in the interwar and post-war years.

As John Pultz notes, since its beginnings photography has played an important part in cataloguing death: 'In depicting the dead with all the absoluteness and finality that secular empiricists said was their state, photography restated its claim to absolute truthfulness.'[52] The American Civil War (1860–5) was one of the first major conflicts to use photography to capture the horrors of death and destruction on an industrial scale, as Lynda Haverty Rugg writes:

> Photographs of the dead have a consuming power – since photography arrests the flow of life and creates memorials to monuments, persons and objects, the medium was from the first associated with death, consumers of early photographs clearly understood it as well, as evidenced in nineteenth century enthusiasm, for photographs of the dead.[53]

This intimation of death with nakedness in the *Gertrude* image resonates with latent anxiety; the gap between what is real and what is constructed, of the brutal realism of the 'found image' and the plethora of signs that can be deducted through its connotative relationship to the text. The prone naked woman, the ambiguity over her fate, and the fictional context in which the photograph is sited creates a moral ambivalence that resounds within the play itself. This photographic meditation on death and the natural world is echoed in Gertrude's final speech to the dying Claudius:

Gertrude   Grey garden
Grey garden
Ashes scattered on it

> Scattered ashes of burned men
> HE'LL RUSH TO FUCK
> HE'LL RUSH TO FUCK
> AND OUR SLIDING HEELS WILL TREAD YOU IN[54]

Susan Sontag has written that

> Desire has no history – at least it is experienced in each instance as all foreground, immediacy. It is aroused by archetypes and is, in that sense, abstract. But moral feelings are embedded in history, whose personae are concrete, whose situations are always specific. Thus, almost opposite rules hold true for the use of the photograph to awaken desire and to awaken conscience.[55]

The binary opposition held for so long in photographic discourse, between the image as a document of time and space (objective reality) and the constructed artifice of the form itself (subjective experience), is disrupted in these programme photographs through the use of fictional contexts and invented personae that intimate an objective reality while subverting the way in which the images can be read. As Geoffrey Batchen writes, 'the meanings of photographs are not determined by, or confined to, the pictures themselves, for meaning is continually being reproduced within the contexts in which these pictures appear'.[56]

Objects

A photograph is both a pseudo-presence and a token of absence.[57]

Susan Sontag

Barker's evocation of an 'actual but hidden past' through the placement of his programme photographs in a fictional but historicized setting of post-WW2 Europe invokes comparison with his fascination for the found object remade as art (the *objet trouvé*), as evidenced through the set and costume designs of Leipzig and Kaiser and exemplified in his play *13 Objects* (2003). In this respect the importance of Benjamin's 'outmoded' object becomes central to the design principles of TWS. Houth relates that Barker

> ... loved relics and remnants even while he knew they defied his curiosity, becoming only the substance of new myths, pretexts for annexations ... In his plays the relic comes to threaten the living with its significance, for it has by virtue of being dead matter a seeming authenticity ... it can no longer be corrupted ... but it can be appropriated ...[58]

Barker's programme photographs are redolent of an 'ascetic formality' (Walker) in their appropriation of everyday objects as a 'pretext for annexation'. *13 Objects*' (2003) programme has a front cover credited as 'Anti-profiteering poster, Hungary, 1943' (see Figure 6). The tone in the programme cover is nostalgically sepia rather than B & W, and continues the themes now prevalent in the photography for the programmes: obscured faces, anachronistic formalism in style and dress (the man wears a bowler hat and the woman a 1940s hat in a style that is now consistent with Barker/Kaiser's costume design, based on Dior's 1947 'New Look'), with the eye being drawn to the importance of the object pinned to their clothing. The play itself takes 13 objects – a spade, a cup and saucer, a medal, a pair of shoes, a rattle, a camera, a ring, a painting, an urn, a postcard, a pair of spectacles, a bucket, a drum – and constructs a very specific 'theatrical milieu', as Barker writes:

> The (theatrical) milieu is not reality but a composition of elements which freely admit their artificiality whilst making every element a cultural sign. Mirrors, you'll have noticed (*Dead Hands*). The white sheet. The single chair. And smaller items, like the gun. The hospital trolley. And the massive photograph of the actor in *Ursula*. The morality of this lies in the abolition of trivial, quotidinal flotsam and the resulting concentration of thought on tragic values, and here the moving body, (naked, at critical times) is a determinant, sculptural and therefore, Hellenic in its origins, so that every form of the body is openly, confessedly, contrived (take the murder in *Gertrude*). This extends to props – a bucket, a chair, a gun, a spade. The spade resonates throughout my work, from *Victory*, to – critically – *13 Objects*.[59]

Barker has described this process as 'film-as-imagination',[60] constructing a compositional frame around everyday objects and re-siting them in an invented world. The composition of figures and artefacts in his photography are extensions of the *mise-en-scene* of his stage worlds. The photographic image for *Dead Hands* (2004) extends this process further; as with the image for *Gertrude*, it is credited to an invented photographer, Jean-Paul Malakoff, with the title '*Non, Je ne suis pas la* (1947)'. The B & W image reveals five single black gloves 'floating' against a white wall, with a pair of hands tied with rope protruding between the far left and second left gloves. The effect is startling on first viewing; a sense of disembodiment, with the five black gloves suspended in mid-air; the bound hands reaching up in the same visual composition as the gloves. Like some of the programmes, it is designed to be viewed horizontally rather than vertically, and the rectangular dimensions of the programmes assist in that regard. There is a hypnotic, almost ghostly presence indicated by the absence of the human body except for the bound hands; as Houth writes, 'The uncanny was routine to him and he included it in his thought as an aspect of things, almost a law'.[61] This emphasis on the 'uncanny' can be detected across all of Barker's artistic outputs, from his painting, to his poetry and drama. It is most apparent in Barker's photography, as the power of the still image, manipulated to seem 'other', of 'the everyday recorded with such understated directness that it comes to seem haunting, somehow inexplicable' (Walker) is carried through into his later incarnation as Eduardo Houth, the inscrutable chronicler of objects and desires, and an exemplifier of 'an actual though hidden past' (Benjamin).

The mysterious Eduardo Houth

Houth's biography reads

> Long resident in Europe, Eduardo Houth was born in Chile of Scottish ancestry. Following the overthrow of the Allende regime Houth travelled extensively in Europe. His first photographic commissions

were for fashion magazines in Spain. Later he diversified into stage photography and creating images for book jackets and theatre posters. His poetry, often presented alongside the sharply focused iconic images for which he is known, include LANDLESS (1989) and IF I CEASE (2000). He is the author of a poetic biography of his friend the dramatist and poet Howard Barker, *A Style and its Origins*. (Howard Barker/Eduardo Houth. Oberon Books, 2007)[62]

Of all the alter-egos created by Barker, Houth is the one that seems most simpatico with Barker's own artistic self, as Houth straddles continents, artistic forms and hybrid identities. First credited in 2005 with the photographic image for Barker's play *The Fence in Its Thousandth Year*,[63] the work of Houth has increasingly become the touchstone through which TWS has formed its latter identity. The images of Houth usually encompass everyday objects re-fashioned into entities of metonymic power; the iron hooks for *The Seduction of Almighty God* (2006); in *Found in the Ground* (2009) the close-up of a hand protruding through the ground, clutching a key, with the transparent dirt acting like an x-ray and focalizing the bullet casing in the soil (see Figure 7); the juxtaposition of a spade (a significant object in Barker's scenic landscapes) with a high heel for the front cover of Rabey's *Howard Barker: Ecstasy and Death* (2010).

These images have moved away from the arch modernist/surrealist style of *Und*, *A House of Correction* and *Gertrude* to photomontages of *objet trouvé*; these photomontages imbue the juxtaposed objects with an almost religious significance, as holy relics that have mysterious secrets, dug up, reframed, reused. Houth writes that Barker 'required the past and its remnants nearly as addiction, but drew out of it an absolute modernity which in a faithless age had faith's exhilarations and its agonies . . .'[64] As Houth, Barker imprints visions of his worldview through these elaborately constructed photomontages, bringing into sharp focus his 'composition of elements which freely admit their artificiality whilst making every element a cultural sign'. These images exemplify an interior existence, as Hirsch has written of the contemporary photographer Lee Friedlander:

... he constructed an interior world that was not apparent until it was organised through his camera ... his belief that the self is the only object of verifiable knowledge, became the benchmark for photographers examining the inner landscape ...[65]

Barker-as-Houth also works within an 'interior world' that is its own referent, a landscape of objects that reflects a circuitous negotiation with reality. Sontag writes that 'photography turns people into objects that can be symbolically possessed',[66] and Barker-as-Houth turns objects into a way of possessing the past. There is something deeply atavistic about the conflation of the everyday object in his work, and the self-portrait in *ASIO* is another form of Barker 'photographing the past', using his photographer alter-ego to imprint images of his experiences through language. Philip Roth writes that 'Memories of the past are not memories of facts but memories of your imaginings of the facts',[67] and in *ASIO* Barker-as-Houth constructs powerful images around memories of childhood that are ephemeral, connected to space and earth and home:

> BARKER SPOKE OF HIS CHILDHOOD but mostly as sound ... with the fall of darkness deep-breathing locomotives slipping on the incline from their too-heavy freights ... the trucks elbowing one another as they clattered back ... over it the screaming of out-late girls ... under it the boy-shouts ... with dawn the plaintive convent bell disputing with the factory hooters calling women workers to the assembly line ... it was profoundly urban yet from his window he saw ancient trees ...[68]

Lynda Haverty Rugg writes of Walter Benjamin's autobiography as being structured in 'images – alluding to the theory that history is experienced in photographic flashes that conjoin and illuminate past and present experience'.[69] Benjamin's autobiography contains no photographs of the author's life; neither does Barker's except for the photograph on the dust jacket: Barker-as-Houth, fedora hat drawn down over the 'high forehead',[70] woollen coat collar turned up, hand drawing a *Gitanes* to the mouth, as if he has just stepped out of a Brassaï photograph of 1930s Paris by night. What Rugg writes of Benjamin's and Wolf's autobiographies can be applied equally to Barker's poetic self-portrait: 'they draw the photographic frame according to their own constructions, challenging the readings imposed on their texts and images (their self-construction) from without'.[71]

In an interview from 1983, the Russian film director Andrei Tarkovsky said

> We can express our feelings regarding the world around us either by poetic or by descriptive means. I prefer to express myself metaphorically. Let me stress: metaphorically, not symbolically. A symbol contains within itself a definite meaning, certain intellectual formula, while metaphor is an image. An image possessing the same distinguishing features as the world it represents. An image – as opposed to a symbol – is indefinite in meaning. One cannot speak of the infinite world by applying tools that are definite and finite. We can analyse the formula that constitutes a symbol, while metaphor is a being-within-itself, it's a monomial. It falls apart at any attempt of touching it.[72]

Barker-as-Houth: the photograph as 'being-within-itself', monomial, irreducible and beautifully excavated from the past. 'In the rehearsal room were faded photographs of dead boy scouts smiling for the camera . . .'[73]

7

Vintage Barker: New Writing in Old Bottles

James Hudson

While it is by now axiomatic to say that Howard Barker does not comfortably or conveniently fit into any generic categorization, dramatic movement or school, the reasons behind this are rarely made explicit beyond Barker's prescription that he would not join any club that would have him as a member. The notion of Barker as a maverick 'modernist theatre *auteur par excellence*',[1] eschewing prevailing dramatic fashions and treading an idiosyncratic path through the margins of recent dramatic history is now very well established. Nonetheless, it remains possible to locate Barker within particular dramaturgical genealogies, specifically considering his affiliation with two of Britain's national theatre institutions prior to the inauguration of The Wrestling School in 1988: the Royal Court in the 1970s and the Royal Shakespeare Company's Warehouse Company in the late seventies and early eighties. So while the notion of Barker-against-the-world is a fairly settled critical perspective, as an emerging dramatist, Barker was nonetheless the beneficiary of producing and commissioning structures that prioritized the playwright as the originary point of creative emanation. In the mid-nineties this approach, notoriously, would become an end in itself, with the phenomenon of 'New Writing' becoming the prevalent determinant of play development processes designed to turn youth, rawness and up-to-the-minute social relevance into marketable commodities.

New Writing is often credited in celebratory terms as being the force that transformed an etiolated UK theatre industry into a thriving, dynamic, and commercially successful culture during the 1990s, and is said to be characterized by 'the distinctiveness of the author's individual voice, the contemporary flavour of their language and themes, and sometimes by the provocative nature of its content'.[2] If this list of qualities seems to be too broad to usefully capture the stylistic dimensions of New Writing, this is because it is: as Aleks Sierz says, New Writing can only be properly understood as the articulation of these traits by 'newly arriving or young playwrights',[3] and it is this strain of 'newness' that proved particularly fruitful as play development and marketing strategies seized on both the novelty and the putative authenticity of the voice of the young writer as ways of valorizing the theatrical event. By the time the New Writing vogue took hold in the mid-1990s Barker had assumed principal directorship of The Wrestling School, all but formalizing his estrangement from the British mainstream theatre ecology, his plays by then rarely if ever produced by the major UK companies. While his formative years as a practising artist were occupied by engagement with British national and subsidized companies, since then he has stood apart significantly from his contemporaries: David Hare and Howard Brenton, for example, enjoyed similar career trajectories, being nurtured by the Royal Court and transitioning swiftly to the National after emerging from the alternative theatre movements of the sixties. It is there that the comparison ends, however, as Barker appears to have followed the path of most resistance: The National Theatre's belated production of *Scenes from an Execution* in 2012 emphasizes the size of the gulf that developed between Barker and the United Kingdom's prestige theatre companies.

Nonetheless, despite his exile from the system, Barker has remained an unabashed critic of the prevailing tendencies, theatrical fashions, and ruling orthodoxies he identifies as governing contemporary dramatic production, specifically on the British stage. Indeed, one crucial way to understand Barker's work is to appreciate how it is animated by resistance to the theatre forms that he considers institutionally sanctioned within the mainstream theatre ecology, and the degree to which his thinking, writing, and theatre practice attacks the presumptions of industry discourses that prioritize social relevance has been a key index of his aesthetic style. Ever since Barker has produced theatre theory, he has been remarkably consistent in his conscious opposition to the theatre of his time, whatever its politico-aesthetic determinations.

The critical document that not only proclaimed Barker's apprehension of radical new aesthetic sensibilities, but also foreshadowed his subsequent ideological deracination, *Arguments for a Theatre*, passionately inveighs against both the moribund paradigms of progressive dramaturgy practised by his contemporaries as well as the damaging influence of Brecht upon British theatrical culture.[4] More recently however, Barker's criticism has tended to elaborate upon the malfunctions of the subsidized mainstream in terms of its reliance on social-realism and Naturalism, which he regards as reductive and redundant aesthetic forms. It is perhaps not yet fully appreciated how Barker's Theatre of Catastrophe is specifically constructed in opposition to these forms, reversing their prescriptions to develop radical new articulations of theatrical expression: a process perfectly reflected in Bianca's observation in Barker's play *Women Beware Women* (1986): 'Catastrophe is also birth. Out of the ruins crawls the bloody thing, unrecognisable in the ripped rags of former life'.[5]

Barker's posture as a critic of these tendencies becomes particularly apt when juxtaposed with the paradigms and politics of dramatic production that New Writing initiatives emphasized during the 1990s. One of the New Writing phenomenon's principal effects was to flood the British stage with a species of dramatic representation that was the result of a deliberate reorientation of the material and discursive frameworks that supported producing structures at the time, where play development processes began to prioritize particular approaches and impose specific conditions on dramaturgical practice. Reframing the politics and aesthetics of New Writing within the compass of Barker's critique consequently allows us to situate his long career in relation to the landscape of a theatre culture predicated on a 'relentless search for novelty',[6] where, as Graham Saunders observes, 'the concerns of young people seem to be the *only thing* worth exploring dramatically'.[7]

Waves and brands

David Edgar has theorized a post-war narrative of New Writing consisting of three distinct generational 'waves' occurring prior to the 1990s boom, specifically identifying Barker as an example of a second wave playwright 'forged in the youth revolt of the late 1960s [for whom] the questions were much more aggressively political'.[8] Early in his career, Barker fell between stools in terms of critical categories, and the work produced between 1975 and 1985, characterized by Chris Megson as 'State of England' drama,[9] saw him crudely but perhaps understandably bracketed within the unofficial confederacy of Leftist writers at the time. Barker's early plays at the Royal Court were readily categorized as emanating from this familiar political position, that of the instinctively Leftist Royal Court coterie, and were represented onstage via the theatre's artistic director William Gaskill's patented distillation of Brechtian techniques. While the Royal Court went on to stage visiting productions of Barker's plays through the eighties from Joint Stock, Barker grew disaffected with the theatre, calling it a 'glorified landlord' with 'an obsession with social realism'.[10] In conclusively repudiating critical realism during the mid-eighties, Barker brought the curtain down on the predominantly conventional forms he had previously tarried with, while the lineaments of what he disparagingly called 'Critical Theatre',[11] clarity and verisimilitude, were to become consecrated in New Writing initiatives during the following decade as governing paradigms that signified the 'authenticity' of the playwright's voice.

New Writing is commonly credited as becoming dominant in two specific periods, with the English Stage Company's early artistic policy of instituting a 'Writers' Theatre' at the Royal Court often perceived as marking its inception as a deliberate strategy for the acquisition of new works, and the mid to late 1990s and early 2000s distinguished by the wholesale re-pivoting of the British theatrical ecology upon new play development and the discovery of new, specifically young, writers. When New Writing recrudesced in the mid-nineties it was again the Royal Court that was regarded as the pioneering force that ignited the boom years, with its daring programming of previously unproduced writers. While the Royal Court's former Artistic Director Graham Whybrow is credited for instituting a 'search for talent [. . .] strategically tracking first time writers in a very purposeful way',[12] Ruth Little and Emily McLoughlan point out that many of these writers were in fact 'opportunistically snapped up'[13] by the Royal Court fresh from their involvement with other theatres, so that they had already, in the words of Jacqueline Bolton, 'benefitted from varying degrees of dramaturgical support from companies that, for whatever reasons, were unable or unwilling to grant a production'.[14] Bolton has written elsewhere that

> The Royal Court's success during the mid-1990s played an instrumental role in the proliferation of literary departments established by theatres across London and the regions to discover, 'nurture' and produce new writing talent.[15]

Not confined to the Royal Court by any means, the total picture is of 'the emergence of a New Writing Industry',[16] a period of vigorous promotion of new writers by artistic directors at major venues and state-subsidized theatres that 'used their funding to stage a critical mass of productions'.[17] It amounted to a huge expansion in new plays being staged, as the figures cited by Aleks Sierz attest:

> Arts Council statistics show that, at the end of the 1980s, new plays formed less than ten per cent of staged work in subsidised theatres; by 1994–96 the figure was twenty per cent. Even more important has been box office success. In the late 1980s, new writing regularly attracted audiences of less than fifty per cent; by 1994, this figure was fifty-three percent; and by 1997, it was fifty-seven per cent, which means that new plays were outperforming adaptations, postwar revivals, translations, classics, and even Shakespeare.[18]

In Sierz's exposition New Writing is 'arguably more of an indicator of theatrical health than classical revivals, physical theatre or live art'.[19] While Sierz readily concedes that because it is 'now thoroughly commercialised, British theatre listens to and follows the money',[20] he rather attributes the upsurge of New Writing,

> more to unpredictable factors than to any deliberate policy by arts funding bodies. Such uncontrollable factors include: a previous period of routine aesthetic dullness which acted as a spur to an oppositional new wave; a sense of do-it-yourself possibility; the arrival of a maverick new artistic director; or a feeling of individual frustration among would-be writers.[21]

While Sierz was one of the very first scholars to lay a critical groundwork for New Writing, in his initial foray into the subject the adventurous tendencies of what he calls the 'brand' were transposed too securely over his most famous and enduring classification, with the bulk of playwrights categorized as the 'avant-garde of "in-yer-face" writers, whose streetsmart sensibility and formal innovations attacked the complacency of the British theatre scene, provoking controversy and encouraging imitators'.[22] What Sierz later recognized with admirable candour was that the provocative content of his 'experiential' theatre was increasingly being mediated by quite primitive dramaturgical means, and that this shock content was little more than a carnival mask worn over lumpen Naturalism. In a retrospective article of 2002 Sierz excoriated the rudimentary scope of the 'conservative and untheatrical'[23] aesthetic palette favoured by young writers:

> Most new British plays remained linear social-realist accounts of the experience of 'me and my mates'. They were timid plays and their timidity was expressed in small casts, small theatrical ambition, and an insular small-mindedness.[24]

The moment that best captures this inertia was perhaps when the judging panel (of which Sierz was a member) declined to award the Soho Theatre's 2002 Verity Bargate award for the best new play by a first-time writer on the basis that no play was considered good enough. Of course, what is described here is precisely what Barker has frequently decried: the aesthetic hegemony of limp realism on the British stage, where plays are anchored in truthful observations of social reality and the playwright is their objective and authentic witness.

This necessarily brief account of New Writing makes it evident that the phenomenon has effected a significant transformation in the way that creation and production in the theatre have been thought about and acted upon. The effects of New Writing extend far beyond economic performance, and obliges us to recognize it as a paradigm that has exerted a profound influence on the theatrical landscape, with identifiable criteria governing the selection and commissioning of material for production, the processes by which this material is developed, the particular aesthetic style to which this material conforms, and, implicitly, the values and attitudes to which it subscribes. Barker's contributions in theoretical writing and theatre work identify him as the self-appointed watchdog of a theatrical culture doggedly preoccupied with the aesthetic postulates that accrued around New Writing play development processes.

The dramaturgy of New Writing

While the phenomenon of New Writing has had its share of scholarly attention, its dimensions as a discursive force and an institutional apparatus have perhaps not yet properly been appreciated. Harry Derbyshire describes Arts Council policy that 'upheld new writing as an ideal . . . making its encouragement a financial necessity for theatres', requiring new frameworks to be established in order to provide 'systematic encouragement'[25] to new writers. The role of the literary manager has been, and continues to be, one of the most important elements within the system of New Writing.

Mary Luckhurst identifies the professionalization of this role and its subsequent proliferation within the UK theatre ecology as being instrumental in making seismic alterations to the fabric of recent theatre production. The strategies of literary management, a profession which Luckhurst describes as enacting 'a silent revolution in the management of play reading and play selection',[26] coincided with the fashion for unearthing young and untested writers at this time. With the dual monetary success of New Writing in terms of increased box office receipts and its useful ability for attracting funding, Bolton describes it as becoming a 'core activity' by the turn of the millennium:

> As more money became available for new writing, an increase in literary management appointments at subsidised theatres and companies was accompanied by a development of the literary manager's remit from the reading and reporting on scripts to the practical, hands-on development of plays and potential playwrights. Scratch nights, workshops, writers' groups, out-reach placements, festivals, competitions, attachments: a remarkable number of access points were initiated by literary managers in order to attract and encourage, or 'discover' and 'nurture', a new generation of playwrights.[27]

It is not, therefore, merely that the neophyte New Writing dramatist was young; it is more that they were inducted into the industry at a time when commissioning and development processes were becoming increasingly refined and specialized, with young playwrights inculcated by literary managers into generating work in specific ways. In effect, Bolton argues, 'contemporary literary management cultures . . . functioned to provisionally stake out and even delimit the imaginative parameters of new and emerging playwrights'.[28] Consequently, the privileging of the 'youthful' 'authentic' voice of the individual playwright inaugurated an era of dramatic work where truthful observations of particular experiences of social reality began to dominate the stage because New Writing dramatists were encouraged to describe their witness of their immediate social circumstances. In this sense New Writing almost represents a system of cultural patronage. It is no secret that playwrights have frequently been championed and selected less for their imaginative capabilities than for their autobiographical credentials, a tendency perfectly crystallized in Max Stafford-Clark's euphoria in receiving the 15-year-old Andrea Dunbar's first play *The Arbor* (1980) written in green ink in a school exercise book.[29] The foundational principles of New Writing were orchestrated around providing a 'clean filter' for the dispensation of this 'authentic' voice of the young writer, something that has emerged via the Stafford-Clarkean objective for playwrights to be the journalists of their time, representing the individual experiences of their own social milieus as honestly as possible, all the way through to a potentially exploitative exoticization where the playwright is recruited primarily as an auto-ethnographer. In an interview with Bolton, Graham Whybrow encapsulates this tendency: 'you're not saying this is a great piece of art, it's not particularly imaginative or adventurous or daring or innovative, but [rather] I've never seen a play about third generation Estonian, mini-cab office in Shepherd's Bush before'.[30] The rise of the verbatim play over the previous decade and a half is a testament to the renewed expectation for drama to manifest authenticity; what is significant about New Writing is the conventionality and prescriptiveness of the dramaturgical means chosen as the vehicle for its investment in the real.

Dramaturg David Lane has noted that the lexicons and methodologies adopted during play-development processes by the New Writing industry cleave to what are surprisingly very orthodox and dogmatic conceptions of theatrical representation, an observation not without a certain irony considering the talismanic posture of provocation often attributed to it:

> The common terminology on offer when developing a play text takes its lead from the realm of psychological realism, where phrases such as character, narrative, language, locations and plot carry particular associations. They are part of a broader understanding of theatre where stories are linear, characters are three-dimensional; dramatic action and therefore plot structure, has a basis in causality; spoken text takes the form of conversations between characters; and locations are part of the material world we recognise in everyday life.[31]

The theoretical co-ordinates described here – mimetic, Aristotelian, accessibly naturalistic – belong to a set of practices that Barker has frequently castigated as impoverished, redundant and even corrupting. It is instructive to note that there is little to differentiate the form of drama that Lane describes above from a reach-me-down Naturalism that adheres to the standard grammar of most television and film. Indeed it might be argued instead that the feature that allows for such discrimination is in fact not the dramaturgical modality of the piece per se but is instead the discursive framing that authenticates the product as a cultural artefact invested with particular significance: an emanation of the young, the vital, the provocative. When contrasted with an artist like Barker, who has always retained an aspiration to push form to its limits, there is perhaps something singularly unambitious at the heart of the New Writing initiative.

This apprehension allows for a few reflections upon how this relates to the aesthetic project that has occupied Barker since the development of the Theatre of Catastrophe. In readjusting his strategies and intentions, Barker deliberately turned his back on the kind of prevailing dramatic orthodoxies that might make his plays accessible to the major stages of Britain, repudiating humanism, deviating from critical realism and presenting countervailing tendencies to traditions rooted in Brecht or Stanislavski. The case is put in *Arguments* that the encroaching commodification and utilitarianism of theatre, and the audience's implied consent to the clichéd dramaturgy used in the manufacture of its populist and propagandist forms, has fettered the capacity for imagination. While these sentiments were advanced in Barker's theoretical work in the eighties, they clearly foreshadow developments in the UK theatre ecology stimulated by New Writing initiatives. Jack Bradley, former literary manager at the National Theatre, has described the 1994–5 season of plays for two-week runs at the Royal Court Upstairs, many of which were developed at the NT studio, as 'stack 'em high, sell 'em cheap'.[32] New plays produced at the Court in the mid-nineties became part of a recognizable 'brand' that shared distinctive characteristics: stories of dissolute and often violent youth, frequently psychologically unstable, who are the habitués of a contemporary urban milieu, authored (and, hence, *authorized*) by playwrights marketed as 'discoveries'. Barker's aesthetic project has increasingly been calibrated towards resisting the kind of commodification emblematic of New Writing ventures, which we might think of as a refusal of assent to the comprehensive reductivities of contemporary society and theatre.

While Barker's theatre shuns both the liberal-democratic political status quo of the empirical world and any notions of progressive or emancipatory ideological projects which might achieve its transformation, Barker's counter-naturalist depictions are subversive along the Adornian lines of 'autonomous art'. According to Theodor Adorno, mass culture's manifestation as a 'culture industry' has pressed artistic production into the service of a consumer capitalism that 'impresses the same stamp on everything'.[33] Against this hegemonic homogenization, it is aesthetics *itself* which constitutes a site of resistance, and in Barker this takes the form of countermeasures against naturalist representation, and by extension, 'the pressures of the market with its insatiable demands for more of the same'.[34] Against a backdrop of theatre-making policies that understand 'authenticity' as synonymous with personal experience and its truthful testimony, Barker's notion is to stimulate and reawaken the spectator's hitherto atrophied capacity for imagination: 'Writing now has to engage with what is not seen (i.e. the imagination) because real life is annexed, reproduced, soporific [...] Everything is possessed except the imagination'.[35]

Barker imagines the Theatre of Catastrophe as a manifestly non-mimetic mode, a species of drama which is productive rather than reflective, 'where theatre is emphatically not the world but a speculation upon it'.[36] The key objection of this non-mimetic drama is to the widespread and automatic conflation of theatre with direct social experience as the norm which governs most theatre production. For Barker this application is manifestly wrong, as 'the condition of witnessing drama [...] takes moral speculation, and not social imitation, as its unfaltering objective'.[37] Rather than assembling a representation of reality providing a recognizable equivalence to lived experience, Barker's Catastrophism refuses to depict anything that might replicate or simulate the 'reality' of our social milieu, withholding recognizable co-ordinates in staging, language and character presentation. Barker's work abhors the quotidian social world as irrelevant to its deeper concerns, and correspondingly avoids the tautologous re-inscription of immanent social reality.

In a paper entitled 'On Naturalism and Its Pretensions' (2007), Barker presents a critique of 'the industrial scale of naturalist drama'[38] that elaborates upon the principles established in *Arguments for a Theatre* (1997), castigating it as 'the official art of late democratic capitalism'[39] and criticizing the lack of imaginative integrity in an ersatz representational form predicated on accessibility and 'unambiguous meanings, usually of a socio-critical kind'.[40] For Barker the association of the naturalistic form with putatively positive values such as 'truthfulness' and 'accessibility' is inseparable from its functional, if not baldly utilitarian quality. These remarks see an extension to Barker's previous critique, where in the United Kingdom the post-1968 Brechtian drive towards enlightening and educative theatre is increasingly seen to be mediated through plays with contemporary relevance via socio-critical Naturalism. This is a theatre that Barker deplores as complacent in the certitude of its liberal attitudes, with specific companies attacked unsparingly: 'the ambitions of the English Stage Company and its priggish child, the Joint Stock Theatre group, seemed to [Barker] patronising, condescending, patrician in effect'.[41] In *A Style and Its Origins* (2007), Barker writing as Eduardo Houth describes 'a calcified but self-perpetuating system which justified itself by its posture of critique but was in effect a redundant, decayed aesthetic ... Barker himself thought such a theatre was sustained only by a Soviet-style bureaucracy and an ingrained anti-intellectualism'.[42] Barker later embroidered this criticism in 2009, with remarks published in the *Daily Telegraph* that the Arts Council of Great Britain was possessed of 'a socio-political agenda which is purely Stalinist'.[43] At first glance this remark might be an allusion to Barker's conception of the dominant aesthetic of watered-down Naturalism representing a cod-Zhadanovian socialist-realism, but in fact the statement is far blunter, depicting the Arts Council as an arm of the state engaged in remedial social engineering to compensate for its failed educational programmes. Barker/Houth alludes to this tendency in *A Style and Its Origins*: 'as society became less effectively educated, it invested more and more in educational initiatives so that the theatre was drawn deeper into rackets of social amelioration.[44] The wider critique intended here is that the Arts Council makes notions such as 'use', 'relevance' and perceived social benefit its dominant calculus in determining the disbursement of funding, proclivities which of course consign an aesthetic predicated on deliberately withholding these features to oblivion (as threatened to be the case when the Arts Council cut the grant for The Wrestling School in 2007).

While we may be used to Barker as a scourge of liberal pieties, there remain salient parallels between his condemnation of the liberal 'agenda' and theatremaking trends and policies that inhered in the heyday of New Writing. David Edgar has mused about the plays of the period being redolent of 'New Labour's cultural instrumentalism – the idea of the arts as a branch of the community cohesion industry';[45] and, writing in 2006, Mary Luckhurst suggested that industry professionals had concerns over play development culture, for some time perceiving 'the rise of literary mangers and dramaturgs as little other than an unstoppable tide of Blairite bureaucrats who implement a particular New Labour pedagogy, driven by a missionary zeal for what they believe is the moral and political enlightenment of their theatre audiences'.[46]

Legacy

Another significant motif that characterized the new drama of the nineties was the treatment of politics on the British stage, where, as Graham Saunders has observed, 'there appeared to be a disengagement and dismantlement from recognisable forms of political engagement by the new generation of young dramatists'.[47] Most noticeable was the falling of the various forms of post-1968 political theatre into desuetude: forms which, by and large, were historicized, analytical, class-based and consciousness-raising. New theatrical orthodoxies swiftly eclipsed these tendencies. Barker's orientation away from a politically committed theatre was a precursor to the prevailing mood of a broad and decisive shift away from identifiably Leftist forms of theatrical expression on the British stage; indeed, Barker had already divested himself of conventional ideological partisanship both in his public persona and his plays by a considerable span of time before subsidized theatre institutions shifted their political optic. While Barker's sternest reprove in *Arguments for a Theatre* is of a British theatre dominated by adherence to Brechtian models and addicted to political panhandling, a gradual reversal saw these tendencies diminish, however much they could have been considered genuinely pre-eminent representational forms in the first instance. However, while by the mid-1990s specific instances of plays that trafficked in recognizably progressive or Leftist tropes became increasingly rare, it has been well established that the drama of the 'Thatcher's Children' cohort was the manifestation of a response to particular ideological developments: globalization, rampant consumerism, the vagaries of neoliberal economic hegemony as an enculturing project. Evidently, Barker's theatre anticipated this discursive shift, presaging the replacement of a theatre of ideological persuasion with a theatre that appeals to corporeal sensation, offering no political frameworks as support or aspiration to its characters. Nonetheless, if Barker foresaw a theatre culture shorn of socialist commitment, while he may have heralded it, he was not its beneficiary; the majority of New Writing was anchored in a type of Naturalism to which Barker professed an allergic reaction as severe as his antipathy to Brecht.

The resulting narrative of a new generation of writers comprising the likes of Mark Ravenhill, Jez Butterworth, Anthony Neilson and Martin McDonagh is now very well-limbed, as is the critical focus that often places particular emphasis on violent content and copious profanity as indexical of their topicality. Ken Urban has argued that 'Barker's essays calling for a "theatre of catastrophe" clearly exert a huge impact on this generation,'[48] though it is an influence perhaps more evident in some of the less enduring nomenclature applied to the group of playwrights than in an examination of their formal elements. These 'New Brutalist', or 'Neo-Nihilist' dramatists, who indulged in depicting various types of stage violence, have been thought to owe inspiration to Barker's prosecution of an aesthetic that unsparingly explores pain, violence and trauma, with the human body a site of dereliction to be frequently despoiled and mutilated, often graphically exposed to acts of extreme and visceral brutality. Early in his career Barker was dubbed a 'New Jacobean',[49] and yet even as Urban argues for Barker's influence upon these playwrights, he concedes that 'some [Ravenhill and Penhall] held onto certain components of critical realism in their work', while 'other "Nihilists" [Butterworth and McDonagh] mimicked film and TV'.[50] Fundamentally, while the master-signifier 'in-yer-face' announced visceral spectacle and a generalized array of shock tactics as the radical gesture that defined the theatre of this period, the epithet often obscured the lack of dramaturgical innovation at the level of representational aesthetics chosen as the vehicle for these topics. Indeed, there is little to differentiate much of the output cultivated by this group of writers from the aesthetic precepts used in New Writing initiatives, with its vocabularies and methodologies of psychological realism, linearity of narrative and social relevance. It is no small irony to note that many of the signatures of Barker's aesthetic project – the transcendence of traditional dramatic categories, innovation and experimentation in form, the permanent contestation with the constraints of Naturalism – are primarily associated with the 'new', the avant-garde and the modern. Yet in the context of the New Writing boom, Barker became bracketed as a mature writer, while the fairly orthodox and conventional characteristics of the drama produced at places like the Royal Court, the Bush, the Hampstead and the Soho was instead granted the sobriquet 'new'. As Sanja Nikčević writes, the so-called in-yer-face plays 'brought some novelty on a topical level, but did not change any previous practised theatrical convention, mainly because realistic and naturalist procedures are usually sustained'.[51] It is probably true that Sierz's original classification overemphasized the content and topics of the plays of these writers at the expense of a truly incisive examination of the dramaturgical workings that underpinned them, and even then it is difficult to credit the articulation and treatment of violence by these playwrights with anything like the sensitivity of Barker's approach. It is difficult to argue with Graham Saunders' assessment that this tranche of plays are characterized by 'the voyeuristic glamourisation of violence, rather than its analysis'.[52]

Nonetheless, if there is a straightforward relationship between Barker and New Writing, it is indubitably in terms of 'legacy'. If the sensationalist strategies deployed by in-yer-face writers constitute a vulgar appropriation of Barker's recourse to the extremities of experience, it has become a critical commonplace to identify Barker as an influence upon Sarah Kane. Frequently described as 'catastrophic', Kane's theatre appears to share the same transgressive theatricality favoured by Barker; Kane's liking for Barker's work is very well known, and her famous remark that Barker was 'the Shakespeare of our age'[53] is instructive as it is salutary, as what it implies, apart from high esteem, is a deficit of contemporaneity. The yoking of Barker with Shakespeare implies a reverential distance, an appreciation of a monumental figure creating precedents, pioneering territory and establishing foundations, rather than one with whom one shares an immanent commune, a sense of participating in the same process, in the same world, at the same time. Kane is perhaps the monolithic figure in the New Writing boom, and it is of course the first production of *Blasted* that is most often identified as the epochal moment that convinced companies that the programming of new plays by unknown writers was a policy worth pursuing. There are many points of contact between Kane and Barker's work: the orchestration of interpenetrating mutilations in Kane's *Cleansed* seem to have their echo in the systematic 'pruning' of Helen's limbs in Barker's *The Bite of the Night*, even reverberating with Bradshaw's progressive reassembling of her husband's scattered remains in *Victory*. The fugue states of subjectivity that characterize Kane's *Crave* and *4.48 Psychosis* find their complement in the restless search for the self that preoccupies so many of Barker's protagonists. Dan Rebellato observes that the most evident hallmarks of Barker's influence upon Kane are detectable in their shared tendency to lace texts with stage directions that are deliberately challenging, perhaps even to the point of unperformability.⁵⁴ In both Barker and Kane, strategies are deliberately deployed to push theatrical representation beyond what is practically and materially possible to such a degree that their theatre resists assimilation by Naturalism's hegemonizing tendencies. Karoline Gritzner calls this collocation between Barker and Kane a 'New Expressionism', and writes that

> Kane's work, manifestly influenced by Barker in terms of the treatment of challenging subject matter and the suspension of readily available meaning, provides theatricalisations of subjectivity that embrace and transform the ostensibly postmodernist principles of uncertainty, irrationality and ambiguity into formal categories without, however, suggesting a compliance with the cultural assumptions underlying late capitalism.⁵⁵

Perhaps the fundamental point of differentiation between Kane and peers is that, as Graham Saunders suggests, 'the plays by Ravenhill and his contemporaries sometimes become uncomfortably close to – the actual point of complicity with – the very aspects of globalisation and consumer capitalism that they set out to critique'.⁵⁶ If sensationalistic depictions of violence are recuperated by the system that they purportedly attack, neither, as Barker has frequently maintained, is Naturalism up to the job of representing or resisting a dynamic and globalized world. Perhaps it is this attitude of resistance that ensures that Barker, while an artist of a certain vintage, will always be 'new'. That is the lot of a figure engaged in the relentless pluralizing and decapitalizing of all the hitherto great concepts, first principles and fundamental axioms that the dramatic tradition has produced.

8

Howard Barker and the Return of Religion

Peter A. Groves

God's silence is too terrible for men.

Howard Barker[1]

An interest in spirituality and theology is clearly perceivable in the plays and dramatic theory of Howard Barker, with Barker himself observing in 2005 that his '*art of theatre* has many of the characteristics of a religion'.[2] Barker's sustained engagement with religious subject matter begins in the mid-1980s when his theatre engages increasingly with European myth and history, leading to encounters with the great Abrahamic monotheistic religions of Judaism, Christianity and Islam. This chapter reflects on some of Barker's radical excavations of moments in Europe's spiritual heritage and how the deconstruction of monotheistic ideas and narratives inform the tragic and atheistic spirituality that Barker offers in its place. Christian clerical characters: priests, monks, popes and prophets, feature in many of his texts. These characters, forced into rigorous self-examination and redefinition by the catastrophe of war or violent social upheaval, emerge (usually momentarily) from the ashes of orthodox Christianity, with a more existential spirituality. A key feature of Barker's spirituality is that conventional morality is unravelled and sexual ecstasy becomes a new and dominant component. Barker defines the sacred as 'the unconscious and the instinctual', 'the uneducated aspect of human nature', and when reflecting on where it has 'migrated to' in contemporary society, he suggests, 'Is it in private life, in what is effectively a religion of sexuality?'³ In order to try and construct what could tentatively be described as the theology of his work, I will examine the influence of sexuality and its interrelationship with religious concepts in Barker's drama.

Particularly significant in this construction are the ideas of a medieval German Dominican friar, Meister Eckhart (c. 1260–c. 1328), who Barker intriguingly refers to as his 'theologian', despite describing himself as 'probably' an atheist.⁴ A study of the appropriation and transformation of Eckhart's concepts of 'the one' and 'detachment', along with other monotheistic concepts and their fusion with a religion of sexuality, offers a potential basis for speculating on the theology of Barker's tragic theatre.

Barker and *Genesis*: Return to the beginning

In Barker's 1978 play *The Love of a Good Man*, set in Passchendaele two years after the end of the First World War, a location described by a character in the play as 'not ground so much as flesh', a Bishop is presiding over the graves of the many dead. He becomes overwhelmed by the horror of so much suffering, leading him to divert from a more traditional sermon to claim that 'God is so very fond of pain'.⁵ The Bishop's attempt to understand why his God must have allowed so much agony to occur during the war does not lead him to posit atheism, but instead he responds with a provocative question, 'I do not deny the existence of the person God. I merely ask what sort of character He has.'⁶ This response to suffering and the trials of existence is adopted by a number of characters in subsequent Barker plays: rather than denying God's existence they instead choose to reformulate and re-imagine the personality of the divine. The result is that their idea of 'God' seems to function as a poetic projection of the complexity and suffering of human existence, leading them away from orthodox monotheism's notion of an ethical God. This is very much in line with Barker's theatrical project, which aims to create 'moral confusion in the audience'.[7] Barker argues that the limitations of the ethical nature of the Christian God are problematic because He fails to encompass all of human experience, 'We have never really come to terms with the Christian god, because he has repudiated malice, it is not part of his will.'[8] Instead Barker gravitates towards pagan and early Jewish traditions that present gods that partially correspond to negative aspects of existence, 'we know the Greek gods were without conscience, that the Old Testament God was jealous and vindictive'.[9]

For this reason Barker is mainly inspired by ancient and ethically problematic conceptions of divinity and their associated myths and literature, 'the great narratives of antiquity – almost entirely tragic in character – possess moral ambiguities.'[10] When looking at the influence of the Hebrew Bible on Barker's drama it is interesting to note that the five narratives he selects, with one exception, come from the book of *Genesis*.[11] There is general consensus among biblical scholars that *Genesis* is composed primarily of three sources.[12] The earliest sections of *Genesis* comprise two contrasting traditions, the Priestly or 'P' source and the Yahwehist or 'J' source. The Elohist or 'E' tradition begins later with Abraham.[13] Ronald Hendel summarizes the differences between the two sources that provide diverse strands from the creation myths onwards, 'P's is a world – and a narrative – of clarity, order, and nested hierarchy. J's is a world of emotions, ambiguity, and ethical complexity. P portrays a transcendental God, a cosmic deity, while J portrays a deity with the human traits of regret, anger, compassion, and delight.'[14] Barker's description of the Old Testament God as 'jealous and vindictive' would seem to be referring to the anthropomorphic and more ethically ambiguous god of the J tradition and it is this idea of the divine that influences Barker's drama, and probably the reason why *Genesis* is where he looks for inspiration. This anthropomorphic conception of God occurs not only through language in Barker's theatre, but also more directly via characterization, either in the form of God himself or an angel.[15]

Christianity and Islam in *The Castle*

Barker's 1985 play *The Castle* offers an example of characters creating new ideas of God that deviate from orthodox monotheism. The play opens with the protagonist Stucley, a knight returning from the crusades, horrified to discover that his estate has been taken over by women, and his wife, Ann, has entered into a relationship with the new religious and spiritual authority, a witch called Skinner. Deeply affected by this challenge to his faith, we are presented with another Barker character concluding that God must delight in causing human suffering, 'Oh, Lord and Master of Cruelty, who has no shred of mercy for thy servants, I worship Thee!'[16] During the crusades, Stucley's love for Ann gave his life meaning among the chaos of war and his commitment to her was absolute, 'I who jumped in every pond of murder kept this one thing pure in my head.'[17] As Charles Lamb observes, Stucley's 'exaggerated veneration of women, within the predominantly medieval context of the play, strongly accords with the chivalric "courtly love" phenomenon, the secular counterpart of the cult of the Virgin Mary'.[18] Ann, therefore, in the mind of Stucley is a fusion of religious faith and sexual desire, so her infidelity with the female pagan usurper of his land understandably derails his core beliefs. It is unsurprising then that when his trauma finally leads to the formation of a new and heretical version of Christianity, it is one that engages deeply with the suffering and ecstasy of sexual experience. Having examined the gospels, Stucley highlights an omission that for him is conspicuous by its absence, 'Christ's cock', and he is convinced that a deity who has experienced 'neither pain nor ecstasy' in sexual encounters is of no use to mortal man.[19]

The medieval setting of the play, a period when Christianity influenced most aspects of society, adds to the heretical charge of this exclamation. Michel Foucault argues that Christianity, in contrast to pagan attitudes, associated the sexual act with 'evil, sin, the Fall and death' and in terms of permitted sexual relationships 'drew the line at monogamous marriage' and 'strictly excluded' same-sex relationships.[20] Stucley recounts a spiritual crisis while in Asia and his expression of what seem to be sexual feelings towards Christ strikes at and troubles the core of Christianity's repression of sexuality, 'longing to know Him, to have some sense of Him, to put my finger into Christ and feel His heat, and what pained me, what agonised me I assure you, was not the absence of a face but His castration'.[21] Stucley's engagement with sexual ecstasy could have led to a freer spirituality, as expressed by the pagan women, but in its insular male bias leads to something even more oppressive than medieval patriarchal Christianity, with obvious phallocentric associations, 'Gospel of the Christ Erect!'[22] Lamb notes how the metaphysical construction is mirrored by the physical development of the castle, 'Both erections – physical and theological – go together to form a system of total psychological and physical domination.'[23] However, for Barkerian characters in later plays, spiritual crisis, with orthodox religion destabilized by sexual desire, will lead to new, mystical and ecstatic spiritualities that transcend conventional morality and ideology rather than intensify it. This process begins when Barker moves away from a socialist political approach to theatre from 1986 onwards, to instead embrace a new form of tragic theatre in 1988 that regards 'all ideology as the enemy'.[24]

As well as the Christianity of Stucley and the paganism of Skinner, a third religious position is suggested in the captured Islamic engineer Krak. He is the most considered and prominent Islamic character in Barker's theatre and although his intention is to destroy his captors through the building of a castle that invites attack, he is not completely unsympathetic because of the terrible atrocities the Christian crusaders enacted on his family.[25] Barker invokes in Krak a particular aspect of Islamic spirituality: the importance of mathematics. Seyyed Hossein Nasr observes that in Islam, 'algebra, geometry, and arithmetic were to possess a contemplative, spiritual, and intellectual aspect, as well as that practical and purely rational aspect, (. . .) developed by the later Western science'.[26] In an interview carried out during the writing of this play, Barker explains that he is approaching 'the issue of mayhem in science by showing the alienation of the spirit of inquiry from the needs of community.'[27] Krak, therefore, represents a negative, excessively rational, and alienated mathematical worldview: presenting a critique of European science rather than Islamic mathematics; and this rationalism is challenged and eventually disordered by female sexuality, 'Where's cunt's geometry? The thing has got no angles! And no measure, neither width nor depth, how can you trust what has no measurements?'[28] It is Ann's seduction of Krak that is finally able to unsettle his rigid belief system, while she remains beyond all ideologies: 'Ann steadfastly refuses to sacrifice any of her instinctive desires in the interests of ideology or even of sparing others pain.'[29] Krak functions both as the religious other to the Christian (and pagan) characters, and as an expression of scientific rationalism, equated with military technology and war due to his design of the castle.

Apocalypse and rebirth in *The Europeans*

One has heard talk of many theatres existing, and of many forms, as if theatres tolerated one another. The fact is that theatres annihilate one another as all religions annihilate one another. Is this because theatre is a religion?[30]

This quotation offers an intriguing insight into how Barker views both religions and theatres and how, for him, there is a clear relationship between the two human phenomena: they are both founded on difference and opposition. This mutually exclusive notion of religion is very much within the tradition of Abrahamic monotheism founded on the principle that only one God should be worshipped to the exclusion of all others, as set out clearly in the first of the Ten Commandments, 'You must have no other god besides me.'[31] The historically exclusive and oppositional nature of monotheistic religions defines the backdrop of Barker's play *The Europeans* (1990), in which he imaginatively explores the aftermath of the 1683 Battle of Vienna, where Christendom was severely tested by the threatened incursion of the Islamic Ottoman Empire.[32]

The protagonist is General Starhemberg, whose ruthless perseverance in the face of overwhelming odds saved Vienna from the siege. *The Europeans*, according to Barker, is the first Theatre of Catastrophe play, and in both form and content it expresses the ideas and approach of this new form of tragic drama.[33] In his 1989 manifesto *Arguments for a Theatre*, Barker asserts that in the reception of his plays, difference and division should be encouraged over unity, 'The audience is divided and goes home disturbed or amazed', offering a challenge to what Barker defines as the humanist theatre's preference for consensus and cohesion in the dramatic experience, 'We all really agree / When we laugh we are together.'[34] When considering his plays from this period, Barker suggests that there are perhaps connections with the subject matter of these plays and the religious tensions of the twenty-first century, 'the rise of fundamentalism in east and west [and] the religious war that's upon us. [...] I wrote several plays about Islam's conflict with Europe long before all this started.'[35] Unlike Krak, who is one of the main characters in *The Castle*, the Islamic characters in *The Europeans* remain largely offstage and are for the most part reported and interpreted by the Europeans, rather than presented directly to the audience. In one particularly telling example, the play's central characters reflect on the expression seen on the dying severed head of an executed Islamic soldier, trying to imagine what he is experiencing. The Turkish soldier is considered by the Europeans but is unable to respond, highlighting the play's avoidance of dialogue with the cultural otherness of the Ottomans. The only Islamic character to speak in the drama is a Turkish official Jemal, who in an exchange with Starhemberg in the final scene seems to be questioning the play's somewhat dubious and stereotypical portrayal of the Turkish army, 'You persist in identifying me with all atrocity which is –' before being cut off by Starhemberg, whose response is perhaps reassuring the audience that references to Turkish cruelty are mainly employed in order to question the ethical principles of the Europeans, 'No, no, I was merely being philosophical...'[36] The play therefore adopts an insular and subjective focus on the Christian experience in its quest to excavate a European spiritual identity.

In *The Europeans* there is sustained engagement with two particularly powerful and related tropes of Christianity, whose interrelationship gives the Theatre of Catastrophe its distinct form. The first of these is Christian eschatology, the belief that history is moving towards an apocalypse and that from this chaos a new divine order will emerge.[37] Philosopher John Gray argues that this idea is so ingrained in the European mind that, 'Secular myths reproduce the narrative form of Christian apocalyptic', constructing a model where they believe conflict will ultimately lead to harmony, as in the Marxist belief that revolution will give birth to a utopian communist society.[38] Although the emergence of the Theatre of Catastrophe is informed by Barker's rejection of socialist ideology, the influence of Christianity and/or Marxism is still apparent in his positing of a theatre that sees a benefit in catastrophic events cleansing society of traditional beliefs. However, instead of a transformation of society Barker focuses on a spiritual transformation of the individual. This leads to the second Christian trope, which the philosopher Slavoj Žižek's finds particularly valuable to culture, 'What Christianity did, in a religiously mystified form, is give us the idea of rebirth. Against the pagan notion of destiny, Christianity offered the possibility of a radical opening, that we can find a zero point and clear the table.'[39]

Barker's *The Europeans* is preoccupied with the idea of rebirth and it is the rise of a new self from cultural dislocation that the play proposes. The primary visionary of this new individualism is Starhemberg, whose conception of a new art reflects this belief in the possibility of rebirth: 'I need an art that will plummet through the floor of consciousness and free the unborn self (. . .) I want to make a new man and a new woman but only from the pieces of the old.'[40] The Christian context of the play highlights the religious origins of these tropes and this is particularly exemplified in Starhemberg's collaborator, the Priest Orphuls. The threat posed by death and Islamic culture has left Orphuls open to the possibility of complete alteration, 'Every morning when we awoke, we felt the possibility of **utter transformation**, rising with the sun.'[41] Orphuls' spirituality shifts from orthodoxy towards what could be described as a religion of sexuality, where ecstasy fills the void created by God's absence. This is succinctly expressed in an exchange with his new lover Susannah:

Orphuls This is not Hell.
Susannah Not Hell. What's Hell, then?
Orphuls Absence.
Susannah I assure you this is absence.
Orphuls Of God. (*Pause*)
Susannah Take me to the café. You said you would, for showing you God's absence...[42]

The influence of Christianity on Barker's drama helps to explain its essential difference from the original Greek model of tragedy. Whereas Attic tragedy marks the limits of human order by asserting divine destiny over the hubristic subject, Barker's new form of tragedy refuses closure in favour of the continual rebirth of the individual as a response to the apocalypse. It is the influence of Christianity that makes Barker's Theatre of Catastrophe a distinct sub-genre of tragedy. As well as the influence of these Christian tropes, a spiritual response to the hell that is the absence of God, as it is described by Orphuls, relates to Barker's description of 'his theologian', Meister Eckhart: 'who knew God was not there and made faith from His absence'.[43]

Meister Eckhart

Although Barker makes only a brief direct reference to Meister Eckhart, it is possible to find evidence of his influence elsewhere on his writings. Eckhart's mystical approach to Christianity strives to achieve oneness with God in a process known as *apophatic* or negative theology. According to the medieval scholar Oliver Davies, *apophatic* theology 'aims specifically to transcend images and to enter the "darkness" and the "nothingness" of the Godhead itself in a journey which leads the soul to the shedding of all that is superfluous, contrary or unequal to God as he is in his essential Being.'[44] Eckhart uses both the terms 'Godhead' and 'the One' to describe the true nature of the divine, and it is the goal of Eckhartian mysticism to move spiritually beyond multiplicity and into this oneness. However, Eckhart's assertion of the extent to which God and the soul of man are able to become one comes dangerously close to removing any sense of difference between man and God, 'We shall all be transformed totally into God and changed into him. [. . .] I am so changed into him that he makes me his one existence, and not just similar. By the living God it is true that there is no distinction there.'[45] By achieving this state of oneness the Eckhartian mystic enters the eternal now, the realm of the Godhead, and thus exists in an infinite present, 'He dwells in a single now which is in all time and unceasingly new.'[46] Within this 'now' he is able to 'live without why', in that, once union with the Godhead is achieved, questions of purpose become irrelevant, as the pressure of the past and future dissolve in the eternal conceptual nothingness of the Godhead.

Eckhart is keen to emphasize that any suggestion of self-directed purpose, even when it is supposedly 'for God', is to some extent self-conscious and not truly living 'without why' and therefore not a complete union with the Godhead in the now. The pathway towards this state of oneness involves one of Eckhart's most famous and influential concepts, 'detachment'. For Eckhart the approach of detachment is the closest way in which man can achieve a sense of divinity, 'should a man wish to become like to God, insofar as a creature can have any likeness with God, then this can only come about through detachment'.[47] He concludes that detachment is the highest virtue because all other virtues, including love, connect us to earthly things and human suffering, whereas, 'detachment leads me to where I am receptive to nothing except God [. . .] detachment approaches so closely to nothingness that there can be nothing between perfect detachment and nothingness'.[48] Therefore, only via detachment can we enter into the void beyond form, the One.

The important concepts in Eckhartian theology of 'the One', 'detachment' and living in the now 'without why' are particularly useful when attempting to trace the underlying theology of Barker's work. However, they are not always immediately apparent, and therefore require a degree of extrapolation. This is probably due to their necessary transformation from Christian theology into Barker's atheistic mode of thought, an atheism that Barker then reads back into Eckhart's theology. The suggestion that Eckhart's mysticism stems, in fact, from an absence of God is not unique to Barker. Schopenhauer, who defined Eckhart as 'the father of German Mysticism', argues that, 'We see all religions at their highest point end in mysticism and mysteries, that is to say, in darkness and veiled obscurity. These really indicate merely a blank spot for knowledge, the point where all knowledge necessarily ceases.'[49] A mystical theology that aims to move beyond images and forms is a useful model for Barker's theatre in its desire to dismantle and move beyond the concepts that construct normative ideology.

The One

Following this identification of *apophaticism* in his writings, another significant Eckhartian concept to be found in Barker is the One, a term he uses in the title of *Death, The One and the Art of Theatre*. This text is a series of thoughts on tragedy and desire, expressed in short poetic sections and aphorisms. With regard to tragedy, the central argument of this text can be partially summed up by this extract: 'Very great plays yield no meanings. They move like the mouths of the dead on the banks of the Styx. "Meaningful" plays are soiled/spoiled by their meanings. What is the meaning of death?'[50] This criticism of 'meaningful' plays is a continuation of Barker's now long standing confrontation with rational humanism, the ideology that he describes as dominating British theatre, and these are clearly the soiled/spoiled plays under attack here. This dismantling of the apparently 'meaningful' forms and ideas of normative society has a similarity of method and outcome with the *apophatic* Christian's journey, a journey that moves away from the more orthodox structures of Christianity to, 'the point where all knowledge necessarily ceases'. Tragedy and mystical theology both yield 'no meanings'. These reflections on death and theatre are interspersed with the author's examination of his engagement with 'the one'. For Barker 'the one' is a female who generates an all-consuming desire in the author and, therefore, like Eckhart's Godhead, extinguishes other attachments and objectives.

No mention of Eckhart is made in this text, so one might initially surmise that 'the one' refers to the idea of 'the only one' in popular romantic expression. However, Barker is very quick to reject the limitations of this populist idea, describing it as, 'a nauseating exclusivity according to democratic ideology, where absolute interchangeability is the rule'.[51] If for Barker, 'the one' of the title is not the 'only one' then in what other sense can this person be 'the one' or have 'one-ness'?[52] It is here that we can usefully draw upon Eckhart's theological concept. In *Death, The One*, the author's search for 'the one' begins when he discovers that accepted ideas of compatibility with 'the loved one' are inadequate and deceptive, 'mutuality was not a sign of the one, that any amount of agreement was beside the point'.[53] The authorial voice, in *Death, The One*, moves beyond these preconceptions and seems to encounter an idea of the female as 'the one' that can arguably be connected to Eckhart's notion of the divine. Like the Godhead and tragic art, the 'female one' also becomes a mystical encounter where meaning and purpose end:

> The one came to exemplify all that could no longer be evaded, she was therefore a recognition that what had seemed escapable was not, and as such, was relief from an enervating and pointless struggle. The one was a joyous yielding to the determinant facts, in other words, the end of the world. In this she possessed an awesome familiarity . . .[54]

The continual meditation on the collapse of all meaning in *Death, The One* helps to generate a worldview that encourages an end to the search for meaning, and therefore living in a state similar to the 'without why' of Eckhart, but admittedly one which is not expressed in the decidedly more tranquil language Eckhart employs. Eckhart's 'Without why'

Figure 1 *Slowly* in rehearsal; 'like taut pieces of wire'. From left to right: Penelope McGhie, Suzy Cooper, Vanessa Ackerman, Megan Hall. Photographer: Maciek Surowiak

Figure 2 Cross lighting in action: Victoria Wicks as Placida in *Ursula* (1998). Photographer: Stephen Vaughan

Figure 3 Jan Maxwell and David Barlow in *Victory* (2011). Photographer: PTP/NYC

Figure 4 *Mental Institution, Stuttgart, 1945*. Programme cover: *A House of Correction*, 2001. Photographer: Eduardo Houth

Figure 5 *Mal de Reine*, Alain Jassy, 1950. Programme cover: *Gertrude – The Cry*, 2002. Photographer: Eduardo Houth

Figure 6 *Anti-profiteering Poster, Hungary*, 1943. Programme cover: *13 Objects*, 2003. Photographer: Eduardo Houth

Figure 7 Programme cover: *Found in the Ground*, 2009. Photographer: Eduardo Houth

Figure 8 Pressure on the body: *Chthonic* space in *The Europeans* (1993). Judith Scott as Katrin. Photographer: Leslie Black.

can be compared to Barker's idea of 'hope-lessness', which is another concept important to the proposition of *Death, The One*:

> Tragedy is hope-less. Death is hope-less. Neither is bereft of hope, rather they have dispensed with hope. They exist in a vortex, not of hopelessness ('the situation is hopeless' always contains the plea for a miracle) but a vortex without categories either of optimism or pessimism (. . .) Hope-lessness is the point of departure, not a closure but new condition . . .[55]

Optimism and pessimism are both perspectives on the future or assessments of the past. The vortex that hope-lessness generates appears to be one in which existence is embraced, therefore, in the present without why; this would seem to be the nature of the 'new condition'. In *Death, The One*, therefore, the configuration of this female or females as 'the one' appears to be due to their own awareness or at least apparent awareness of hope-lessness, which then acts as a window into, and doorway to, the abyss. In Barker, 'the [female] one' becomes a symbol or personification of oneness/nothingness and consequently hope-lessness. For Eckhart, living in a time where Christianity unquestionably predominated, the journey beyond form to the now is expressed, instead, through the Godhead as the One. What separates Barker's 'the One' from Eckhart, is the same element that transformed theology in Barker's 1980s dramas. By combining the idea of oneness with the 'female' Barker allows sexual desire to enter this mystical encounter, a desire that would have been foreclosed to Eckhart in his encounter with the Christian God.[56] This focus on an actual female as a symbol of nothingness means that something in fact does remain, the female body, which, therefore, allows a powerful sexual dimension in an environment where all else is eradicated.

Rome: On Being Divine

Barker's play *Rome: On Being Divine* (1993) is his most detailed dramatic engagement with conceptions of divinity. Although the

Eckhartian terms 'the One' and 'detachment' were not given full prominence in Barker's work until they were used in book titles in 2005 and 2009, respectively, it is possible to observe, retrospectively, their influence on this epic religious drama.[57] This text also provides a clear example of Barker's interest in the more anthropomorphic and ethically complex portrayals of God in the Hebrew Bible, with two versions of the famous Binding of Isaac story from *Genesis* 22 punctuating the main action of the play. In this biblical narrative that can be seen as expressing monotheism's rejection of dark pagan practices, God commands Abraham to sacrifice his only son Isaac before dramatically halting the proceedings in the climatic moments of the ritual to accept a ram instead.[58] In Barker's first version of the story, Abraham seems to be struggling with the transition to an ethical monotheism, singing a frenzied song to an animal deity, 'Oh the sunset is an insane bull / Which bellows as it mounts the clouds / Oh see the blood run down the sky / I am God's waterfall.'[59] This savage expression of the divine relates to Barker's own scepticism towards a concept of God that fails to represent the cruel and irrational aspects of existence. When challenged by Isaac to why he is doing this, Abraham's response shows his desire to embrace the irrational, '**no reason**'.[60]

When God, in the form of 'a vagrant' called Benz, finally appears to change the command to a ram instead, Abraham vents his deep frustration at this ethical compromise to his act of faith, 'You ask for everything. And I want to give you everything. (*Pause*) And now you say, not everything, after all . . .'[61] In Barker's Second Abraham, we are given an inversion of the first episode with this time Benz giving 'no reasons' for his actions and rebuking Abraham for failing to submit unconditionally, 'in all clarity, in the fullness of understanding, to the wholly irrational act. You were to kill your son without the benefit of philosophy. You were to make no sense of the deed, but to endure the purest pain. For my sake.'[62] This terrible demand is too much for both Abraham and Isaac who attack and kill Benz.

Despite this death of God, Benz is an irrepressible force, 'I am will. Will only', and therefore is still active in the play's main location of

Christian Rome, where monotheism is under threat by a barbarian incursion.[63] Beatrice, the lover of the dying Pope Pius, is established at the start of the play as a possible rival for God, with the Pope's religious devotion intimately bound up with his desire for her: 'When I first saw your arse, I yielded you my life. One look, and I was altered. Its poise, its pride, its plenitude, its pity and its vigour, I saw God in its motion!'[64] When Benz first enters the main action of the play in Scene 3, following his introduction in the first Abraham scene, his opening line shows that he is, like the dying Pope, powerfully drawn to Beatrice: 'When I look at you I know that love is not to do with pleasure.'[65] Benz's attempt to describe his response suggests an uncomfortable level of anxiety and perhaps ecstasy when looking at her. The subsequent and various encounters between Benz and Beatrice are dominated by Benz's simultaneous sexual desire for her and frustration at her lack of belief in anything. In these encounters we are offered a complex expression of mysticism and sexuality that Barker will reflect on in *Death, The One*. In one such encounter, Benz pleads with Beatrice to adopt some form of faith:

> You are quite without belief. Political. Moral. Social. Theological. Teleological. Philosophical. Anything! And it is unforgivable! [. . .] Please have belief. Let it be wrong, let it be foolish, reprehensible, misguided or malicious, but do have one please.[66]

Beatrice recognizes that both her power and attraction lie in this refusal to submit to belief and that it is Benz who is in fact so desperate to submit. The encounter ends with Benz kneeling at her feet and clinging to her shouting out enraged 'Emp-ty! Em-pty!' His desire for, and desire to submit to Beatrice can be seen as a clear expression of this shift from the male Christian God, who is historically affirmed by morality, philosophy, teleology and theology, towards Barker's deification of the female as oneness/nothingness in the absence of any other ideology. For Benz, the emptiness of belief in Beatrice seems to initiate a similar crisis and abyss in him, resulting in an explosion of emotion: a mixture of rage and ecstasy.

At a later stage in the play there is an attempt to examine more closely what makes Beatrice the object of such desire, and even an attempt at a definition of the nature of her divinity, and therefore divinity itself. As the new barbarian (secular) ideas seem to be taking hold of the populace, Benz appears on stage with their baby. This is shortly followed by the appearance of Beatrice, who is 'revealed naked' and 'resolute'. Beatrice makes an announcement that shows a detachment that even exceeds her previous rejection of ideologies and beliefs. She confesses to herself and others that she is 'incapable of love' and is therefore 'impervious'.[67] After inviting all to worship her, she turns to Benz and announces that his desire for her means that he has ceased to be God.

Beatrice's confession that she is incapable of love seems to be a final freeing moment that leaves her fully detached from the world, as she simultaneously recognizes how the desire of others for her is what restricts them: when God desires he ceases to be God. The fact that the performer playing Beatrice is naked during this revelation allows the female body, separated from any cultural codes of costume, to act as a signifier for this higher state. Barker has referred to the unclothed body in performance as a mobile surface that can adopt new modes of signification and 'which, no matter how overwritten, still has the power to be discovered *differently* . . .'[68] It is the 'mobile surface' of the naked female body, representing a person in a state of complete detachment, that the other characters and the audience are invited to worship. After covering herself again, Beatrice reflects on her new state of complete detachment, which she defines as divinity, 'I have ceased to apologise even to myself. Can you imagine the freedom of that? [. . .] I am divine, therefore. Divine!'[69] The connection with Eckhart's argument that it is in the nothingness of detachment you become closest to the Godhead is apparent here. Barker seems to be expressing a similar idea by having Benz, the emotional and anthropomorphic male God of history, greatly diminished in importance when he is placed alongside Beatrice: a human in a state of perfect detachment. Beatrice's detachment makes her the new divinity, or a higher divinity, in the same way that for Eckhart the Godhead exceeds God.

Even when Benz returns with their child, that he has now killed in a final challenge to her authority, her response to this harrowing event is one of supreme detachment. Beatrice '*controls every emotion in her stillness, under* **Benz**'*s gaze*' and '*takes out a cigarette, and lights it.*' Benz is left speechless as Beatrice observes: 'I am greater than you / Lonelier and greater than you.' In this moment the shift from the male God of history into the deified female, a symbol of mysticism and ecstasy, is complete, as '**Benz** *falls at her feet, rocking to and fro on his knees*'.[70]

The submission of the male God, previously supported by the belief systems of Western theology and philosophy, to a female who stands for radical detachment and absence of belief, is an effective concentration of ideas that are more fully explored and expressed 12 years later in Barker's *Death, The One and the Art of Theatre*. The dramatic shift from Eckhart's Godhead as a symbol of absence and detachment, to the deified female as such a symbol, allows Barker to combine both *apophatic* and mystical theology with sexual ecstasy.

Conclusion

Whereas the central male characters in Barker's theatre are often driven by will, including divine characters, significant female characters that correspond to the archetype of 'the one' seem to exist primarily beyond the realm of will. They are often passive in their responses to the world, allowing themselves to be seduced or not, and rarely proactive in pursuing the male. This stillness and detachment is exemplified in Beatrice who defines her divinity as no longer requiring love. Benz, the male god, wills, but Beatrice, the one, transcends will. The new condition of hope-lessness without why, appears to be the highest point in Barker's theology, but one that the female usually occupies and the male protagonist is drawn ecstatically towards.

9

Going Underground

James Reynolds

This chapter explores the work of Howard Barker and The Wrestling School through the lens of space. The spatial is marginalized in conversations about this practice, but considerations of space and its effects nevertheless saturate the work of Barker and company. My exploration is focused in three areas, drawn from Gay McAuley's *Space in Performance* (2000), namely, 'stage space', 'presentational space' and 'fictional place'. As McAuley says, to investigate space meaningfully requires 'a minimum of three terms'. Investigating space is problematized by 'blurred distinctions', so distinct areas are needed. McAuley's terms create focus, assist us in appreciating the 'spatial system' or 'thematic space' at work, and facilitate a contextualized reading of an evolving theatre practice.[1] Consequently, by reading space and spaces in this way, the evolution of The Wrestling School can be understood more fully, as can Barker's forward momentum as a writer of spaces. These dynamics produce plays which Barker describes as existing 'in that territory of tragedy which creates its own emotional and physical milieux'.[2] Ultimately I characterize the theme and system of Barker's tragic terrain as utilizing *chthonic* space. Barker acknowledges the *chthonic* roots of theatre, but a full reading of his work through the idea is undertaken here.[3] This is a practice moving towards the dark, a literal and metaphorical 'going underground', in keeping with Barker's rejection of naturalistic dramatic forms and the enlightenments they seek to impose.

'Stage space'

The history of Barker's work, both before and after the founding of The Wrestling School [henceforth WS or TWS] by Kenny Ireland in the 1980s, is saturated by considerations of stage space. Here, I focus mainly on the spatial demands of the Barker text, and the ways in which those needs were met – or not met – in terms of 'access' to 'prominent' stage space of an appropriate scale for his writing.[4] There are other drivers – Barker says his 'favourite actors led him from one phase to another'.[5] Here, I argue for recognition of the spatial as another key driver.

Barker's relationship to stage space is summarized in his remark that while he wants 'theatre to be a place for a poet', theatres like the Royal Court 'squirm at poetic discourse' and at 'tragedy, which must also be poetic'.[6] It is revealing that questions of language and place are intertwined for Barker. The poetic, tragic dramas of the Elizabethan/Jacobean period, and Shakespeare in particular, are served by expensive, often purpose-built theatres, ranging from the Tokyo Globe, to that of the Royal Shakespeare Company in Stratford-upon-Avon [henceforth RSC]. But when contemporary writers produce a poetic drama, and seek access to stage spaces suitable for such work, the same level of support is not available. There is a paradox in this public hunger for a poetic theatre, and the theatre industry's apparent preference for the historical voice of the antique text, leading to overreliance upon a relatively small number of plays, and the overlooking of contemporary poetic drama.

The dynamic of this cultural paradox lies in questions of spatial economy, and in Barker's case, the spaces his work accessed prior to TWS. Although the community play is not typically what scholarship associates with Barker's work, *The Poor Man's Friend*, a commission written for Ann Jellicoe in 1981, was at that point his largest scale piece, involving 150 performers. Barker noted that an irresistible, 'overpowering emotional state' was generated through 'powerfully ritualistic and mythical' mass images; Jellicoe writes that this 'overpowering emotion comes partly from scale'.[7] Barker's interest in extremes of scale continues to the present day. Barker wrote to Ireland after *Seven Lears* (1989) that

> We should expect to work with small audiences, in such a way that the audience is possibly outnumbered by the cast, and is drawn into the scene as a privileged observer, and because of its smallness, able to attend the most intimate things. It is a catastrophic loss for us if the perfection of small scenes like the dinner in SEVEN LEARS, which depends for its power upon the proximity of the audience, is abolished by big house theatre. With a carefully conducted audience we can move from the spectacular to the minimal without loss.[8]

Barker shows significant interest in space and scale here, but the 'spectacular' and the 'minimal' were embedded in his writing much earlier, in distinctive objects and places – most notably the exhumation of corpses from the battlefields of the First World War in *The Love of a Good Man* (RSC, 1978). The mid-to-late-1980s saw Barker working with equally precise coordinates, but moving towards a monumental scale of theme and image. *The Castle* (RSC, 1985) and its vast buildings reflected the arms race of East and West: *Scenes from an Execution*, set in Renaissance Venice, explored the fallout from Galactia's giant canvas commemorating the battle of Lepanto (BBC Radio, 1984); and *The Bite of the Night* (RSC, 1988) experimented with time and structure through different layers of 'Troy'. Barker was, then, well supported by the RSC, but his dramatic imagination was continuously increasing in scale.

In interview, Colin Chambers, RSC literary manager in the 1980s, says that over a eleven-year period of commissioning and production, seven Barkers were staged by the company, including the 1985 Barbican 'Pit' Season (*Crimes in Hot Countries*, *The Castle*, and *Downchild*), and Barker remains the only living writer to have ever been given an RSC season. Barker's *That Good Between Us* (1977) had opened the RSC's new writing venue, the Warehouse Theatre, and he became identified with the venue,[9] benefiting from the company's 'new play policy' – even as artistic director Trevor Nunn edged the RSC towards his personal vision of a populist theatre.[10] Twin tracks, then, led to 'one of the defining moments in contemporary British playwriting', where

Barker's 'spiky' Pit plays[11] had *Les Miserables* being sung overhead in the Barbican's main house;[12] by 1998 'such a combination was absent' from the RSC. Writers like Barker 'who wanted to see their plays on the RSC's big stage[s]' could not.[13]

The Barker plays the RSC rejected in the 1980s are also telling in regards to stage space, first *Victory* (staged by the Royal Court, 1983), and secondly, *The Europeans* (rejected 1984, staged by TWS, 1993). Both have the scale to succeed dramatically on the Barbican main stage, but both were refused this prominent berth. Chambers relates how the fate of these plays became intertwined. Barker's first submitted draft of *The Europeans* (1984) was seen as a lesser work than *Victory*: previous Barker submissions had had the strongest sense of artistic completion, and *The Europeans* seemed unready by comparison. Interestingly, even the theatrical anecdotes that have sprung up around *The Europeans* – particularly that the rejection was given emblem by the script being thrown across a room – are spatialized. The play is not so much refused in this anecdote, as much as it is physically and spatially renounced (Chambers, however, questions the anecdote, being present at each literary management meeting, and recalling no such event). Having rejected *Victory* as a main stage production, the company were bound to refuse *The Europeans* that slot, as it was perceived in relation as weaker.[14] Warehouse productions like *The Hang of the Gaol* (1978) had shown 'how the energy of a writer could be released through the discipline of a small-space production', but although discussions about staging *The Europeans* in The Pit took place, the RSC never staged it.[15] Barker was writing on a scale that could work in either a studio or a main house, so the prominence of the stage space itself should be considered.

A key difference between the plays was that *The Europeans* was an RSC commission, and its production would also have been a public statement accepting Barker as a writer for the main stage.[16] Questions of access to prominent stage space, therefore, play a significant a role in the trajectory of Barker's writing career at this time. Richard Boon and Amanda Price summarize this neatly: 'the breadth of [Barkers] work demands the perspective offered by the large auditorium, while the form and content of his plays refuse to supply the commodity packaging upon which the audience that fills that auditorium is built'; his work, therefore, has been 'duly consigned to the studio spaces that, while guaranteeing limited exposure . . . also bound its ambition'. In not gaining access to prominent stage space, they argue, Barker became a 'rootless playwright'.[17] Consequently, after the relationship with the RSC broke down in 1984 (Chambers remarks that the already-scheduled Pit season was a footnote to the relationship, with *The Bite of the Night* being its coda, and certainly not a way back into partnership) the question of 'where' Barker would 'go' next to find a home for his work became most pressing.[18] As Robert Shaughnessy remarks, neither the National Theatre, nor the BBC, were hospitable to Barker in the 1980s.[19] 'All credit to Howard', says Chambers: unlike many of his contemporaries, 'Howard didn't go under' when institutional support was lost.[20] Instead, with Arts Council support, The Wrestling School was born.

Having been denied access by the RSC to the kinds of stage spaces capable of realizing the scale of his drama in literal terms, Barker responding by writing into imagined spaces, which are, of course, limitless in their scope and scale. With Ireland as director, and with the professional relationships and networks Ireland brought to TWS, Barker steps towards a catastrophic re-imagining of the world, perhaps most noticeably in *Seven Lears* (Royal Court, 1989). Having accessed the Royal Court stage, however, the relationship was short-lived. When the Court rejected a proposal to re-stage *Victory* in 1991, the question of a home for the work once more arose. Max Stafford-Clark wrote to Ireland personally:

> I don't want to be thought of as having disenchantment with Howard's work. Clearly he is a major writer, a talent of our time who will always have a place on the Royal Court stage. Your own work has done much in the past few years to put him in that position. At the same time I think it would be very unlikely that we will wish to commit to a new production of a play we produced comparatively recently [1983].[21]

Barker, however, wrote to Ireland, with a strong feeling that

> the loss of the Royal Court (as co-producer) is profoundly to our advantage. The problem with presenting work there is that it becomes Court work, even if they don't give a damn for it. It is breathing pure oxygen not having to communicate with those manic depressives grudging us every success and affecting amazement that any public can be found for our work. Above all, our entire method is the negative of all the Court stands for in aesthetic terms. I feel this separation is a liberation for The Wrestling School.[22]

Given the pattern that emerged, it is unsurprising that TWS adopted a comment from *The Independent*'s review of *Judith* (1995) to banner their work – 'the most important buildingless company in Britain'.[23] In interview, Ireland confirmed that the possibility of a permanent location for the company was discussed in the early days, but that the complexities of running a building were prohibitive. Rather, TWS established its identity through a national network of theatre venues (particularly, the Leicester Haymarket and Sheffield Crucible, but including Derby Playhouse, Plymouth Theatre Royal, Birmingham Rep, Colchester Mercury, York Theatre Royal, Oxford Playhouse, and Gardner Arts Centre in Brighton), and later through international touring (to countries as varied as Latvia, Italy, France, Germany, Denmark, Holland, Ireland and Australia). But it was always seen as essential to have a partner venue in London to take these productions off tour. The Royal Court and Greenwich Theatre initially fulfilled this role, and then 'for many years that [venue] was the Riverside'.[24] Ireland 'left' TWS in 1993, and Barker drove his work even further towards imagined worlds, taking the reins as director and designer, and bringing the company into a sharp antithesis with the dominant, naturalistic mode of theatre. Plays such as the episodic *Wounds to the Face* (1997), and epic, mythical works such as *Judith* (1995) and *Ursula* (1998) spearhead this antithesis, which is given emblem in the company's production of *(Uncle) Vanya* (Sheffield Crucible, 1996), Barker's radical reworking of a canonical text of Naturalism, in which the walls collapse to let in the sea, as well as Chekhov himself. By the time TWS lost its Arts Council funding in 2007, their work had achieved major international renown, even as their sphere at home shrank. Private finance enabled TWS to continue production in following years, but touring has not been sustained.

At the same time as the company's geography at home shrank, Barker began to abstain from providing localizing references to place and time in his writing, taking WS productions still further away from possessing specific spatial coordinates, and making them deracinated. This, perhaps, has a peak in *Blok/Eko* (Northcott Theatre, 2011), which 'has no place or time'.[25] The 'spatial system' of the typical dramatic text, including 'geographical and other place names, reference to objects, descriptions of place and space . . . and other indications of proxemic relationship' is nullified.[26] The effect, as Roger Owen describes, is that Barker's characters become 'part of the scenography, growing into the stage rather than being projected out to the audience': action is 'not tied to any social milieu', existing 'on the theatre stage' only; with spatial references acting as a 'poetic effect rather than as a "locating" device'.[27] Increasing abstraction takes Barker well beyond the 'rhetorical scenery' of Renaissance drama, where language creates worlds through description; indeed, Barker's combinations of writing, direction and design move towards what Bert O. States describes as 'the idea of theatre as a complex appeal to the senses', whereby 'scenic illusion' is not a question of description or image, but is the overall effect of all elements combining to produce the theatrical moment.[28] As the possibility of access to prominent stage space in Britain recedes (in counterpoint, we should note that one of the most prominent theatres in Europe, the Odéon Théâtre de l'Europe in Paris, mounted a full season of Barker's work in 2009, in the same year that his writing was the subject of a major international festival), the degree of imagination required in building the worlds of Barkerian drama increases, almost as if in an equation.

Material access to space is but one element in Barker's evolving spatial aesthetic, but nevertheless an important one. Another element to consider is Barker's painting. From the Pit season onwards, Barker's artwork has appeared regularly in public on marketing materials for his plays: furthermore, the 'links between the development of his writing and his art are multifarious'. Barker:

> I am very specific in my placing of the actor in the space of the stage, and the relationship between what is spoken, and the movement, or shape of the body, is of critical importance to me and to the success of the undertaking. My pictures, therefore, are something between a theatre situated in a landscape, a landscape almost featureless, and a film still, and it is possible film might have been the integration of all those aspects of the drama that preoccupy me . . . But no, these paintings can only be paintings, for they make no claim on reality and show no real space. Nothing in my plays or my pictures ever pleads for recognition, they exist in that territory of tragedy which creates its own emotional and physical milieux, where the cry or the howl comes to the relief of a language silenced by pain.[29]

As Owen notes, character and scenography are intimate – one, even. Barker perhaps exemplifies what Nick Wood describes as 'the work of the theatre-maker', occupying 'space, deeply, completely but also ephemerally and surprisingly; looking to purify it to a degree of worn out or corrupted "space-filling" conventions, and always seeking a new and better understanding'.[30] The sense of space that emerges from Barker's history of practice is not grounded in considerations of the real, but in *tragedy*, which creates its own context – made up of emotion and physicality – and thereby generates its own *territory*. It is telling that Barker characterizes his chosen genre in spatial terms, as a 'territory'. And it is unsurprising that, in attempting to express tragic space, he has pursued the deepest possible integration of theatrical elements, a pursuit of an imagined space which has in turn formed a dynamic that now helps to shape his writing.

'Presentational space'

Having considered a dynamic that connects issues of stage space to the development of Barker's aesthetics, we can now reflect on how Barker physically organizes what he presents in his theatrical spaces. There is a key relationship between body, space and object here, which creates testing conditions for the performer. As noted, characters are embedded in Barkerian scenography, and sink into it, rather than standing separate; this is facilitated by the front-facing spatial configuration Barker typically employs. In *I Saw Myself* (RADA, 2008), a group of women produced a tapestry commemorating their lord's life, and their lady's infidelities; hanging across the front of the stage was a series of thick wooden tapestry frames. The visual obstruction was marked, and imposed upon the performers. Similarly, both the catafalque in *Dead Hands* (Riverside Studios, 2004), upon which lay the dead body connecting each of the characters, and the hanging bed in *A House of Correction* (Riverside Studios, 2001), compressed the performing space, pushing the characters together and imposing nearness. These features ensure that the 'bonding of scenery and character, environment and psychology' which takes place in naturalistic drama, and which externalizes character interiority, cannot occur here: Barker's characters connect to, but are dislocated from, their environment.[31] The Barkerian stage is never a *home* for the character, but rather an ordeal, and the lack of potential for stasis communicates that ordeal visually to the spectator.

The body often describes the world of a Barker text, sometimes viscerally. Ball in *Victory* (1983) has his tongue cut out: Skinner in *The Castle* (1985) has a corpse strapped to her body in punishment; and Holofernes in *Judith* (1995) is beheaded. Later works are less physically violent, but nevertheless inflict excruciating pain, whether it is Und's inability to leave her home and save herself (*Und*, Sheffield Crucible, 1999), Eff's incarceration with his father's corpse in *Dead Hands*, or the barber in *The Dying of Today* (Arcola, 2008) being cajoled into conjuring the death of his only son into a narrative. Here we see what Stanton B. Garner describes as 'the world-constituting abilities of the bodied subject as it interacts with its environment', with the 'disruptive presence of the suffering body' giving expression to the 'realities of embodiment'.[32] Barker uses the suffering of the individual body in describing tragic territory. Indeed, Barker recognizes the centrality of the body, saying that 'Theatre is body-in-space', while noting that in plays like *Judith* and *The Europeans*, 'the sexual body and state power' come into conflict, producing 'a grand struggle between state and private will'.[33]

Here, then, we might read Barker's politics of the body, which becomes the site of ideological struggle in his work, particularly over the capacity of the individual to define their own identity. Once more, it is telling that Barker's ideation is spatialized, here through the performer's physicality. As Boon and Price argue, a theatre such as this, which links 'stage-space to concepts of identity' reveals the 'ideological structuring of the self' that takes place in the world: Barker's characters 'wrench' themselves 'into being without the safety net of a consciousness administered by the certainty of consensual truths', and in this they represent a 'desire to be free of the self-defining dialectic offered by the state'.[34]

The same principle can be applied to Barker's distinctive mode of pre-performance – the *exordium* – which can be seen as a breaking away from a 'state-sponsored' dialectic, in this case, the mimetic form of Naturalism and its ideological compliance with order. 'Exordium' originally described 'The introduction of a speech, where one announces the subject and purpose of the discourse, and where one usually employs persuasive appeal of ethos in order to establish credibility with the audience'.[35] Essentially, this is how it is used practically by Barker – as an introduction, statement of intention and formation of relationship with an audience. But we might equally think of it as *initiation*. Barker:

> The exordium is my substitute for properly possessing the performance space. I have often said that the foyer is an obstacle to a spiritual experience, an area of trivia littered with the destructive detritus of entertainment. I cannot own a theatre, so I am compelled to create the conditions for my work in that critical time lapse between the auditorium doors being opened and the beginning of the performance.. . . it is a necessary break with the normal continuum of street-foyer-performance-street, an admonition that [the audience] will not be seeing or hearing according to the conventional rules.[36]

Usually, the *exordium* is formed at the end of the creative process from elements of the performance that will follow it – elements that are organized musically, often repetitively, and typically without narrative or dialogue. States encapsulates how important such a ritualistic strategy is in radically shifting the 'ground and conditions of our perceptions of the world. In a stroke [the dramatist has] altered our customary orientation to time and space'.[37] This is particularly important for Barker because, as McAuley notes, theatres provide 'audience space' for their patrons, which affects 'the way performance is experienced and interpreted'.[38] The exordium can produce what David Shearing describes as 'an imaginative arousal . . . which can further entwine the participant with the scenographic world'; Barker thus initiates 'a process of incorporation', producing 'a scenographic landscape' which folds the spectator into the work.[39] Fundamentally, the exordium is Barker's means of shaping both auditorium and presentational space into a territory for tragedy. Barker notes that 'These rhythms in a fixed space immediately call up certain ritual processes', reminding us of the origins of tragedy in ritual, and recalling initiatory rites like the Eleusinian mysteries.[40] As Shearing writes, '"scape" comes from the old English sceppan or skyppan, meaning "to shape"', and this 'shaping of the land' means that landscape is not necessarily 'a pictorial representation', but something that creates an 'embodied understanding' – in this case through the suffering body, object, action and image.[41]

This is not, as Michael Evenden writes of *Ego in Arcadia* (1991), 'the placidity of a Steinian landscape', but rather a 'demonstration of the decay of order and . . . convention', where characters 'stumble through the unavoidable rubbish of culture and history'. The idea of detritus is important. Evenden notes how Barker's text 'strains to free itself from . . . specific historical panic' and the presence of objects with relic status in Barker's spaces reveals that both the collapse and persistence of culture dislocate us from identity, albeit in different ways.[42] But this is not a landscape of waste; rather, it is one of tragedy, where, as Karoline Gritzner suggests, Barker 'locates the possibility of authentic individual experience', because only the tragic is 'powerful enough to act as a counterforce against the dominant liberal-humanist ideology of mass culture'.[43] Nevertheless, the 'relics and remnants' which Barker so loves[44] fracture his landscapes, and ensure that 'there is no escape from the problem of the self' and its similarly fragmented nature.[45] The degree to which Barker roughs up his theatrical landscapes in order to problematize the identity of the figures who populate them is indeed extreme. Disharmony in landscape is often accomplished by sound: Barker states that 'dissonance' is where he feels 'at home'.[46] Adrian Curtin notes how Barker's 'subtle-but-insistent sonic accompaniments, in concert with the ideational worlds of his plays, work to transport his audiences to a perceptual landscape of catastrophe'.[47] Barker's characters also transport through this landscape, often towards their destruction, which Alan Thomas suggests parallels the 'journeying downward' of the 'progress' narrative found in mediaeval allegory. In such stories, there are 'no natural limits of duration; once the actions are initiated they may be arbitrarily extended or curtailed'; this occurs in *The Bite of the Night*, where 'the survivors of Troy [journey] through a succession of different political orders', and in *Seven Lears*, where Lear journeys 'along life's path in a progress that is decidedly a reverse of growing up'.[48]

Reviewing this selection of qualities found in Barker's use of presentational space – ordeal, the suffering body and its world-description, dislocation between identity and environment, the need for self-definition above social definition, the bringing together of spectator and figure in a catastrophic landscape haunted by relics, and journeys towards destruction – encourages me to describe Barkerian space as *chthonic*. In using this term, I am *placing catastrophe* – 'placing' as in positioning, but also giving it place. *Chthonic* is a Greek term adopted by Carl Jung in describing the 'dark' element within the unconscious, appearing positively as an animating 'spirit of nature', or negatively as a destructive 'spirit of evil', spirits which in reality 'belong together' as dual aspects of the unconscious, and which mankind must become aware of in order to grow.[49] Barker's work continuously explores the edges of morality, and we might begin by characterizing this speculative endeavour as *chthonic* in the sense that such drama stares into the potential for wrong action each individual holds within, rather than looking away from it, in denial. This long stare into the 'dark', perhaps, helps to explain the often profound affect of WS performances, as confronting the full psyche might be said to produce a particular mode of cathartic response from spectators.

Here, however, my focus will be on *chthonic space*, typically thought of as 'of the earth or under the earth'. Incarnated in 'ancient, infernal, carnal, gods', ranging from Set to Dionysus, the *chthonic* is 'connected to the blood and to the soil. To be *chthonic* means to be rooted in the ground, sunk into the earth where all things die, decompose, and rejoin the primal elements'. The *chthonic* realm 'is depicted in all myths as the Underworld, Hell or Hades', as 'the place the hero must descend in order to find his essence', and provides the 'primordial material that the psyche needs in order to evolve and grow'.[50] A *chthonic* landscape, therefore, we might read literally as one where the predominant colours would be brown or black: where there would be no sunlight, electricity, or plastic; where people might have to travel long distances, perhaps underground; where the dominant themes of existence would be sex and death; where characters are likely to die, perhaps by the spilling of blood on the ground (adding some red to the colour scheme); where characters and objects are broken down into their elements; where people go after their lives have ended, and struggle to remember their past identity, but also, and in balance to the darkness, where a process of spiritual renewal can regenerate the psyche out of the ashes of the old.

Returning to the question of diminishing access to prominent stage space, and the parallel increase in the imagination required to create the worlds of Barker's plays, we can now characterize the tendency of that imaginative increase as one of 'going underground', an inexorable movement towards depth and darkness. Barker acknowledges this almost directly in remarking that he calls 'his poems excavations', and sees his birth city of London as not 'wide but deep' – writing also that 'his sense of the dispersal of all things runs through his work', and that neither spiritual nor material can 'resist decay'. This extends even to Barker's preferred rehearsal space in Pimlico, a 'chaotic and incongruous building, old and choked with its own detritus'. In his drama, this sense of the *chthonic* space re-occurs, as in *The Castle*, where 'the witch Skinner envisions the casual ignorance of the future as it treads over the sacred sites of the past', with all being 'subject to the law of oblivion'. It is also revealing that Barker describes his plays of imagined history as 'excavations of the buried or concealed'.[51] I am not seeking to present this as a totalizing description, but I am arguing that the *chthonic* has increasingly informed Barker's theatre practice, and is distinct within the fictional landscapes of both text and scenography – and therefore needs to be considered fully in order to realize the full expressive potential of Barkerian space in performance.

'Fictional place'

In McAuley's terminology, 'fictional places' describes the 'places presented, represented or evoked onstage and off'.[52] In much of Barker's work, as noted, the body and its suffering serves to describe the nature of place. First, we might consider the exhumed corpses of the early to mid-1980s – *The Love of a Good Man*, and more particularly *Victory* and *The Castle* – as emblematic of the physical decay typical to a fictional *chthonic* realm. Secondly we might recognize both the decay, death and the blood of *chthonic* space in plays from the late 1980s and early-to-mid 1990s, notably Katrin's mutilation in *The Europeans*, Helen's progressive dismemberment in *The Bite of the Night*, Holofernes' beheading in *Judith* and as a continuous theme in *Wounds to the Face*. Continuing, we might also consider that the chorus of the gaoled in *Seven Lears* effectively occupy a subterranean space, as do Dancer and the Romanov family in *Hated Nightfall*; indeed, the subterranean gaol is also present as a space in scenes from *Wounds*, and also in *Scenes from an Execution* (the irony of Barker being accorded a season in 'The Pit' should not be lost on us here). We might think of *Und*, and her entrapment in her home preceding death, and Barbara's candlelit library in *The Road, The House, The Road* as different kinds of gaol. In the Depths of Dead Love provides a more recent example (2013) of the subterranean, but an exterior one, being focused around a village's favoured suicide spot of a bottomless well.

The side-lighting characteristic of Ace McCarron's lighting designs for TWS certainly assists in creating the sense of travelling through the tight corridors of an underground space, as well as creating pressure on the figure due to minimal overhead lighting (see Figure 8). The colour schemes of both Barker's paintings and theatre designs rely heavily upon earth tones, 'consigning colour to the edges of the palette' with occasional flashes of red, and with pure white occasionally deployed for its premium contrast, or 'as an immaculate commentary on the sordid facts of the social world'.[53] Nearly all of the objects in Barker's designs are made from natural materials, and he rarely, if ever, uses devices requiring obvious electrical sources on the stage. This includes the screen, which is effectively excluded from his aesthetic. Nowhere is this more pronounced than in *Blok/Eko*, where the execution of the medical profession in its entirety by the same token banishes its technologies. The notable exception would be the camera in *13 Objects: Studies in Servitude*, but this favourite device of Barker's remains resolutely celluloid. I give the piece its full title from the production programme here to remind us of Barker's use of the object as detritus, and of its dislocating effect: each object 'evokes disturbing memories and extreme feelings', bringing the past into the present and destabilizing identity.[54] Indeed, Barker writes that 'the material detritus of society' is 'imbued with suffering or loss', and in this play 'the relic comes to threaten the living with its significance', with 'each object being a focus of painful speculation but also a means of demonstrating the laws of Coercion and Decay'.[55] This, we should note, is almost diametrically opposed to the naturalistic use of stage objects 'to implement the individual's self-projection through space . . . and to ground the individual, as body, in its material surroundings'.[56] Where the emblematic space of Naturalism might be thought of as the living room, the emblem of *chthonic* space is probably the boneyard – in both senses – as graveyard, and as collecting place for lost or unused objects. From the late 1990s onwards, the themes of sex and death increasingly dominate Barker spaces, combining in the beheading of an entire chorus of virgin nuns in *Ursula*, sexual murder in *Gertrude – The Cry*, erotic encounters with a deceased father's mistress in *Dead Hands*, incest in *The Fence in Its Thousandth Year* and a series of mysterious fatalities in *The Seduction of Almighty God*. In the late 2000s, death is environmental, with characters in *I Saw Myself*, *The Dying of Today*, and *Slowly* contemplating destruction in the light of approaching violence, and seemingly unable to fly from it. The onstage-offstage relationship, a key feature in the fiction of space, is exploited to the full. Barker employs what McAuley calls the 'unlocalized off'; places that do not connect directly to the physical world onstage, but which nevertheless impact upon it.[57] In these three plays, war is a remote, but ever approaching fact of life, placing immense pressure upon the fictional space. Even notable exteriors, such as those of *The Fence in Its Thousandth Year*, or *The Road, The House, The Road*, are brought into a *chthonic* register by night settings, or howling winds. Thomas suggests that the 'wind of desolation' which penetrates *Seven Lears* places no less than 'a cosmic frame of anxiety' around the stage;[58] similarly, Barker's desire for 'the longest possible entrances' in staging creates a foreboding sense of things to come.[59]

These landscapes sweep away complacency; as Evenden writes, this is 'a theatre that dwells in a preternaturally extended moment of radical transformation', revealing that 'Political stasis and aesthetic morbidity are one'.[60] Resistance to, or embracing of change, destroys some, but renews others. Whereas in Naturalism, 'the fateful participation of the setting' creates 'epics of claustrophobia', with characters wishing themselves elsewhere, and effectively imprisoned without possibility of change, the *chthonic* landscape, while ostensibly more destructive, nevertheless unleashes characters into transformation, ensuring that we witness their lives very much in the present tense: in Chekhov, 'Space is destiny'; in Barker, space is risk.[61] His rejection of 'domesticity' in theatre is passionate,[62] and settings for pieces such as *He Stumbled* (2000) epitomize his intention 'to create acting environments that repudiate[d] all compromise with naturalism', instead creating 'startling, active settings for voice and movement'.[63] In performance, WS performer Julia Tarnoky felt that *He Stumbled* 'seemed possessed of a darker narrower atmosphere, set, as it were, at great depth', whereas 'the panorama of *The Ecstatic Bible* . . . felt like a great wasteland and an open excavation'.[64] Gerrard McArthur notes how each Barker 'character is a per-sona ("through sound")': in 'sounding out Barker's language', the actor must engage in the 'drama of psyche . . . arising from the catastrophic landscape'; David Ian Rabey illustrates the importance of this 'sounding', writing that it is the means by which Barker characters 'plumb fully' – ascertain the depth of – their situation.[65]

I have not mentioned *Found in the Ground* because this play exemplifies a fictional *chthonic* landscape most obviously, and before discussing it in detail, I wished to demonstrate the relevance of the principle generally, which hopefully I have. First, the play's title indicates its relationship to the *chthonic*, hinting that its contents are buried, or to be excavated. This was consolidated pre-performance by the programme photograph, a muddied hand emerging vertically from soil, holding an antique key, and accompanied in its burial and/or emergence by a spent rifle cartridge (see Figure 7). The simplest inferable meaning is that the dead of war hold the key to understanding the past. Although not announced in the programme, the character list of the first published version includes a judge of Nuremberg, the spirit of a war criminal, a former prisoner of war, Hitler, and Macedonia – a headless woman whose speech throughout consists of listing Holocaust victims.[66] The Second World War provides a temporal anchor for understanding, although in performance the effect is of timelessness.

Throughout, Toonelhuis, the judge, dines on '*heaps of earth or peat*' which represent the war criminals he sentenced to death, and whose bodies have been rejoined to the primal element.[67] Barker puts the metaphor in some context in his programme notes; information about the past cannot assist in digesting 'all that is terrible in human experience'. This role falls to art, which routinely disinters 'those briefly consigned to the silence of the grave' in a 'restless, tidal habit of covering and uncovering' which provides only 'exquisite irresolution'.[68] The figures attached to the retirement home which connects them are effectively sunk in the earth, already dead perhaps, and they must be uncovered through art in order for us to apprehend atrocities past. It would seem we are in an underworld, where Toonelhuis seems to reign over the drifting fragments of existence confined to dwell there; he is even in possession of three ferocious dogs, reminding us of Cerberus, the three-headed hound that guards the entrance to Hades.

Toonelhuis has passed the judgement of death like a god, and is ancient, and infernal indeed, but his carnality is faded, his erotic capacity limited to recalling memories of unexpected intimacy in a forest. The carnal theme is more strongly set by Burgteata, his daughter, whose vocation is to lie naked with the dying, in sleep and/or sex. She is a source of fascination for three men, Denmark, the Workman, and Lobe, her father's valet. Lobe similarly propels the erotic onto a heightened level, in his remark that 'Intimacy is awesome', and that if god is anywhere – 'He's there'.[69]

The forgetfulness which accompanies passing over into this 'underworld' is exemplified in Toonelhuis's burning of his library of 40,000 books, which takes place throughout, and in Denmark's (a librarian) inability to name a single book he has read. Typically to a *chthonic* landscape, the one book Toonelhuis owns that Denmark can name, 'De Logico et Theologico 1683' by 'Haaken', is 'bloodsoaked'.[70] It is not only books that are blood-soaked; Lobe slits the dogs' throats at the end of the play, and *'The black blood drains onto the ground with a characteristic sound'*.[71] This sound is the same as the pissing of Macedonia and the chorus of Nurses which has punctuated the play – directly onto the floor, but also onto Denmark's body. This draining of bodily fluids into the soil repeatedly connects body and earth viscerally. This connection is also accomplished by characters being brought physically closer to the earth. Toonelhuis is wheelchair-bound: Denmark begins to lean until he is prone and lies on the floor before crawling onto the book bonfire; Hitler walks into the scene having left his car, and finishes the play rolling on the floor and 'covered in mud';[72] and when the chorus of Nurses lie bikini-clad on the ground to sunbathe, Nurse 'C' reprimands the sun as 'a lout'.[73] At Riverside Studios, the floor design was a covering of riveted metallic sheeting, making the surface hazardous for walking. This was further accentuated by the wire tracks which pulled the mechanical dogs, and which passed from upstage to downstage on a diagonal. The physical challenges of the playing space, combined with the text, established the testing nature of the environment. The landscape Hitler walked through to arrive was 'pleasant', 'Undulating' and without 'steep climbs', but on stage, Toonelhuis's wheelchair-bound body, Denmark's physical collapse and burning, the Workman's continuous dumping of books from a wheelbarrow into the fire, and Macedonia's continuous walking in heels, each demanded a complex negotiation of small but nevertheless physical obstacles that cut the space. Furthermore, the characters travelled in pathways particular to their journey of self-discovery, demanding a choreography of body which illustrated the environmental conditions in full. Toonelhuis nearly always went from upstage to downstage and back in a straight line in his motorized wheelchair, the exception being the dance of death that was his ultimate exit: Macedonia cut across the stage from left to right and back in a similarly direct way; the chorus of Nurses walked in regular procession; and Knox drifted in and around the space and other characters, ghost-like, in much more fluid and circular patterns. The continuous variety in traffic was intense and illustrative of spatial quality, in particular the long pathways which the characters travelled: there was an imagined vastness in the scale of what was presented. The bare walls of the stage space itself were exposed, its blacked bricks and visible pipework entirely appropriate for the scene. Enhanced by sound – much barking, the *'sound of infinite distance'*, the *'repetitive sound of an industrial process'* – space and figure were joined in a *chthonic* landscape.[74]

Going underground . . .

What I have attempted to trace here is an equation between the material circumstances of production of Barker's texts, a movement towards imagined space, and, ultimately, the realization of a *chthonic* aesthetic of spatial fiction particular to that imagination. Barker's drama has with very few exceptions (and these are mostly revivals, and not new work) receded from prominent British theatre spaces, but in an inverse process, this has helped move his work 'underground', towards a unique practice of writing tragic space through its *chthonic* properties. This, of course, is but one way of reading the 'thematic space' and 'spatial system' of Barker's work, nor should we forget that his work is staged prominently abroad.[75] In finishing though, we can note the various significances that this dynamic recognizes. First, this movement has helped facilitate Barker's abandonment of Naturalism, allowing him to express 'another form of reality' through the form of tragedy, 'which by its autonomy expresses [that which] is concealed by empirical reality'.[76] Secondly, in Nietzschean terms, this analysis positions Barkerian tragedy firmly in the Dionysian camp, and as antithetical to the illuminating, more Apollonian impulses of scientific Naturalism and its theatrical offspring. And finally, given Barker's repudiation of the theatre industry and its cult of celebrity, we might speculate (after Jung) that in this dynamic of 'going underground', his work has come to resemble what we might think of as the unconscious of theatre itself – all that the theatre industry might seek to repress, but without an awareness of which, its 'light' entertainments are fundamentally empty.

Part Three

Other Barkers

Introduction

In this section of the book, the staging of Barker's work outside of the context of The Wrestling School, both nationally and internationally, is investigated. The following chapters can be read, straightforwardly, for contrast to, and comparison with, the accounts of Wrestling School practitioners in Part One. There is, indeed, a sense of balance between this final section, and where this book started. However, Part Three offers more than just a counterpoint; rather, by providing accounts of alternative methodologies and performance approaches, and harvesting the experiences of directors with a prolonged engagement with staging Barker's work, this section enhances not only our understanding of Barkerian theatre practice, but also serves to nullify any reductive impression that the challenges of staging the Barker text will be met by a single, fixed method. On these terms, *Other Barkers* also interacts with Part Two in reinvigorating the existing critical conversation, by providing alternative discourses and readings. However, whereas the inclusion of alternative readings of practice extends both our focus, and our breadth and depth of contextual understanding, the inclusion of alternative practical perspectives may be expected to reveal contrasting, and even antagonistic, ideas. Yet what this section of the book shows, despite the diverse accounts of practice that it contains, is that there is a considerable core of shared concerns stretching across both The Wrestling School and other practitioners – shared concerns which effectively over-weigh any differences that are expressed. Fundamentally, this core derives from the need to mediate the Barker text to its greatest effect, and yield performances from it which harness and deliver its considerable power to affect audiences. In this regard, the search for a coherent, non-naturalistic style of performance is the most significant, and naturally common, element of this shared core. Notwithstanding, Part Three is distinctive and revealing on its own terms, combining perspectives informed by practice abroad, in Scotland and North America, with formal research into performance methodologies such as Viewpoints, and with the perspectives on performing Barker of high-profile professional actors like Fiona Shaw, with those of student actors from drama school and university. As one might expect, by working in different contexts, different results are produced. Part One gives us a good sense of continuity in practice; this section adds to that sense of continuity a sense of difference.

We begin here with *Acting Barker*, which sees Wrestling School associate and director Hanna Berrigan in conversation with Fiona Shaw. In 2012, Shaw played Galactia in the National Theatre's production of Barker's *Scenes from an Execution*, directed by Tom Cairns. Notably, this was the first production of a Barker play at the National Theatre. In this chapter, Shaw discusses her experience of playing Galactia, touching on language, characterization, technique, rehearsal and the themes of the drama. Berrigan draws a detailed portrait of an actor and her role from Shaw, and Chapter 10 thus reads well against the writing of Wrestling School actors on performance in Chapter 2, 'From the Actor, to the Actor'. *Scenes from an Execution* is but one example of a recent high-profile staging of Barker's work. His plays are staged across the world, perhaps most prominently in France, but we continue Part Three by exploring the staging of Barker's work in North America. PTP/NYC is an Off-Broadway theatre company founded in 1987 by Co-Artistic Directors Cheryl Faraone, Richard Romagnoli and Jim Petosa. PTP/NYC's purpose is the production of politically and socially acute work with a company comprised of veteran artists and emerging talent. From 1987–2006 Potomac Theatre Project produced in DC and Maryland. In 2007, the company relocated to New York and became PTP/NYC. Two of the company's artistic directors, Faraone and

Romagnoli, are also Faculty at Middlebury College, where every season the company begins its rehearsal process before moving to New York City for the summer. The company has produced the work of a number of contemporary playwrights, chief among these being Howard Barker. Since 1987 the company have produced nine plays and poems by Barker (many in multiple productions), more than any other professional theatre company in the United States, and in the summer of 2014 performed *Gertrude – The Cry* in New York City. In Chapter 11, 'Staging Barker in America', the founding members of PTP, Cheryl Faraone and Richard Romagnoli, discuss with Andy W. Smith the importance of Howard Barker's theatre to their company. In doing so, they also reveal affinities and subtle differences in practice, not only in comparison and contrast to The Wrestling School, but also in relation to the work of Hugh Hodgart and David Ian Rabey – whose work is discussed in this section, and who also direct Barker's dramas regularly. *Other Barkers* also presents the findings of emerging practitioners, however; in Chapter 12, Sarah Crews discusses how the application of Viewpoints to the rehearsal process of a production of Barker's play *Ursula* affects both the actor's relationship to the material, and the overall dynamic of the text in performance. Furthermore, Crews offers an interrogation of sound and image in *Ursula*, exploring how the structural and rhythmical articulation of elements is facilitated through the unique relationship between director, ensemble and text. Drawing on how emerging theories of scenography, ensemble studies and authorship are challenging traditional understandings of the role of theatre director, Crews shows how Barker's plays provide not only critical evidence for contribution to these debates, but also fertile ground for theatrical experiment and exploration. 'Barker from a Viewpoint: *Staging Ursula: Fear of the Estuary*', therefore, is a chapter that might be equally at home in Part Two of this book – offering as it does an unexpected reading. However, while a methodology such as Viewpoints may seem contrary to the strong textual focus Barker's work seems to require, what Crews reveals here is considerable, fruitful space for innovation in staging his plays. Chapter 13 reveals similarly keen perceptions while exploring the staging of Barker's work in Scotland, and accounting for Barker's continuing appeal in that country. In conversation with Mark Brown, Hugh Hodgart discusses the considerable history of his Barker production work at the Royal Conservatoire of Scotland, Glasgow, harvesting his substantial experience of staging Barker with acting students, while offering reflections ranging from the challenges of language and ambiguity of meaning, to Barker's role and position in the contemporary theatre landscape. As elsewhere in this volume, Hodgart speaks from a continuity of experience, but not to describe a practice that has ossified over time, but rather to account for the ongoing excitements of staging the Barker text. Both Brown and Hodgart show that stimulation through the charge of their conversation, and, similarly to other contributors to this section, communicate a vitality of engagement undiminished over the years. The harvest of a similar engagement concludes the volume in Chapter 14. Here, in 'A Gallery of Images': From the Aberystwyth Students, David Ian Rabey draws upon what might be described as a back catalogue of Aberystwyth University students' work on the Barker text, bringing together their testimony of experience in order to express practical understanding that is both expert and diverse, as well as personal values gained by engaging with Barker's drama. Unsurprisingly, what Hodgart and Rabey both communicate is the considerable level of expertise in performing Barker's writing that university and drama school students can attain. Rabey's chapter concludes the book, and in a sense, forms a natural Afterword, responding as it does to Barker's poem *To the Aberystwyth Students*. Barker ruminates upon the challenges of performing his dramatic writing in the poem – contradiction, discomfort, reluctant meaning – and Rabey's chapter, and indeed much of this book, is an articulation of how those challenges have been met in different contexts, and of the unique values of such engagement.

In conclusion, then, *Other Barkers* builds on Part One of this book by providing a further platform for new voices, new readings and new appreciation of Barkerian theatre practice. This section of the book also develops what is offered in Part Two, by further extending the frames of reference that are positioned around Barker's theatre with The Wrestling School. Part Three reveals many similarities between theatre makers tackling Barker plays in different contexts, but also differences that add nuance to our understanding of Wrestling School practices. Finally, this section of the book in particular shows the enduring appeal of Barker's drama, and demonstrates a strong appetite for his work at many levels – thereby throwing the under-representation of his oeuvre in the contemporary theatre landscape into sharp relief.

10

Acting Barker

Hanna Berrigan in Conversation with Fiona Shaw

HB: How did you come across the play, *Scenes from an Execution*?

FS: Well, I was asked to do it. I was asked by the National to do it, and actually by Tom Cairns. I was delighted, on more than one count. I had seen a lot of his [Howard Barker's] work earlier on. I had seen some of The Wrestling School stuff way back, and when he was at the Almeida – 20 years ago.

HB: How did you come to it?

FS: It was very famous. When I was at Stratford, *Victory* was very famous, but also, *The Castle*, and I remember being very envious that I hadn't been in it. I was at Stratford actually – I wasn't in the running for it, but I would have loved – I think *The Castle* is a wonderful *idea*. So, when I was asked to do this, there was no *question* of my saying yes or no, you just knew you were going to say yes. You sort of don't mind what the play is.

HB: Do you know whether Tom brought the play to the National or the National brought the play to Tom?

FS: I think it was a list of plays, that Tom wanted to do, and I think the National felt it was time, and they predicated it on my doing it. I say that with no self-trumpet, merely that you do need someone who has done a lot of those big things to do it, because whatever Howard Barker says about his own writing, there is a lot of 'filling in' – and whatever the theatre is, however discursive, however political, or not political, you do need to fill those characters up with three dimensional being. He's written brilliant contradiction in the personalities which is really good, but you just need to navigate around it, and I did feel in the production that those who were able to get beyond the *sometimes* delineated silhouette of some of the speakers – they did better.

HB: It's interesting, if you look at the actors that Howard works with again and again, they are themselves, *massive* characters, so what they end up doing really, I think, is filling the words with *themselves*.

FS: Well that's good isn't it? Like Shakespeare.

HB: Absolutely, so he's asking actors to bring a lot to the table.

FS: Yes, and it also needs a certain fluency with the language, that many people find hard to do. But it's not the language, it's fluency with the thought.

HB: Yes!

FS: That you can hold big thoughts in your head, while being *deft*, is it not?

HB: Yes, and you're holding one thought here, and tinkling away over there.

FS: And I think that's classical acting actually. So you need good classical actors, and even although the plays are modern, they are classical in that technical sense.

HB: Can you explain what it was that made you want to do it?

FS: Howard Barker, he is a *marvellous* writer, and by that one means, that we have suffered, for economic reasons, or staging reasons, with smaller plays, and he writes big plays, with big themes, with big characters, and that is, the best of the tradition in this country. And he is, in that way, very necessary. He's like Poulenc in the opera, or Bizet, you know, he actually has looked back at what goes before and *matched* it and not many people have done that.

HB: How does playing Barker's poetic language compare to playing the language of Beckett, Shakespeare, Brecht, others?

FS: Brecht often has power in silence. In *Mother Courage*, when her dead son comes out and she doesn't speak, that's probably the most powerful moment in the play. In Beckett, the fragment has got a huge lot of meaning in it, so that you know that the other side is the real meaning. And Barker – in a funny way he's kind of more romantic or more extravagant. And sometimes he indulges his extravagance. And I don't think that's a bad thing.

HB: What's your favourite moment in the play and why?

FS: I loved the scene, scene 4, where she says to her boyfriend, you know, stop being whingy, just stop whinging, because she's so *careless* ...

> *Wonderful, idiotic crushing in the night. Can't you just crush me in the night?*

Lovely. And however careless she is, she *does* love him. She does panic when he goes. She believes art is more important than love but doesn't live like that – she lives as if love is just as important. She's a hopeless mother which is true of so many great people. But she is charming, by virtue of her drawbacks. Now, I think that's fundamental to the theatre. I would say it's fundamental. He [Howard Barker] would not. She's a terrible person, and we're absolutely delighted by her, and I was delighted playing her – because there's an honesty in the unapologetic.

We also like people with big intellects, with big brains. The Doge is interested in her because she has a big brain. Now, it's a selfish brain, and a decadent brain but he's impressed by her. Look, it's great fun to play impressive people. She's up there in my mind with the Rosalinds and the Portias and the great heroines of Shakespeare, because there's a certain muscle you have to use to play that you very rarely have to use otherwise.

HB: And what would you describe that muscle as being?

FS: Large arcs of thought, deftness of wit, huge contradiction in the personality, and what you said, room for the performer to fill the airbag of the character with their own imagination. I designed the costume, with Hildegard [Hildegard Bechtler, designer]. We were looking at white T shirts, T shirts with paint stains on, Francis Bacon meets modern person, maybe mini-skirt, maybe surprisingly Hoxton, we were playing with all of those things, and while we were up trying on various T shirts and combinations of cardigans, there was just this red rag shirt on another trolley, on another rack, which was for some other show. I said, 'Shouldn't it feel something like that?' It was a *man's* shirt, and, you know, my breasts fell out of it, and I put it on and the colour was so like something from a Caravaggio, it was washed pink (washed red actually that was heading towards pink), so it was a really dirty Renaissance colour – suddenly this frumpy sack – was perfect. And my breasts kept falling out of it, and I thought *that* was perfect. And it had no period in it, I mean, it could have been something an artist would wear now, and it had an element of a smock about it, it certainly had an element of not-dressing-up about it. It had nothing cool about it. And that was *found*. So, I was delighted with the costume. Anything else would have said something.

Artists being characters is a very exciting thing in the theatre because it's someone without boundary. Obviously we all joke about the bohemian element of artists . . . but it's partially that there isn't time for them to conform. And conformity is another set of rules, another ladder which you climb, and they have to climb outside it. And actually, I think, actors fall somewhere between the two, as I discovered when I went to Buckingham Palace the other night for a RADA do. The actors are incredibly well-behaved when they're around the Queen, they're over excited actually which is rather lovely because there's something about the courtier desire to please that's inside them. On the wall was Gentileschi's self-portrait, and it's a wonderful painting, and actually I think Howard has very much got her in the writing. [Galactia is thought to be based on seventeenth-century Italian painter Gentileschi.]. She's a kind of chubbier woman than I am but she's full of energy in the painting. Very good self-portrait. Funny angle. Very exciting picture.

HB: How did you prepare the role imaginatively? Through research? Do you have a method?

FS: Well, I'm all for the drive-the-car-straight-at-the-kangaroo kind of method.

HB: What do you mean by that?

FS: Well it was something that Bruce Chatwin wrote about chasing kangaroos in Australia with Aborigines. He was invited out to join them, and he thought there were going to be huge rituals, you know, and bamboo pipes and fellows getting ready going 'doing doing doing', and he met them in the morning and he was ready, he was ready to take off his clothes, to wear whatever they wear when they go hunting . . . and they all get into a van and drive out to the desert, and when they see a kangaroo they just put their foot on the accelerator! [Laughs].

HB: I love it.

FS: I love it! Because there is no path that will easily make the end come to pass. Now, you might mutilate the poor kangaroo. You might damage it. But you can reverse back up and try another method then if that doesn't work. But at least you've hit the thing. There was a lot of research done, we'd wonderful assistants, but actually, Barker has alienated it slightly – which is good. Some things were useful and some things were not.

HB: Were there points in rehearsal where the character started to arrive for you?

FS: Late. But I am often late. I've good ideas at the beginning, and I charge in – kangaroo. Tom Cairns was incredibly kind to me because I am used to working really long hours you know, and very 'toughly', and doing extra hours. And I think it's the extra hours that give you the confidence to be wrong and know you've time to get right. The National only allow actors to do two-session days. If you're playing a big part then you're tended to be in most scenes, so it's hard not to want to do a three-session day (the director can have a third session but not the actors). Tom would always say at 5 o' clock: 'Give yourself a break'. And I've always felt, you know, keep at it, till the last second. But Tom saying 'Give yourself a break' – what he was saying really was, that the air of the character was coming through any way – let it – don't make it, don't fight it, don't insist on it. But I'm always so frightened about the clock, about getting ready on time, being somewhere I didn't know I'd be. You know, it's not that you can't put on the costume and try to do it but . . . there were very challenging things in it. Jamie [Jamie Ballard] who played the lover, he was quite shy you know, he had to be naked in the beginning – these things are hard to rehearse – they're vulnerable. The scene in the prison was very hard because you were raised up on a lift, but also you're on your own. In fact, it's a radio play, and that's when you feel the radio play – it's the manic thoughts, sometimes random thoughts of a woman who's been imprisoned. The fact that she was imprisoned at all means that the play takes a tilt where the audience assume she's going to be killed – which would be the Saint Joan version. She should be killed – instead she's set free, and then goes to the party with the Doge. So Barker has this way of stealing tragedy from the jaws of tragedy, and turning it into the tragedy of the non-event. And that's really exciting. That's hard to pull off actually – because the audience rhythm is tuned to the catastrophe tragedy. And you can't fight that easily. It's not the audience's fault. Barker challenges them. So, those scenes were hard. Oh I know, when I began to get it! There was a big high scaffolding thing that I wheeled on (because she used to have to climb up, Gentileschi, onto the paintings that were so high), and as I wheeled it on myself, I felt finally that me and the production were meeting. It was a huge thing, and I enjoyed wheeling it on and climbing up it. And I felt suddenly as if I owned the architecture of the piece. And I think, as a leading actor, you do have to do that, or you're in someone else's concept.

HB: What technical challenges did you face in terms of speech and voice in the space?

FS: Hildegard and Tom had created a very open set, so that the rooms would just collapse away. Big walls would just shift. These walls were very clever, they looked like paintings themselves. They looked like sort of Mondrian paintings. You have an archbishop or a cardinal sitting next to a tall wall, and suddenly you're in a Francis Bacon, or you were in something more classical, something renaissance. But vocally, I do seem to remember that you do need to speak out in the Lyttelton, and some of the scenes are intimately written because they were for radio, so I'm sure we had our challenges. Lying on Jamie's back and playing a love scene while making EVERYONE hear what you're saying was one.. . . But they're the usual challenges.

HB: How did the role change during the run?

FS: Well, Phoebe became much more confident. And Phoebe Nicholls is a very good person for the role. And Tim McInnerny, was magnificent. They're both zany. I think by zany I mean *profoundly* imaginatively articulate, illogical, oblique in their choices, self-deprecating, kind off the wall – both of them for different reasons. So I couldn't have been with better colleagues, who carried a lot. Tim's Doge was so selfish, so witty – Tim can make me cry laughing. Phoebe had to come in and do this big scene where she had to climb this ladder up to me, and then go back down again. She would talk about the nature of criticism or the nature of what a critic does to survive. Now . . . that pedantic language in the mouth and being of a red-coated glamorous and zany imaginative actress, was really delightful to be with. I could really relax up in my scaffolding, and know that the play was being *held* by a richly tapestried group of people.

HB: So in a sense, does that mean perhaps that over the run you relaxed more into the role?

FS: Yes, so I began to really not worry whether you liked her or not, and began to not feel I had to hold the scene in every scene. Tom saying: 'Just give yourself a break' was also helpful with that – to insist that there be air that floats around these scenes – that is everything opposite to what we're trained to do. We have to HOLD THE SCENES and FINISH them, and then we MOVE ON to the next one, KEEP the ball in the air.

When actually, we have to *not* keep the ball in the air. You can only do that, it only works, if there is a confidence.

HB: I think it's interesting in the light of what we were talking about before the interview. That we have to stop telling the audience stories they can understand. Often as a director, you know, you're saying: 'Where is this scene going? What kind of a scene is it? We must get to the end!' And actually, that air in between, where we don't know what kind of a scene it is – is the exciting bit.

FS: Yes. I mean I'm sure you find this as a director, that actually, being exposed to Barker, will make you look at other scenes with a much more *aerating* possibility. You *don't* need to lock them all up neatly. And I *would* say that the National Theatre has begun to lock things. I think there's a conservatism that has come into the National Theatre's playing of scenes, that slightly *solves* the scenes. Now, of course you want to fulfil the audience, and give them a *feast*, but you don't need to *solve* it any more than a dream when you wake in the morning is solved. I think there's something about schedules and timings (and technology perhaps, even) that is slightly *solving*, that frames around things that need to be open-ended, and he's [Barker] very good at leading us away from that.

HB: The play was written as radio drama, and radio has a balancing effect in giving attention across characters. How did the ensemble meet the challenges of work like this – where the lead can dominate?

FS: Well, there's a man with an arrow through his head. I mean, that's a wonderful gift, to play. This is a man who was in the battle of Lepanto, and who, in his attempt to feel less about his trauma, goes a bit bonkers in the play, and I would say it's a *starring* role. There's an admiral who is homosexual and who is worried that his homosexuality will appear obvious in the droop of an eyelid – that's another *starring* role. So, in a funny way, just given our conversation, I felt for the first time in many respects that my leading part was to be a sort of master of ceremonies for the night – to celebrate these characters, to welcome on these characters to *fly* – and I was often *not* speaking in the scenes. And that's very nice for me too, not to be always saying the *bons mots* but to welcoming the peacock-feathered characters, who are in themselves celebrations of *life*. She [Galactia] does go on a bit but you know, the choice for the leading actress who is playing one of those roles is not to dominate too much, but to try and welcome everybody else.

HB: How does she compare with other female leads you've worked on at the National?

FS: Well, as I think as mentioned she's something of Portia, I don't know why, I suppose maybe having to be in a court case. When she gets arrested and she's defending herself there's an element of Portia. I was always searching for her vulnerability because – whatever Howard Barker says – without that you can't really stand as an actor on the stage. You need to know the vulnerable point of the person. The audience do not want the strength – well, only the strength in the face of opposition. And for that, you have to find that the person is only brave because they are frightened. Bravery if you're just foolhardy has got no value in it, for the audience or for anyone.

HB: And elsewhere?

FS: She's like Medea before Medea starts the play. She's a gifted human. We have a culture – I think every culture is like this, it urges women to homogenize themselves, to confirm to a sort of feisty yet passive function so that they can be wooed and married. I think I am saying something quite big actually, about thank you Howard, but also, it is part of the job to remind people you don't have to be the conforming heroine, and maybe too many plays that are modern plays, start from the typical rather than from the extraordinary.

HB: You've played many great female roles, but she is possibly the most sexually powerful. What difference does desire make to performance?

FS: Huge actually – brilliant question. The other sexually charged person I've played was Medea, who fundamentally, for sexual reasons, kills her brother, runs away from her father and runs off with Jason. And runs to so many places – she runs out of road and can't go anywhere else. And at the moment, her husband's desire changes, she is sexually involved with him and trapped. Very bad position to be in. But it *charges*, what is otherwise, a terrible play about killing children. It makes it understandable – because sexual desire is the great unlegislatable part of us. But this woman's [Galactia's] sexual desire is only interesting if it's not acceptable. And I had a problem, which was that any sexual desire in a woman would have been a scandal in the seventeenth century. Because that wouldn't be the case now, I had to flagrantly make it more so for the audience, hence I allow the breasts to fall out as someone who genuinely didn't care if her breast was out or not, who was offensive to the audience in the way that she would have been offensive in wanting to go to bed with some guy then. So you have to translate sexual desire and you have to communicate, and it's quite hard to do. That's why I had that breast falling out. It wasn't to show off my poor breast but to make it that she *really* didn't care. Sexual desire really charges things – it charges evenings. And I often get to play the moral centre to the thing, which is the goddess Athena fundamentally, which isn't sexual.

HB: So was it more enjoyable to play?

FS: I think sex is a really big part of acting. And so whatever part you play, it's a great place to be sexually free, the theatre. I'm much more sexually free on stage than I am in life – it's fantastically freeing. And I remember when I played Electra who was in despair – it was sort of erotic the grief. I felt as if the grief had become erotic because there was a sort of abandonment in her body as one would have in sex, to that grief. I communicated that at the time, I was much younger. Finding the sexual, unnamed part of the person, but their unnameable part that the audience can find like a lover can find, is very important.

HB: Some reviews made a fuss over the partial nudity. We're surrounded by images of bodies. Why do you think the naked body on stage still has the power that it does?

FS: Because people find it hard to listen when they're looking at a naked body. If you're completely naked they can't hear a word you're saying. They're just going: 'Please put your clothes on!'. Mine was merely unlegislated. The lover was naked too. I think probably Barker put it in to show that – that we need the shock of the real. I think nudity is very important on the stage actually, for *a* moment. I think it's not unimportant that King Lear, to be really good, *should* be naked. What a piece of work is a man? You almost want to get down to the sculptural fact of us. Like Antony Gormley's figures. That is who we are. And I think it's really good, nudity, just for a moment.

HB: The 'yes' at the end of the play is pivotal, because it can be delivered as a definite acquiescence or a kind of defiance. It can be ambiguous. The play finishes with this forward-looking moment which casts its eye back over the play, and to some extent, decides the interpretation of the whole work through a single moment. How did you tackle it?

FS: Maybe it's too hard for the play to ask for it to be reassessed in relation to one word. Where it is surprising I suppose is that this woman is saying yes to an invitation to dinner with a man who had not only tried to interfere with her painting but who had arrested her. And maybe Barker is onto the fact that by saying yes, when an artist comes in out of the cold, they have a more comfortable time – everyone likes a more comfortable time finally. They've fought their battles. She can either go on fighting them or come in out of the cold. *The Taming of the Shrew* has a very similar ending. She says: 'My hand is ready, may it do him ease.' There's a thing about ease that brings a lot of us in. The audience probably wish that not to be the case because they're hoping that art will remain high by being forbidden when it cuts across the needs of the politic.

HB: So as you said yes as her, what were you thinking?

FS: What I was trying to think, was that I didn't plan the yes, that it's whatever comes out. She could have said no. Actually, it's incidental. It's not: 'Well I'm going to change the history of my life by going yes'. He says: 'Would you like to have dinner?' He dares to say it, and therefore he knows that he's got a chance that she will. She's not going to go: 'Fuck you, I'm going off to fight another battle'. People get very weary from fighting battles. That's what Barker's on to. People don't want to be in prisons for days on end. I mean, when she leaves the prison she says: 'I'll be back! I'll be back. Don't worry I'll be back'! But she doesn't come back. Because she sees the success of her work, and people are looking at it. People say it's a huge hit, people like a hit – I think even Howard Barker's been challenged by that. He says it's terrible to be abused, and not to have a hit, but in fact it does keep you very safe. Beckett had the same idea – that if you stay slightly outside the popular praise you do better, and it *is* worth noting I think, that Picasso's paintings that appeared in the 1900 Exhibition at the Royal Academy, didn't sell. They were nothing. So often the person who's praised in the moment is not *the thing*. When she's finally praised, she's the thing, and it softens you. She might be less of an artist after that.

HB: Do you think that the role of the artist in society has changed since the play was written? And how do you see the timing of the revival in relation to that?

FS: I would say a lot of our artists are not attempting to really deal with the situation we're dealing with. Art is a point of view. Artists remind their audience that you can look at a tree this way *or* this way. Art reminds them that they can look at themselves this way *or* this way. It's a way of seeing. When I saw the Bailey photographs the other day I thought: 'Gosh, he really *nailed* the 1960s'. But I must say that Barker must be disappointed by the role of the artist. The success of the play did not have in it the scandal of my being the artist and playing the artist in that way. We have absorbed so much. I wish the play had been more controversial. I wish it had been more upsetting for people. It wasn't upsetting enough. But it wasn't to do with my being charming – that's not the reason why. We packed as many punches as the play could hold. We don't live in a time when art is allowing itself to make a difference. But it's not the artist's fault. Maybe it's us.

HB: Well there are certain people who get through, aren't there?

FS: There are popular artists and I'm sure the really great artists are not, as I say, above the parapet. They will come. But at least your question is about that. At least he's writing a play about that. You and I have worked together – I feel very strongly that you are the next generation. What can we do except offer you skills of what we've done? I'm such more interested in what *you're* going to do.

HB: What do you think of the significance of her being female is, in terms of her being an artist?

FS: Very big, isn't it? It's still very big. I've just done a programme about Eileen Gray the architect, for the radio. Another disappeared woman. I have to say Gentileschi was pretty disappeared when we were growing up. Learning the history of art, I learnt *too* little about women artists, and there were not so many of them. But, one sure way of having fewer of them, is not to tell us about them. Purely on a feminine level, as a woman, I think it's incredibly important. The Greeks often chose women as their heroines – the Clytemnestras and the Electras and the Medeas, because they felt that the gods treated women worse. So I think it's very good when there's a woman artist because she's up against more things and that makes it more interesting. It also means that she's having to deal with the world as the world, not dealing with world as her family. The domestic world is not her only world. And I think that this century is the first time that women have been able to do that. We live in a marvellous time. You're not identified by the man you're with. You're identified by what else you do, as well as being a mum. That is a *huge* shift compared to your grandparents, my parents.

HB: The play was the first by Howard Barker to be staged at the National. What is your take on why it took so long for them to stage one of his works?

FS: I'm not the sure The National Theatre was necessarily the natural home for his work, but it does surprise me a bit. It's not that there's been a conspiracy against Howard Barker. I think it would be nice to believe there was because it would be more exciting. Maybe they should have invited The Wrestling School in before. They probably should have. Maybe they wouldn't have gone? Maybe it's a bad thing it's gone there! But what do we mean by the National Theatre? Being allowed into 'the Cathedral of Culture'? Well, if he wants to be, maybe it's a sign of him becoming acceptable. I think the plays appear, whether he likes it or not, mixed in their content. I think some of it is genius and some of it isn't. Shakespeare's the same. They do need big legs to stand up on. I'm thrilled however, that the National did it, and I hope they do more.

HB: Is there another Barker play you'd like to perform in?

FS: Yes!

HB: Which one is it?

FS: *The Castle*!

HB: Of course. Why is that?

FS: I just find it sexy. There are so many. So many deep in my subconscious. I don't need to be in them all, by the way.

HB: Are there some you'd like to see?

FS: I'd like to see all of them. If there was a festival of Barker it would be very good. It's time for a festival of Barker, definitely.

11

Staging Barker in America

Andy W. Smith in Conversation with Cheryl Faraone
and Richard Romagnoli

AWS: It might at first be useful to contextualize the production history of PTP, its origins as a theatre company and the sort of work that it is dedicated to producing, particularly in relation to Barker's theatre. It is interesting to note that PTP have produced plays from Barker's contemporaries in post-war British theatre (Brenton, Hare, Churchill, Wilson) as well as writers he has influenced (Kane). Is there a company focus on contemporary texts that explore issues around national identity, gender, sexuality and politics?

RR: Actually the company's origins go back to my dissertation research on the Old Vic Theatre School, and its predecessors the London Theatre Studio, the Compagnie des Quinze and the Vieux Colombier: the building of a theatre company made up of artists with a shared theatrical aesthetic. Certainly, PTP produces mostly contemporary plays but I can't say, categorically, that its three directors share the same political agenda. I don't bring politics to my directorial work and shun political theatre. And virtually the only other contemporary playwright whose work I've directed multiple times was Snoo Wilson and he was more of a fantasist than a political ideologist. I'm interested in long-term relationships with specific writers, and believe that I've had one with Howard through his plays.

CF: To the question of the company and its aesthetic and political choices: when we first produced, in 1987, we specifically termed ourselves a political theatre company for the nation's capital – there were certainly no theatres of this description or anything like it in Washington DC at the time. Of course there was the occasional disparaging 'sixties lefties' comment tossed at us, which had no actual foundation. But as the years passed, our definition of political expanded (and it always had social and cultural components), until it gradually became clear that the three co-directors of the company (including Jim Petosa) who do virtually all the directing (there have been three others briefly over the years, including Chris Hayes, from the UK) were simply directing their preferences. I am very engaged with the work of Sarah Kane and Caryl Churchill; this season (2014) I am directing David Edgar's *Pentecost*. We opened our first season in New York City (as another company, the NY Theatre Studio) in 1977 with a far too ambitious production of Snoo Wilson's *The Beast*, but out of that Snoo became a friend – in our ten years in NY pre-PTP, Richard directed his work almost as frequently as he now does Barker's. Jim works frequently with the American writer Neal Bell, but he is also a Hare fan – he has done his work both with PTP and other companies (although we were refused rights to *Slag* in the 1980s on the grounds that Hare no longer recognized that voice). So there are personal focuses – sexual identity, women's issues and various political strands – which are a part of the company's DNA. We are directors who are very engaged with plays that exhibit linguistic complexity and interest.

AWS: The focus of the company has (up until 2014) been on Barker's work from the 1980s and early 1990s – *No End of Blame*, *The Castle*, *Plevna*, *Gary the Thief*, *A Hard Heart*, *Scenes from an Execution*, *The Europeans* and *Victory*. Is there a particular rationale in choosing to stage these plays of Barker's, which in most cases pre-dates Barker's later work as a writer/director/designer with The Wrestling School?

RR: I guess I'm slow to catch up. But yes, *No End of Blame* takes place in multiple locations across Europe and England but the arresting visual element isn't a scattering of chairs, tables or even the empty stage but those wonderful Gerald Scarfe cartoons that explode even a limited naturalistic environment, however spare. Howard rejects those earlier plays as ideologically black and white but I don't agree. In *Scenes from an Execution* I think Galactia is a brilliant artist but a horrible person who manipulates others (such as Prodo) for a glimpse into their pain and to gain a visual angle with which to justify her general preconceptions, of war, authority, leadership. I believe here that Howard totally subverts the traditional view of the martyred artist. Audiences don't always get that, having been trained to believe that the artist must be clothed in virtue and selflessness. The Admiral Suffici must be evil because he's patrician and isolated from the horrors of war, what could he really know about his sailors' horrible fates until he sees the painting? His anger (ego) melts into guilt, even despair, when he sees beyond his own grotesque representation as a bird of prey and recognizes the degree to which he betrayed the trust those men had in his judgement as a leader. I think Howard has written many subversive and disarming moments. The play continually subverts the formula. Galactia's opening monologue is:

> Dead men float with their arses in the air. Hating the living, they turn their buttocks up. I have this on authority. Their faces meanwhile peer into the seabed where their bones will lie. After the battle the waves were clotted with men's bums, reproachful bums bobbing the breakers, shoals of matted buttocks, silent pathos in little bays at dawn.[1]

I think that is brilliant. It isn't satire or politics, it's elegiac poetry. The play is filled with great writing. Yes, he's written more complex stories but his talent as a shaper of utterances is beautifully demonstrated in this play. But it's one of many.

No End of Blame is a compelling story about the artist having to continually review his motives, mindful of back sliding into positions of privilege. I remounted the play during our first season in NYC (2007) because I knew it well and could assemble a strong cast of actors who would be committed to the play. And most importantly, it was a good re-introduction for NYC audiences to Howard's work, despite how far he's distanced himself from the play. A great actress, Jan Maxwell, then wanted to play Galactia, the protagonist in *Scenes from an Execution*. By this time the Barker ensemble grew stronger having been amplified by other actors who had done Howard's plays with me while in college, or in PTP's earlier incarnation in Washington DC.

Victory and *The Castle* gave the ensemble the greatest opportunity to utilize all their technical skills and their emotional powers (see Figure 3), with Maxwell playing Bradshaw and Skinner and Robert Emmet Lunney as Ball and Krak (although he had to withdraw at the last minute from playing Krak). The company hosted the best Barker actors from earlier productions, including Englishman Stephen Dykes who was in The Wrestling School's production of *(Uncle) Vanya* (1996). Other actors include David Barlow, who played Carpeta in *Scenes from an Execution*, Charles in *Victory* and Stucley in *The Castle*. Emmet Lunney was my original Bela in *No End of Blame* in 1987, Alex Draper played Grigor in the same production, the Doge in multiple productions of *Scenes from an Execution* and the speaker in *Plevna*. Meghan Leathers from *The Castle*, Pamela J. Gray from *(Uncle) Vanya* and Bill Army from *No End of Blame* and *The Europeans* are the PTP veterans in the current (2014) production of *Gertrude – The Cry*.

In those plays, a large part of their narratives are contradiction, the suspension of accepted moral predicates, speculative morality and the transgression of principles that are celebrated in plays produced by most theatres large and small. The protagonists are anti-heroes who reject that description as reductive, even redemptive. I'm not too keen on satire either, but I'm high on wit and other forms of verbal humour, even physical humour that avoids the sophomoric and easy targets. The character of Holiday in *The Castle*, is a brilliant conception: a builder whose neck, because of his fear of heights and of objects being dropped on his head, is permanently crooked. I think that's brilliant both for its humour and the physical manifestation of his inner anxiety, a Jacobean visual that is terribly smart and his lines are brilliantly structured. Howard is the funniest writer I've read. There, I admit it. Even *Gertrude – The Cry* is full of wit. And although Howard may reject portions of those early plays, happily the production rights are still available.

I'm very familiar with Howard's theoretical writings; I picked up the first edition of *Arguments for a Theatre* around 1990. There are two books that I consistently reference: *The Empty Space* [Peter Brook,

1968] and *Arguments for a Theatre*. I'm delighted that others have begun to write about Howard's plays, although most are preoccupied with those he has written in the last 15 years. I enjoyed staging his long prose poem *Plevna* many times. My first take was to make the speaker into a Beckettian character who had experienced all that he described, but the last iteration of the poem was spoken by a character at cocktail party, maybe a war correspondent, who has too often experienced what he describes to the other guests who happen to be the audience.

I think that PTP, over time, has developed a specific production style with respect to Howard's plays. That said, I reject the exclusive application of any one, specific style when staging his plays. More important, the company seeks to create an alchemical relationship with the text regardless of when it was written, an organic style that will best serve the play.

AWS: What is the company's approach to staging the work of Barker in terms of rehearsal process? What problems do Barker's plays present for the actor, director and designer in PTP?

RR: Each play presents different design challenges. I hate blackouts, so my productions of his plays are usually linked by visual or aural (sound) connections. I love Viewpoint exercises and always use them when I'm directing. With professionals, the process is quicker with less rehearsal time but those actors have much more experience with Howard's work. The company does table work but formal approaches such as the Method or other psychological approaches are avoided. Table work exists to familiarize the company with the play, not specifically with performing it. Any internal work an actor may do is homework. Occasionally, when working with 'new' actors, I've seen them initially make hash of Howard's syntaxes – turning them into Chekhovian chicken soup, turning the poetic phrase into prosaic banality. Howard's writing is difficult and challenging for directors and actors as well as for audiences. I resist working with actors who are completely unfamiliar with his plays. I once cast an actor who had never worked on or seen a Barker play. The actor exclaimed about Howard's work, how wonderful it was. Two weeks into rehearsal, when none of his naturalistic tricks worked on a language driven text, more verse-like than prose, he, alas, blamed the text, when not two weeks earlier he thought the writing was brilliant. His first reaction was correct but for multiple reasons his creative resources were irrelevant. We parted company a few days later.

AWS: What is the impact of staging Barker in North America, with respect to a writer whose contexts and histories appear so specifically European? Are there challenges around the voice and accent, given the settings and Barker's own preference for actors trained in Received Pronunciation?

RR: To the last question, no. The PTP actors that perform Howard's work have all the necessary technical tools. Audience reactions have been mostly positive. I've been more impressed by actors' reactions to the plays. They've been mostly amazed. I'm disappointed that his work isn't produced in more regional theatres or university stages.

CF: It has become apparent over the years that American actors are either deeply enamoured of Barker's work, or mistrust and shun it (although I assume that may be true in the UK as well). Richard has managed to form a fluid company of four to six actors, most of whom have performed in four to five of the productions. Of course among the best interpreters of Howard's plays is Jan Maxwell, who played Ann in the 1989 production of *The Castle*, Skinner in the 2013 production and Galactia and Bradshaw in *Scenes from an Execution* and *Victory*. So there is a shared understanding and empathy among cast and director and a deep appreciation of the material that is completely evident in the production.

AWS: Much of *The Castle* and *The Europeans* deals with the aftermath of war with Islam and the return of soldiers from conflict. How have these themes impacted (if at all) in an American context given the current social-political milieu (noting of course Barker's dislike of 'relevance' in theatre)?

RR: The tensions that exist between Islam and western culture, particularly in *The Europeans*, must have had an impact on some members of the audience: resisting personal and cultural reconciliation, being defined by one's anger, transgressing liberal-humanist principles – the great hypocrisies of history. I loved Katrin's hatred. It takes courage to portray that on stage, in opposition to the Empress's efforts to enforce reconciliation, wiping away all that pain. So many plays are palliatives, analgesics made for audiences who want to feel good, reaffirming their righteousness. Those plays are hoaxes. A theatre that Howard called 'crates of shame'.

AWS: Barker has noted his on-going battles with English theatre critics to have his work acknowledged and accepted in the UK. How have American critics responded to your staging of Barker's plays?

CF: What I think may have sparked our ongoing exploration of Barker's work (which eventually took on a life of its own) was a critical reaction from our first Barker production in 1987 which was overwhelmingly positive, especially on the part of two important Washington DC critics – Bob Mondello of *The Washington City Paper* and National Public Radio, and Joe Brown, then a critic for *The Washington Post*. Now as then, *The Washington Post* is the unchallenged leader in forming public artistic opinion and Brown's wonderful review, along with Mondello's explosive and even more laudatory one, made an enormous impact. This was especially true since it was our first season, and we were artistic unknowns in that area; although all three of the company's directors had gone to university in DC, we had not until that time been practising artists there. Brown left *The Washington Post* shortly after, but Mondello continued to heap intelligent critical praise on all our Barker productions and even spent time advising us how to educate less informed members of the theatre press about Barker's formidable history and presence in the UK and the rest of Europe. Of course, not every critic was overwhelmed; when we produced *The Castle* in 1989, the first string critic for *The Washington Post*, David Richards, was extremely critical of the play (we always felt this was in some sense a response to the fact that he had been on vacation during *No End of Blame* and thus had not written the initial review. In any case, his taste leaned more to American domestic drama). His successors, Pamela Sommers and Lloyd Rose, were as enthusiastic about *A Hard Heart* and *Scenes from an Execution* as Brown had been about *No End of Blame*. When we relocated to New York City in 2007, Richard had directed seven of Barker's plays (some more than once) over 20 years of residency in Washington DC. He had also directed them with undergraduate students at Middlebury College so had a consistent and deep and very profitable immersion in Barker's work. We started the New York residency with *No End of Blame* once more and then Richard made the decision to do one of Howard's plays every season that he directed for the company. Fortunately, *The New York Times* has reviewed every one of those productions; while all the reviews were positive, critics have clearly had varying understandings of the work. Some reviews spend more time with the productions than the play. The strongest reviews have been two of the most recent ones – *Victory* (2011) and especially *The Castle* (2013). Alas *The New York Times* did not like the most recent production *Gertrude – The Cry* (2014), though most of the other responses were very laudatory. Ben Brantley, the chief critic for *The New York Times*, was reviewing his first Barker play in 2013; as, ironically, he spends much of the early summer in London, reviewing 20 or more plays, he had never previously been back in the US in time to see the work. Last season, however, we opened later and this proved very fortunate.

RR: Critical response to every season is an unknown. Fortunately, thus far the major press has responded very positively to both the plays and productions, but it's always a crapshoot . . . 'Presume not, one of the thieves was damned.' Of course favourable reviews will bring in audiences to see actors work their magic performing in risky, difficult plays. Short term positive reviews draw audiences: long term more people become aware of Howard Barker.

CF: Audiences, I would have to say, seem in the majority primarily to most readily respond to the productions, although there are some absolutely committed and deeply intelligent Barker fans – in fact, one man wrote to say he was coming from California this summer (2014) since he knew this was the US professional premiere of *Gertrude – The Cry* and he was unlikely to see it in Los Angeles.

AWS: As already mentioned, PTP's 2014 Barker production is *Gertrude – The Cry*, which is very different in tone and style from the earlier Barker plays that you have become well known for, like *Scenes from an Execution* and *The Castle*. Is there a sense of the company wanting to engage with Barker's more recent Wrestling School material?

RR: The Wrestling School has its own particular style, one which I very much admire, but PTP's production style is different. Of course the plays dictate the style, but so does the culture. You mentioned that Howard's plays and their productions are distinctively 'European'. I'm not sure that I agree, having seen Robert Wilson's work, and the Canadian Robert Lepage's, but also, years ago, the productions of Mabou Mines, Joanne Akalaitis, Richard Foreman's *Ontological Hysteric*, Martha Clark's *Vienna: Lusthaus* and *The Garden of Earthly Delights*. I think all these artists share a sense of formalism, at least generally, with the conflation of Installation and Performance art and dance. The PTP company finds Howard's work to be visceral and passionate, sometime raucous and cacophonous, and sometimes quite still and quiet, surgically executed. Like his writing, the PTP style is without formal punctuation. The PTP style, and I hesitate to say what it is, but when it works best, as I have said, is born from the creative alchemy existing between the text and the company. When that happens I am transported to places I never thought existed. I think the audiences are too.

CF: It is fair to say that we have, primarily in our positions as professors of theatre, 'spread the Barker gospel' pretty far and wide. *Arguments for a Theatre* is a regularly used text in our version of a senior seminar; most students who graduate from Middlebury College's Theatre Department have appeared in a Howard Barker play (sometimes in Vermont and in the NY professional production, in much smaller roles), all have seen a Barker play. Our graduates over the past 25 years have gone on to teach in colleges and universities themselves and to found their own theatre companies. I can think of six such companies, all of which include Howard's plays in their seasons. One Boston based company, founded by three graduates, was in fact named *Whistler in the Dark*. They closed this year after seven seasons and had over that time produced three of his plays (one directed for them by Richard). And all of our graduates in higher education have taught and directed his work. So, the work is indeed spreading.

12

Barker from a Viewpoint: Staging *Ursula: Fear of the Estuary*

Sarah Crews

This chapter addresses the demands of creating and directing gesture and movement in Barker's Wrestling School texts.[1] My intention is to offer a series of reflections on the process and production of staging Barker's 1998 play *Ursula: Fear of the Estuary*, which established a successful working methodology through collaborative practices. I will address the complexities of staging the theatricality of Barker's texts, overcoming anxieties in rehearsals, and exploring the freedom and constraints of the written text. Barker's plays are complex: the term 'wrestling' in The Wrestling School – the name of Barker's company – implies struggle to meet the demands of staging his work, whereby actors unfamiliar with his writing find it hard to maintain the rhythmical quality of the language and develop the physical expression that defines a Barker character. While 'school' implies a particular method or discipline for staging these texts, TWS company declare that their working methods cannot be defined by these traditions; rather the company was formed through the desire to produce Barker's plays and subsequently work under the direction of Barker himself. Barker recognizes that 'not all actors [possess] the capacity or the will for this practice, for its disciplines [are] severe'[2] and this complicates the approach to staging Barker as there is no specific system disclosed by the TWS or production practices for rehearsing his contemporary plays. However, by placing the actor at the heart of the creative process and emphasizing the freedom to explore Barker's text through the body,

I discovered a working methodology for rehearsing and staging *Ursula* that can be applied to Barker's contemporary texts. I discovered the intricate relationship between ensemble, text and performance when I directed a cast of undergraduate students in a production of Barker's *Ursula: Fear of the Estuary*.[3] My intention was to investigate whether the multiple demands of Barker's play could be addressed through a Viewpoints methodology. Viewpoints and Barker could be seen as incompatible within theatre studies, because Viewpoints is commonly associated with improvisational performance practice. I argue, though, that the contemporary application of Viewpoints techniques responds to the demands of Barker's writing: they share a philosophy for artistic practice that resists rational and psychological exploration of character. Barker's work challenges traditions of theatre that are dominated by moral-driven characters and instantly recognizable situations – what Barker refers to as 'Humanist'[4] – in which he has criticized English theatre establishments for promoting Liberalist theatre that is governed by reason. In their 2006 publication *The Viewpoints Book*, directors Tina Landau and Anne Bogart sought to move away from rehearsal practices that prioritize psychological intention: Landau and Bogart appropriated Viewpoints as an alternative way of creating text through the body, which was collaborative, original and non-hierarchical. Recognizing these commonalities, I wanted to use Viewpoints to investigate whether its qualities could provide a practical solution to staging Barker. My experience, I will explain, uncovered a series of findings which suggest that the application of particular Viewpoints, together with a collaborative methodology, demonstrates that a more open approach to staging Barker is possible – an approach that makes Barker accessible outside of the TWS without compromising its power in performance. Barker's writing has the potential for a powerful impact on the actor: Julia Tarnoky argues that 'in Barker the word has the force of the wave itself',[5] suggesting that words 'constitute actions',[6] but I argue here that the *relation* between Barker and Viewpoints facilitates a transformational but *tangible* process for the actor who is experiencing a Barker play for the first time. The interplay between

Barker and Viewpoints conceives of rehearsals that enable complete ownership and embodiment of the material by the individual actors – this subsequently reverberates through the collective, creating a body through ensemble.

A physical tension

Barker's construction of poetic language on the page is inextricably linked to its physical manifestation when spoken. Reynolds's observation that while 'Barker directs the ensemble [. . .] language functions as a second director for the actor'[7] points to an active separation of movement and language; this acknowledges the actor's responsibility to prioritize the particular form of expressing the language as laid out on the page. Embedded in the visceral quality of the language is its primary function; the poetic construction has the ability to transform characters and situations, and as both the form and function of the language can appear intimidating to actors not familiar with Barker's work, my purpose for investigation was to emphasize the physical articulation of the play.

Prioritizing a bodily exploration of text meant the need to temporarily suspend the vocal expression and address this separately; the embodiment of Barker's language does constitute a direct physical effect as the plethora of poetic discourse manifests a certain 'physical tension',[8] as described by Melanie Jessop. For Gerrard McArthur, however, this 'self-defining psyche'[9] enables the creation of Barker's characters through language but the characters also articulate themselves through precise physical gesture. McArthur refers to Barker's characters as 'stage figures',[10] indicating an aesthetic quality that has a controlled and deliberate expression of movement: crucial to the rehearsals for *Ursula* was discovering the correct vocabulary that generated an acute sense of awareness of the body and bodily perception. According to Charles Lamb, Barker's texts 'run completely counter to most of the orthodoxies of received directorial wisdom',[11] so production practices need to resist traditional rehearsal approaches that are dominated by an exploration of subtext and uncovering meaning. The following section reflects on my rehearsal process for *Ursula*, which responded to the text through the lens of Viewpoints and emphasized the body of an ensemble through a collaborative approach to creating image and choreographing movement.

Setting the tone

Viewpoints is a system of actor training that has continued to evolve mainly in America in the past 25 years. Viewpoints was originally created by dancer Mary Overlie, who devised a vocabulary of six techniques that addressed issues of space and time in choreography. For the purpose of this essay I refer to Viewpoints as documented by theatre directors Anne Bogart and Tina Landau in *The Viewpoints Book*; Bogart and Landau state that 'Viewpoints is a philosophy translated into a technique for (1) training performers; (2) building ensemble; and (3) creating movement for the stage'.[12] This practical philosophy systematically prepares the actor to explore rehearsals predominately through the body via a series of exercises. By recognizing and breaking habits, working to overcome inhibitions and orchestrating an environment for disciplined engagement, the Viewpoints methodology enables a multisensory exploration of written text.

As the introductory rehearsal sets the precedence for the process that follows, my priority was to construct a rehearsal environment that could encapsulate practices for staging a Barker text. This required using Viewpoints to move away from traditional table work and towards encouraging performers to focus on the voice and body. The complexity of Barker's plays can often harbour an anxiety that, when harnessed, can generate the creative energy required for exploring the text. From my experience, the Viewpoints preparation created a shared space for exploration in rehearsal which, by encouraging self-reflection through the particular vocabulary, enabled the actors to accept their creative anxieties and share them. The combination of this support system and training exercises established the collective recognition of the physical and psychological complexities of creating character, and developed an approach to creating highly theatrical movement and sound without inhibition.

Barker's work with TWS in recent years always features an exordium that is intended to establish a theatrical atmosphere for the audience entrance; the combination of repetitive sound and movement is choreographed to immediately distance the audience from the outside space. The desired effect of the exordium is to confront the audience with the visceral landscape of the play world and this same technique can be employed for entering the rehearsal space for actors. The group of actors I worked with formed a routine of leaving all belongings outside of the room and entering a circle to engage with a physical warm-up that consisted of repetitive movement and a focus on breathing; a form of ritual was created through sun salutations which were performed in unison. Conditioning the working environment was mandatory to seal the rehearsal space and encapsulate only the text and creation of the play world at all times; this then establishes a similar distance in the process as the exordium does in the performance. The repetition of sun salutations immersed the actors' bodies in the creative process; the series of postures are choreographed to flow and focus the actors' attention inwards, creating an awareness of the body as a platform for multisensory exploration. The initial exercises were instructed with *Soft Focus*,[13] a habitual gaze that facilitates the use of peripheral vision and creates a wider scope of awareness by emphasizing full body listening, which involves softening our more dominant senses of sight and sound in a bid to 'receive information from levels we were not aware existed'. According to Bogart and Landau, 'Viewpoints awakens all of our senses', highlighting 'how often we live only in our heads'.[14] The series of sun salutations then result in preparing the body and mind though physical exercise, 'cultivate wakefulness and a collective, shared present'[15] and emphasize repetition and unification of movement.

Beginning rehearsals with this unification became a ritual for the company that drew the members into the world created through the play text and the process. Encouraging ensemble dominates the philosophy of Viewpoints as it puts the performer at the heart of the process, which is essential when approaching any Barker text. Our rehearsal process drew from several aspects of the Viewpoints preparatory rehearsal exercises and adapted them to fit the unique demands identified in the text. Introductory rehearsals explored the sense of establishing a group pulse through a series of exercises that aimed to initiate movement via shared consent rather than from the leadership of any individual. Reflecting on these exercises encouraged the company to respond to each other and acknowledge each other's physical presence in the space and in the present moment. The collective engagement in rehearsals then prepared the company for the work that followed which applied the Viewpoints techniques to the play and formed a technique for building character. Creating this shared space for creative exploration of movement opened a forum for more rigorous responses to Barker's text; the subsequent stage involved creating gestures and encouraging individual investigation of shape and tempo when generating movement.

Gesture

Viewpoints gesture exercises provided actors with the confidence to experiment with generating abstract movement; gradually introducing the concept of *expressing* ideas with the body provided a way into deconstructing some of the more obscure stage directions in Barker's play. Expression became a key term for our approach to the play and resonated with the cast of actors. The difference between Behavioural and Expressive gestures is illustrated in a series of exercises that instruct the actor to create improvisational movement and then, through a process of reflection, recognize their habitual use of the body and become aware of generating stereotypes. Bogart suggests:

The problem with clichés is not that they contain false ideas, but rather they are superficial articulations of very good ones. They insulate us from expressing our real emotions. As Proust himself put it, we are all in the habit of 'giving to what we feel a form of expression which differs so much from, and which we nevertheless after a little time take to be reality itself'. This leads to the substitution of conventional feelings for real ones.[16]

For Bogart, then, the rehearsal process must encourage the acknowledgement of certain stereotypes; in order to subvert the conventional terms of definition, our process began to consider the physical manifestation of the landscape through creating gestures that later translated as a series of images. Barker's play *The Forty* explores the notion of gesture to an extremity by removing dialogue almost entirely; the theatricality of the play unfolds through a series of gestures and images using similar aesthetic principles to Goya's Sketchbooks, whereby bodies are suspended in a landscape and emotion is conveyed through gesture. Students and staff at Aberystwyth University first staged the play in 2011 and their experiences, processes and reflections were collated as a series of journal entries for *Studies in Theatre and Performance*.[17] Phoebe Patey-Ferguson, assistant director for the production, confirms the importance of definite gestures in Barker in a way that echoes Bogart's point regarding the avoidance of stereotypes. Ferguson's section on the body cites Lorna Marshall, who suggests that 'shadow gestures; (often unconscious) [. . .] habits and default postures' are avoided through a process of 'stylization' which makes the 'shape more defined, the rhythmical pattern stronger' and 'the spatial relationship clear[er]',[18] the consequence of which is that 'you eliminate everything else'. The stylization as described by Marshall can be explored and ultimately achieved through the refinement and reconsideration of gesture that the Viewpoints method outlines; indeed, through drawing on the separation of behavioural and expressive notions of gesture, the 'habits and default postures' can be acknowledged and removed.

The key point here is that Barker's characters reveal themselves through an extreme sense of emotion and a state of heightened anxiety that remains when manifested physically, which requires what Marshall describes as 'removing distractions'.[19] Barker confirms that 'The art of theatre [. . .] disposes of the self-evident with every gesture';[20] consequently, the construction of image through gestures in *Ursula* required the same level of interrogation and precision as the dramatist has composed through the language.

The text revealed key indicators about the women's physical presence: Placida, for example, is described as *a Perfect Liar* and it is evident that she is obsessed with her image and formulates her physical presence accordingly.

The *vagrant* Leonora acknowledges the power of Placida's physical and vocal presence. When speaking with Lucas she states:

> The Mother is a
> Oh, she has this studied possibly artificial I don't know
> each syllable is grave and measured oh and this reflects
> her whole appearance she is in every aspect not young still
> beautiful even the way she lifts her hand closing her eyes
> crossing one leg on the other all utterly
> I LIKE HER ALSO
> False you'd find it comical whereas[21]

Leonora observes the stark contrast between the 'falseness' of Placida and the 'naturalness' of Ursula, and these binaries formed the basis for a more concentrated focus on developing gestures for these characters in our production. Viewpoints suggests that behavioural gestures are *prosaic* and that expressive gestures are *poetic*;[22] here, I was able to draw on these distinctions and the introductory exercises that involved expressing abstract ideas and ask the actors to explore how one might express the concept of naturalness or falseness with their bodies. Immediately the participants could identify any stereotypes they felt had emerged and through subsequently refining their gestures to something less improvisational the process also acknowledged a slippage into natural movement. The company of actors established a reflective discourse that highlighted gestures they felt belonged to the play world and those which appeared behavioural and belonging to the natural world.

Source work

Both form and function of the language reinforces the text's demands to resist the urge to naturalize or normalize gesture and movement; therefore it was essential at an early stage to introduce a less improvisational vocabulary and concentrate on replacing the vocabulary of expressive gesture with something more definitive. The references made particularly to the physical presence of Placida led to a collective agreement that photography of 1950s *haute couture* would provide a visual source to stimulate more fixed gestures.

Instilling the concept and stimuli of high fashion images provided a point of reference for choreographing the physical relationship between Placida and the novices; this inspiration was initially drawn from Barker's costume design, which is heavily influenced by Christian Dior's post-war 'New Look' collection. Among several high-style fashion designers, American photographer Lillian Bassman was highly regarded for capturing Christian Dior's 'New Look' aesthetic for *Harper's Bazaar*. Dior's collection included *couture* garments that featured a highly constructed silhouette to exaggerate the female form. Bassman's stills from the late 1940s are documented in Deborah Solomon's book *Lillian Bassman: Women*; Solomon highlights Bassman's composition of women who 'belong not to our world but to the world [. . .] of red lipstick and lacquered hair, of heels clicking on polished floors and pocket books snapping shut . . .'[23] Solomon's description of these women is reminiscent of a Barkerian woman, none more so than Placida.

Focusing the collective source work on Bassman's imagery and other relevant high fashion stimuli became a breakthrough concept in rehearsals for sharing a collective understanding of the aesthetic importance of creating gesture and choreographing movement. Rabey identifies that a Barker actor 'through his/her diction, rhythm and movement, has to mesmerise and fascinate the audience to continue and extend their considerations of possibilities';[24] this emphasis on the Barkerian actor's strive to fascinate echoes Lamb's definition of the power of seduction in Barker's drama, which is underpinned by Baudrillard's claim that 'Seduction is that which extracts meaning from discourse and detracts it from its truth'.[25] For Lamb, to determine the actor's responsibility is not to search for their character's truth or a cognitive, meaningful understanding of their actions, but rather to comprehend their physical and vocal capabilities – requirements that present themselves through a controlled execution of the rhythm and choreography of language and movement. Lamb's thesis insists that this requires the removal of theatre practices that employ a 'jargon of authenticity',[26] principles belonging to Stanislavski, Brecht and in some cases Grotowski, furthermore demonstrating the urgency to develop a vocabulary for training actors' vocal skills and bodies. Instilling these principles in rehearsal is the very same thing that directors Bogart and Landau were responding to in their approaches to theatre rehearsals in America, in which their development of the Viewpoints methodology as outlined in 2006 facilitates more abstract theatre practices and reacts against the 'Americanization of the Stanislavski system'.[27] For our rehearsals, a unique system was created for actor training that provided a supportive platform for exploration and evidenced a transformation of the company, whose individual members embodied Barker's play based on their own experience. The cumulative effect of this resulted in the company becoming a collective life-force in which the material was executed with confidence and precision through a profound awareness of ensemble rhythm and timing.

Inspiration for gesture and movement for our production was drawn from 1950s *Vogue* editorials and firmly instilled an aesthetic appreciation of the power of gesture and precision in movement required in staging *Ursula*. The aforementioned differences between Placida's 'falseness' and Ursula's 'naturalness' were playfully highlighted by Audrey Hepburn's appearance in the 1953 film *Funny Face*, but it is Solomon's suggestion that Bassman's photographs depict women who 'tend to be tall and attractive and [. . .] have the kind of seductive expressions that come from keeping secrets'[28] that points most specifically to the seductive performance style required when performing Barker. Subsequently, the world described in *Women* captures the same secretive and seductive qualities that Placida's character presents us with; nuances that manifest themselves equally through gestural and vocal articulation. Rabey observes this in Victoria Wicks' performance as Placida in the original production of *Ursula:* he states that she moved 'from one state of tensile poise (anxiety, effortful courtesy, command, abandon, elegant murderousness) to another'.[29] The seduction translated through the physical tension of the actor playing Placida in our performance is an immaculate construction of a sculptural gesture that can be defined by Bassman's image *Across the Restaurant*.[30] The image, like Placida, conveys a delicacy and femininity through model Barbara Mullen's hand position and, as Solomon's commentary reinforces, Bassman's women are not of 'this world': there is something mesmerizing and seductive about their gesture that compels you to look. This particular still of Mullen also features a 'balletic pose [. . .] Her left arm, extended behind her, is long and languorous', and again her face is concealed. Solomon's description of these 'balletic postures' reinforced the style of movement and chorography in our production; the quality of the movement was disciplined and each of the women maintained a sense of poise. The 'balletic precision of the performers' physical presence' was noted by Rabey in his comments on Victoria Wicks' demonstration of 'a "flickering" state of delicate off-balance'[31] – a description that is again echoed in the composition of Bassman's image and Mullen's posture.

The landscape Barker's characters inhabit is formed through this particular construction of image and gesture, so the seductive quality communicated through Bassman's photography reinforces the concept of the actor performing a seduction for the audience. Furthermore, the state of tensile poise is communicated and reinforced through the impact that Placida's physical presence has on the novices, as they too become perfectly constructed through their physical composition. One of the opening stage directions following the novices' entrance states:

> (*Pause . . . on the slightest signal from* **PLACIDA** *the class sits. They adopt various postures of concentration . . .*)³²

The directions above evoke a series of gestures, and when we explored these in rehearsal we discovered that the physical and spatial relationship between Placida and the young women could be defined. Placida's *signal* articulates the power of her physical presence, which then produces a very deliberate and somewhat formulaic reaction from the novices. Barker's use of stage directions provides a guideline for the character's level of anxiety or state of mind; this is an indication for the actor rather than directions for action. When discussing his use of stage directions at a WS workshop, Barker confirmed that instructions such as '*(He Frowns)*', should 'communicate a graduation of emotion'³³ and should present an insight into the character's emotional state. This is evident in the opening of *Ursula* as Placida's declaration, 'Ursula is marrying . . .!', is followed with the direction '(*She gnaws her hand*)'.³⁴

Placida's level of anxiety was also communicated through the following stage directions: '(*The sound of chairs dragged over flagstones. A class of young women enter, pulling wooden chairs behind them . . .*').³⁵ This was achieved in performance by isolating the image of Placida gnawing at her hand, as the chorus of novices moved in unison in an extended entrance that generated an atmosphere by suspending an image of Placida in isolation to emphasize her provocation. This is evoked in Barker's text by the directions above but was realized in our production through a unique pulsating soundscape that was created by the novices' movement. The performance space featured a steel deck and upon the unified movement of the novices produced an industrial quality from the repetitive striking of their feet on the decking. The key point here is that through the combination of expressive gesture from Viewpoints and postural imagery from high fashion photography sources, a unique vocabulary for choreography was created that emphasized the precision required in the movement and acknowledged the architectural rhythm, enabling a seamless delivery of ensemble rhythm and timing. This performance style was described as sculptural in stillness and choreographed in movement; as McArthur suggests of Barker's language, 'Nothing is "something like"',[36] and this is also true of his characters' physical expression and movement. The following section will offer an insight into how objects and props detailed in a Barker play illustrate essential information for character's actions and emotional state.

What is the hat?

The significance of objects described in a Barker text implies their significance to both character and situation; the visual composition of contemporary productions by TWS is highly stylized with specific use of props and in some cases, the removal of set almost entirely. Placida's *small neat hat* is introduced at the beginning of Act Two as the novices begin their journey to Lucas and communicates information that is integral to the character's actions, specifically for performing her seduction. As Placida enters wearing the hat, she is first provoked by Ursula: 'the hat the hat what is the hat?'. Ursula then declares, 'as I am near to Christ I tell you Christ abhors the hat',[37] and announcing her criticism of Placida's vanity who earlier declared, 'how well it suits us all to wear no shadows, gems . . . we wear the perfume of our own virginity'[38] it becomes evident that the mother superior is concealing something. Leonora affirms the seductive quality of Placida's accessory as she indicates her approval on how the hat frames her face: 'the hat is perfect mother and reveals your mouth'.[39] Leonora's comments suggest that in 'revealing' Placida's mouth, the hat therefore veils the rest of her face, confirming vital information about her emotional state; our decision to use a fascinator and half veil for the *small neat hat* was informed in part from the play text and from the distinct use of this accessory in 1950s editorials *Vogue* and *Harper's Bazaar*.

Solomon observes in Bassman's photography that: 'More often than not, the hat is an instrument of concealment and veiling, a place to hide, a room of one's own'[40] and in this sense, Placida's hat becomes 'less like a fashion prop' and more 'an extension of a[n] emotional state'.[41] The revelation of Placida's emotional state is realized the moment Lucas '*draws her to the floor*'[42] as the hat is discarded and left as evidence for her sexual transgression, thus suggesting that the hat had previously concealed her ecstasy. This convention is repeated and reinforced throughout the text and the hat becomes a central device for revealing Placida's secretive sexual desire as '(*Flinging it off her head*)' she proclaims to Lucas: 'Time for another . . .!'[43]

Future considerations

Our rehearsals for *Ursula* addressed the dominant complexities of staging Barker by applying the Viewpoints. Conceived in this way the process encouraged collective authority of the material by emphasizing ensemble training, creating an original and stylised visual aesthetic reinforced by collective source work, and, through a Viewpoints vocabulary, successfully avoiding any attempt to reduce or humanize the process of expressing the physical and verbal articulation of the character.

In performance this translated as a visceral theatricality through the arrangement of ensemble movement, which through its synchronicity created a unique musicality in combination with the rhythmical quality of Barker's poetic discourse. The visual components were realized through a series of gestural images creating a pictorial composition reminiscent of Bassman's aesthetic qualities. In *A Style and Its Origins,* Barker conceives of theatre as 'a place of struggle and domination, as the playground is a place of fear and noise'[44] and a company staging a Barker text unequipped and intimidated can cause this anxiety to manifest and grow. The relation between Barker and Viewpoints demonstrates that by confronting the creative inhibitions of individuals and avoiding any attempt to reduce or simplify the task, a working methodology that emphasizes collectivity can respond to the unique complexities of staging a Barker text.

This chapter has demonstrated a methodology unique to the process of staging *Ursula* that responded to the challenges that the play presented for the actors and director; by carefully selecting and applying the Viewpoints vocabulary, I was able to encourage a creative ensemble and reveal an openness in Barker's texts, and create unique and independent work that facilitated the text and avoided an empty imitation of style.

The rehearsal process began as a journey with a sense of not quite knowing where the production would end, but by reciprocating the text's uncompromising demands of physical and vocal dexterity, and responding to a company of actors through the lens of Viewpoints, a successful vocabulary was conceived for rehearsing and staging the play that provided a collective sense of ownership.

13

Staging Barker at Scotland's Conservatoire

Mark Brown in Conversation with Hugh Hodgart

The following interview was conducted at the Royal Conservatoire of Scotland in Glasgow on 17 May 2013, ahead of the opening of the RCS's productions of two Barker plays, *Victory* (directed by Hugh Hodgart, the Conservatoire's Dean of Drama) and *The Possibilities* (directed by guest director Guy Hollands).

MB: The forthcoming productions of *Victory* and *The Possibilities* will be the thirteenth and fourteenth Barker plays presented by the Conservatoire, and *Victory* will mark the twelfth which you have directed. Why do you keep coming back to Barker as a writer whose work you want to produce with student actors?

HH: This production of *Victory* is the first time I've returned to a Barker play which I've directed before.[1] In fact, *Victory* was the first Barker I directed, and only the second I directed at the Academy,[2] as it was then. The year before, I'd done Edward Bond's *Narrow Road to the Deep North* with the final-year acting students. I was looking for something that was similarly out of the ordinary, in terms of standard drama school fare, and which was going to be a challenge and needed hard work, in terms working out what it was about and how to play it. What I found with the Bond, and I wanted to find again, was not to come in and be interesting as a director, but to have something that really engaged the students, that challenged them. I saw the original touring production of *Victory*[3] at Theatre Workshop in Edinburgh, in which Kenny Ireland[4] played Ball. I thought, 'I like this, it's really intriguing. I don't understand it all, but I'd really like to have a go at it.' So, that's what

I did. The year group that I worked with included Kathryn Howden, who played Bradshaw.[5] What I really enjoyed about directing the play, and continue to enjoy, is that you walk into the rehearsal room, and, although the designer and you as director have done a certain amount of work on it, you still have unexplored territory. You really don't know all the answers. For me, that was something I wanted to put before the students. I wasn't disposed to be a guru. It was about saying to the students: 'Here we are, we're at the beginning of a journey, we all need to work this out together. We can't make any assumptions. Read it, look at it.' Usually, on the first day, there'd be big eyes, because everybody is slightly 'rabbits in the headlights', thinking 'what is this? How's this going to go?' Then you begin the process of exploration. Of course, that means using all the usual tools of analysis. However, you can't just sit down and analyse it round the table, it's absolutely about getting it on its feet and exploring it in a very active, physical way. The actors have to start to make connections between each other.

Barker plays are poetry as well. The man's a historian and a poet in his dramatic writing. You have to consider the poetry of it, and approach rather like you would approach Shakespeare. There are rhythms and tunes there. You've got to pay really close attention to the language, and there's so much in there. Once you start to value the words, and the emotions and aspirations that the words represent, you find that the action is embodied and encoded in the words. When you start to find that, like we're finding just now [in rehearsals for the RCS 2013 production of *Victory*], it all just starts to bubble up, and it becomes increasing clear. You begin to find your way through it. Acting students these days want to work, and, with Barker, they have to. There's nowhere to hide. You can't make easy assumptions about how you are, what you want, and all of those fundamental Stanislavskian kind of questions.

MB: Barker is anti-Stanislavskian and anti-Aristotelian. He's also anti-Enlightenment, in terms of its implications for art. Anish Kapoor suggests that the antipathy towards the arts from within the British establishment is to do with their attitude to the Enlightenment. This is Barker's argument as well, isn't it? As soon as you say that an art work has to have a function, you're actually putting yourself at odds with the arts in a way that other European cultures don't do. I find this interesting. It's also interesting, in this context, that Barker said, in this very building, 'I always think of Scotland as a European country, and England as, unfortunately, not one.'[6] In this context, Barker says the actors don't need to be intellectuals. He doesn't mean that in a derogatory way. He says that it's not about intellectual analysis, first and foremost, for an actor, it's about feeling the rhythm of the line.

HH: That's absolutely right. It's one of the reasons why it's absolutely legitimate to link Barker directly with Shakespeare. You might say, 'but Shakespeare writes in verse'; but so does Barker, in all kinds of ways. He organizes the language very carefully on the page. In some of the plays it's highly organized. He's writing short lines, and longer lines, and monosyllabic lines.

MB: And his use of repetition and silence.

HH: Yes, and, in the published texts, the way he uses bold and capitals, and, as you say, the pauses and silences. So, there's a whole array of, if you will, technical signs, signals and offers in the text. I absolutely agree with Barker that too much thought of the wrong kind can simply get in the way and can sidetrack the actor and the director. And, of course, too much talk can also get in the way, because people are avoiding, in a strange way, the most important thing, which is that visceral moment, finding that feeling, that impulse which the line generates. I think, often, the best way is absolutely through the words, without a lot of intellectual analysis. There's a Canadian acting teacher based in the US I've been reading, his name, strangely enough, is Madd Harold. The book's called *The Actor's Guide to Performing Shakespeare*. It's a very good book indeed. One of his phrases that sticks with me is: 'The emotion is that particular word at that particular moment.' I think that's the key to unlocking Barker, and unlocking Shakespeare. You should pay attention to the words, and allow them and the structure of the language to support you, rather than fighting against them or not really understanding them. Punctuation is profoundly important.

MB: In Barker's case, punctuation is important even when he doesn't use it. Sometimes the lack of it demands that the actor finds her own punctuation.

HH: That's absolutely true. Which takes me back the search Barker requires of actors and directors. It's not all on a plate for you. You have to find your pathway through the work. There's this paradox, where Barker's concerned. People accuse him of being too clever for his own good; that notion that he just wants us to feel stupid. Nothing could be further from the truth. I've heard it from friends of mine, people who I respect. They just see a kind of intellectual arrogance. Yet, the reality is that the plays are incredibly visceral, emotional and mythic.

MB: They're also very open, aren't they? There's a difference between that and the obsession in our culture with 'accessibility', by which the London critical fraternity mean ease of understanding, moral purpose, message, and massaging the shoulders of the National Theatre audience. That's not what I mean by 'openness', Barker wrote a series of theatrical vignettes called *The Possibilities*. That's openness, when a dramatist gives you a series of dramatic opportunities and possibilities. There's that great line from Barker's 'Fortynine asides for a tragic theatre', which I think should be emblazoned on the wall of somewhere like this Conservatoire: 'It is not to insult an audience to offer it ambiguity.'[7] We live in a society that's hostile to metaphor.

HH: Chekhov would agree with that, as well. He totally refused to plough the liberal furrow, you know, that liberal humanist, anti-Czarist position. He was looking at life and presenting it in a more 'problematic' way, and when I say 'problematic', I mean that as a positive attribute in his work. I think there are similarities between that and what Barker's doing. I was re-reading *Victory* again the other day, and the speech of Milton's, when he finally speaks in Act Two, and he talks about the revolution. It's one of the most terrifying, bleakest pronouncements.

Scrope has asked him where the revolutionaries went wrong, and Milton says: 'When the war is won, wage war on the victors.'[8] It's an absolutely terrifying comment on the unending nature of the human struggle. I've always loved the challenge in Barker's work. I'm a rather classic, *Guardian*-reading, left-of-centre, liberal humanist. I absolutely thrill at the challenge that Barker puts up to that.

MB: Yes, I know what you mean. When I first saw *Victory*[9] I found it incredibly invigorating. You describe yourself as a liberal humanist. I would describe myself as a revolutionary Marxist. In some ways, there's an even greater challenge to me in *Victory*. To see a revolutionary, like Bradshaw, in an act of fidelity to her husband, become an infidel to the revolution, to transgress all of her religious, political and moral principles, is extraordinary. Barker is not hidebound by history. He's a historian, or at least he was; he talks nowadays of elements of the historian being left in him. He has this incredible capacity to take the historical moment and reimagine it, without any concern for Naturalism. In his play *The Dying of Today*, an ancient historical reference to the news of a coming military cataclysm being divulged to a barber becomes the basis for a highly imaginative dialogue between the bringer of terrible news and the barber. It only takes one small piece of information from a historical record, then the dramatic possibilities belong to Barker. He's not interested in writing history plays. Likewise, *Victory* isn't a history play.

HH: I wholly agree with that. Although, when you're working with young actors, the history is a good place to start. There's still a lot of stuff in Barker's text to support that investigation. That said, you're right, in lots of areas, he's absolutely going his own way. It's fascinating to ask yourself why he chose the Restoration [in writing *Victory*]. The subtitle of the play is *Choices in Reaction*. This is classic Barker. Nothing's stable. There's a realignment happening politically. The ones who were in charge, now are not. Everyone's readjusting, rebalancing and having to make choices.

MB: It's like what Marx and Engels write in that famous line about the onset of capitalism in *The Communist Manifesto*: 'All that is solid melts into air, all that is holy is profaned . . .'[10] That's what it's like in *Victory*. The Restoration of what? It's not the same monarchy, it's a monarchy which accepted its defeat, and accepted that it will now be secondary to the rising mercantile class. That's why we have that wonderful moment in the play, when Ball shouts at Charles II, 'be a fucking monarchist'.[11]

HH: Yes, it's a wonderful line. One of the things we're finding, doing the play now, is that we're loving the dynamic between Charles and Hambro, the banker. We're finding some great detail in it. It's such a power struggle, but Charles is losing all the way, and Hambro knows that in every moment.

MB: Just going back to what you were saying earlier about Shakespeare and Chekhov. It's interesting that we're not sitting here comparing Barker with his contemporaries. We're talking about him in relation to great, classical dramatists, because that's the pantheon that he belongs to. Given that, how do you explain the years of hostility Barker has faced in London?

HH: I think there's one basic explanation. It's not so much about the hostility, but about a fear of loss at the box office. I would challenge that, and Barker's continually challenging it. People are frightened they'll drive their audience away. He writes about this in the prologues to *The Bite of the Night*,[12] in which he suggests that, if companies and artists would just take the leap of faith, they will find that audiences are prepared to do that. I think there's a lot more excitement about and love of Barker's work around than appears to be the case, given the number of professional productions he doesn't get. I think the commercial factor, wanting to get, maintain and grow your audience, that stops a lot of people doing Barker, when, under other circumstances, they would. Of course, that's the great privilege I have in directing at the Conservatoire, because that isn't a factor. Nobody's going to tell me not to do Barker out of concern for the box office. To be honest, in terms of my own professional journey, when I was at the Lyceum,[13] we couldn't have done a Barker. We did some pretty radical stuff under Ian Wooldridge's regime, but it didn't go down well, and it kind of emptied the house.

MB: The irony of people thinking Barker's bad box office is that his work is invigorating for audiences, because it's so different from the naturalistic drama that dominates on television and in the movies, and it's so different even from the pseudo-naturalistic stuff that dominates in contemporary theatre, too.

HH: Unquestionably so. It's interesting, presenting *Victory* and *The Possibilities*. There's a few years between the plays, and there might be a thesis in arguing that *The Possibilities* represents Barker emerging just on the other side of a watershed where his writing has changed up a gear, and he's presenting a greater challenge to the audience. Maybe it's my familiarity with the play speaking here, but *Victory* has a quite straightforward chronology and it's a picaresque journey. I said, jokingly, at the first production meeting [for the 2013 staging], 'it's like *The Hobbit*', in the sense that it goes there and back again. Bradshaw leaves her garden, she goes to London, she collects all the 'bits' of her dead husband, and she goes home again. It's not conventional, but it's quite understandable. I think it's very accessible. It's classic Barker, because it's funny, I hope, the audience will be the judge of that. There's this dark humour in it. There's a great shock in some of the moments of bleak comedy. It's visceral, dynamic and exciting. Also, there's not an ounce of spare flesh on it, so it's constantly involving. You can't get bored with Barker.

MB: This despite the quantity of language. You could say of Beckett that he's a great remover of words, and that shows up in the brevity of his plays. With Barker, there's not a word in excess, even though there's this tremendous volume of language.

HH: Yes, that's right. You do kind of bathe in it, as an actor or director, as well. Its also a sensual experience for the audience, because of the abundance of the language. Working with the actors, you draw their attention to the poetry and to the lyricism, not because they should be consciously poetic or lyrical, but simply so that they feel that he's not frightened to paint pictures or to play with words. You also want young actors to realize that his characters aren't frightened to play with words; that's the other key thing. It's a rather obvious truism about Barker, but one that we can forget. It's really important with Shakespeare as well. These are your words, Hamlet, or Bradshaw, or Ball. You've chosen these words. You are that witty, or that dark. These are the words that are coming out of you. Obviously, that's the same with any play and any character, but actors can forget this, and that's when they can slip into automatic pilot, or just be a little bit off.

MB: You can't afford to do that with Barker.

HH: No, you have to be right on it. Again, rather like with Shakespeare, and you see this more often than is comfortable, if the actor doesn't really know what they're saying, we, the audience, don't know what they're talking about. I've found that in the past, even directing the most familiar Shakespeare plays, if the actors up there haven't done the work and don't know what they're talking about, I don't understand what they're saying.

MB: Another interesting thing about the hostility to Barker is that it's a defensive hostility. The irony of that is, he's a poet. The hostility comes from the fact that theatre is perceived as an entertainment industry. You wouldn't get a poet being condemned for being metaphorical. It's poetry, so feel it, the same way you feel the effects of a poem.

HH: You're absolutely right. It's the dead hand of a kind of cinematic realism. Something has happened in the last 100 years. Of course, I'm not blaming people like Ibsen or Chekhov. It's something in cinematic culture. We've become fearful, or find it distasteful, if something is poetic.

MB: Yes, it's more the fault of Hollywood than of Ibsen or Chekhov.

HH: Hollywood, in particular, has had an appalling effect, because it has flattened everything. If our theatres are playing safe with regard to Barker, they're infected by the toxic effect of Hollywood.

MB: Contemporary theatre has taken on the insidious myth that the advent of cinema and television has shrunk the possibilities of theatre. That simply is not true. In fact, if anything – and Barker proves this and, in a different way entirely, so does Teatr Pieśń Kozła[14] – anything that can really rise to the possibilities of tragedy – whether, as in the case of Pieśń Kozła, through the body and song, or, in the case of Barker, primarily through language, but also through imagistic imagination – precisely because TV and cinema are predominantly naturalistic (although there are exceptions, of course, such as Tarkovsky[15]), it is all the more important that theatre doesn't capitulate to Naturalism.

HH: Absolutely. Barker is surprising, daring and true, but not necessarily 'real', if that makes sense.

MB: Take *The Possibilities*, for example. The play in which Judith[16] chops off the woman's hand. In cinema, that's easy to represent. You simply ask the special effects people to do a hand being cut off, naturalistically. It's much more shocking and invigorating in the theatre, because it presents theatre makers with a problem as to how to represent it. You, as a director, have faced such questions with Barker many times. Such as in *Wounds to the Face*; how do you represent a man who has had half of his face blown away? Barker says that he never stops himself writing something like that based on a concern about how it can be represented, because he knows that a good director will find a solution.[17]

HH: Well done Howard, on that score. I agree with him absolutely. There need be no limits, because theatre is storytelling. You have to find the best means to tell the story, but there's no story that you can't tell in the theatre. To look on the positive side, there is, around and about, a lot of theatre which, and theatre practitioners who, are happily breaking the boundaries all over the place. Perhaps that's less true of the writers. Most of the writers are holding back. But there's been a real flowering of theatre being made in non-traditional spaces, different kinds of interactive theatre and so on. Of course, these are the positive sides of theatre movements that can have their ugly aspects, as we know.[18] However, if you look at the collision of theatre and live art, the use of media, site specific theatre, devised work and all of the new, experimental forms, while a lot of it ends up on the dross heap, as with every other theatrical form, they produce the nuggets of gold and the diamonds as well. Our theatre has been heavily influenced, over the last 20 or 30 years, by this kind of work, and also European tradition. I think Polish theatre has had a huge impact over the last generation. People like Staniewski[19] and Song of the Goat have definitely had a powerful influence. In certain respects, I think we're in a very dynamic time. However, if you take Barker out of the writing equation, and I don't wish to damn every other writer in the UK, but maybe we could have more invention.

'A Gallery of Images':
From the Aberystwyth Students

David Ian Rabey

To the Aberystwyth Students

It is hard to get a hearing
And the educators lie willingly
And unwillingly
As do the poets

It is hard to get a hearing
And everything's sewn up
Sewn up as usual
But more sewn up than usual now

It is hard to get a hearing
But like the dew which falls in the dark
And the slow journey of rain through faults
The words seep down

Aberystwyth is so very chaste
Only Victory emerging from the dead
Looks flagrantly naked
But in such fractures it occurs

How far from the beat of mechanical
Art and oiled acting
How far from the centres where the
Secretaries yawn and discard their shoes

We gather round a text which yields
Meaning reluctantly

We try to perform the contradiction
We do not smooth and it occurs

That must be the purpose of art
That must be art occurring
Its discomfort is considerable
And yet we return

Howard Barker[1]

Welcome stranger

As I enter my thirtieth year teaching Drama at Aberystwyth University, it seems an appropriate juncture to glance back. The activities of studying, rehearsing and staging the work of Howard Barker have been centrally entwined with my work here, and with most of the primary intensities of my life. These include the forging, through challenge, of some mutually formative creative relationships. This essay gathers a selection of testimonies based on experiences, in partial response to the spirit of Barker's ever-inspirational and profoundly discriminating poem, and of his wider work.

Aberystwyth seems a splendidly *unlikely* location for these, or many, undertakings (notwithstanding its occasional description as the Brighton of Wales). However: Caitlin Moran aptly observes that Aberystwyth is 'near to, and on its way to, nothing' (except perhaps time purposefully spent); 'there's a quiet, stubborn, time-biding self-contained Welshness to Aberystwyth that makes the idea of being "ruled" over laughable': rather, the place 'simply disbelieves it belongs to anything but itself';[2] from this perspective, it seems an entirely appropriate crucible for Barker Studies, with the associated compulsive questioning and uncompromising resistance of both enlightenment values and utilitarian values, and all ideological prescriptions for centralized power and 'progress', and what is perpetrated in their names. Barker's speculative theatre interrogates the received terms and conditions: his plays activate their characters in a counterfactual context in order to speculate on social and cultural possibilities that do not currently exist, to defamiliarize and subvert aspects of our presumed recognizable reality. The ensuing reflections on practice refer principally to the Aberystwyth productions of *Victory, The Castle* (both 1986), *The Europeans* (1991), *Gertrude – The Cry* (2007) and *The Forty* (2011 and 2014).

The 1980s

In my first year of arrival at Aberystwyth, I encountered those who would join me as founder members of Lurking Truth/Gwir sy'n Llechu theatre company, and who are still involved at the heart of its activities 30 years on: Richard Lynch and Roger Owen. Owen's essay, 'Demolition Needs a Drawing Too',[3] presents a succinct perspective on the company's first 16 years of engaging with Barker's work. However, other testimonies based on Lurking Truth's first three productions (1986–7) identify aspects of the appeal of Barker's work for those dissatisfied by the terms of what was designated available, both socially and theatrically.

First words to Richard Lynch:

> I first saw a play by Howard Barker in 1983 when I had just turned eighteen. It changed me. I have been returning to the cause of this change for over thirty years – sometimes sporadically, always compulsively. Indeed it is this compulsive need to strip away the crusted layers of self that lies at the heart of my relationship with Barker's work. His work has taught me to become a better actor: to trust myself and my native intelligence above the learned; to let the work guide the instinct; to let the language inhabit the self, for it is the language that is the crucible through which the actor is enabled and emboldened to reach the emotional self-conscious which is the beginning of discovery.[4]

Barker's work continually brings all involved into forceful contact with an evocative indeterminacy, the tension between the definite and the indefinite. This is extended by what Barker's texts challenge the performer, director and scenographer to achieve; for example, the stage directions to *The Castle* which stipulate a fall of suicidal women from the castle walls (Rabey: 'How *exactly* are we going to achieve that?'; Lynch: 'Faith!'). Moreover, each Barker play(let) seems to evoke *hinge moments*, the end of one era and the beginning of another: small wonder that prolonged commitment to a Barker text in rehearsal and performance often feels as if it is opening up just such a moment in the life of the practitioner, a sensation which might ideally extend to the audience member.

Ian Cooper notes the startling self-reflection this may provoke:

> Each line encountered in Barker's work provides me with an opportunity for the moral, spiritual and imaginative exploration of choices made, irresistible desires and roads not followed. I am profoundly grateful that I encountered this with a group of like-minded outsiders/outliers who were morally and intellectually courageous enough to pursue this at a pivotal moment in our (then) young lives. Some have since made these discoveries their life work. All were miraculously tainted by it.[5]

For several, the tensile nexus of terms at the heart of Barker's play *The Castle* crystallized a crucial dialectic: as identified by Ian Lucas, as he reflects on cultural contexts, in the mid-1980s and now:

> Politics and Desire: I'd heard the words before. But grappling with them onstage, in a text, was something new for me. Previously, most of my theatre experience had been amdram panto (oh yes it was). Then came Barker: the stage, the imagination, and the body became the battlegrounds of desire and politics. I was Coming Out, there was AIDS, Thatcher, and Section 28 in the background; and cunt, argued and portrayed onstage. These battles continued as I became a 'homosexual terrorist' in struggles reclaiming words like Queer, (re)discovering and reclaiming queer history and culture, and (re)creating sexual identities. It continues through my work as a psychotherapist (the importance of personal power and change) and writer (reimagining history and narratives through the filter of desire). During the week in which I write this, a prominent equal marriage proponent argues for the closing of gay saunas on the basis that we need to 'behave'. Politics and desire, ladies and gentlemen. Politics and desire.[6]

The 1990s and 2000s

The theatrical activities of Lurking Truth were subsequently complemented by my forays into directing departmental advanced production projects (principally comprising, and providing assessment for, final year undergraduates) at Aberystwyth from 1990 onwards. In 1991, I co-directed, with John O'Brien, Barker's *The Europeans*: the first British stagings (with the dramatist's permission) of a version of this text, featuring Eric Schneider, a recent graduate (and founder 'Lurker') in the central role of Starhemberg, who went on to direct a further production of the play in 1995 in his native Luxembourg. Schneider recalls advice from the dramatist on how best to prepare for the role:

> 'Read *Beyond Good and Evil*', was Barker's wry answer. We were sitting across each other on a table, his piercing blue eyes and high forehead exuding intelligence and mischief in equal measure. 'Yes, you must read Nietzsche. It's all in there.' For someone of my generation, whose close and extended families understood the sinister consequences of the master race ideology and its deterministic slogans, Nietzsche's reputation was such that it spelt dread and discomfort. Reading, I began to understand a totalitarian dogmatist, like Hitler, who reduces complex ideas into thought-terminating clichés, could not hope to fathom the difficult intricacy of Nietzsche's utopian vision, whereas a man like Starhemberg, who is free of all received notions, moral, artistic, social and political, might therefore invent his own set of values based on deep introspection rather than noisy public demonstrations. This would indeed ask a lot; from the actor, the directors, the backstage team, the audience, and the whole theatrical world.[7]

Aliya Whiteley reflects, from her academic study, on other aspects of the daunting power of this play:

> The first time I read *The Europeans*, I remember being struck by the possibilities of the blank page and also of the empty stage – the threat it presents as it fills. Not so much the threat of violence, which is easier to conjure, but the threat of peace. Peace in Barker's writing does not mean moral resolution (for me), but the sense of delicate accord built

with full awareness of situation, and is in itself a self-destructive act. Nobody forgets and there is no catharsis; only an agreement to live with, or even embody, the knowledge of what has gone before.[8]

Schneider recounts how his own knowledge, based on previous experiences with Theatre of Catastrophe, formed valuable deductions on embodiment. On performing the role of Milton in Lurking Truth's inaugural production of *Victory*, Schneider identifies the inappropriateness of a naturalistic approach to performance, which would involve a flinch at Bradshaw's slap, and a loss of focus on his soliloquy, the epicentre of *Victory*:

> Instead I made my Milton as still as possible, ignoring everything that was happening around him, until the fateful slap that makes him spring into action. With Starhemberg, I found myself in a strange predicament. I was able to visualise him moving askance, with other characters surrounding him, by taking the cue from his numerous non-sequiturs. Barker's systematic use of ellipsis, which is the heart of plot and character – leave them out, or wipe them for the sake of clarification, and you'll lose the entire dramatic impact, and indeed the essence of the play – suggested holding gestures in mid-air, half-finished and not expressed, finding eloquent and statuesque stillness like the eye of the storm unleashed.[9]

Schneider's further reflections on his development of the role also refract intimations of wider situations of exploratory interaction and individual charisma:

> Elements of rehearsals proved extremely valuable in that they assisted me in discovering for myself that, besides his Nietzschean quest for purity of character beyond the confines of mediocrity and nihilism, itself based on an acute sense of the European culture in decline, Starhemberg carries anarchist transformational powers as well, which are realised whenever he encounters other characters in crisis who are receptive: Orphuls, throbbing, cogent and distended; Susannah, hungry and jilted; the Beggar who wants to be taken; or indeed the Officer forced despite himself to tell his invented story. And they in turn transform him. As he reveals them, they in turn reveal him, or

at least fragments of himself. Yet, but for one significant exception, Starhemberg never reveals to them to what degree these characters transform him, nor to what extent he intends to transform them. He remains obscure and aloof at all times and that, to me, engenders his power over others. Most importantly, the characters he meets rarely question him or his intentions; and if they do (the Empress always and relentlessly does, for instance), we are never quite sure what effect their questioning has on him.[10]

The Europeans is one of Barker's highly suspenseful, yet ultimately mysterious, inductions of the audience into a hunt, moving through layers of detail and indeterminacy: Schneider notes how, as Act 1 unfolds, the audience is forced to follow Starhemberg's lead, through gothic motifs (the derelict house, an old woman forever strapped to the memory of a traumatic event, the dank cellars, dark alleyways and frigid park of a broken city); yet they remain 'one step behind in his quest, much like the reader of Arthur Conan Doyle's mysteries.'[11] These events lead to three crucial challenges of staging a kiss (the recurrent motif of *The Europeans*, aptly for a play with the subtitle *Struggles to Love*). Schneider:

> Each of three kisses between Leopold and the Empress, Starhemberg and Ophuls, and Katrin and Starhemberg has a different quality, and we, that is, the actors and directors, were struggling to define their quite disparate aspects. All three kisses are premeditated, they're not spontaneous; rather, they're constructed and planted by the characters who initiate them. The more we rehearsed, the more it became clear we were at an impasse; 'they kiss' say Barker's instructions, yes, but how? Eventually, one of the production assistants came up with images of three types of kisses: the demonstrative, passionate Hollywood kiss (Leopold and the Empress), the private Judas kiss sealing a pact (Starhemberg to Ophuls), and the public, the statuesque kiss of Klimt's Lovers (Katrin to Starhemberg).[12]

Characteristically, Barker's evocative rather than prescriptive stage directions involve the practitioners in negotiations of nuance. Just as the vocal delivery of Barker's language demands the steady discovery of a singer's artistry – pitch, tone, rhythm – so the implied physical score demands a dancer's exploration of the precarious. If student actors with less development of conscious technique sometimes find it difficult to achieve a consistency in 'hitting the beats' from one rehearsal/performance to another, they can demonstrate, at best, an openness to exploration and experimentation which is exemplary to some less flexible professionals.

If you take a tour through the photographic archive of Aberystwyth photographer Keith Morris, you will see how other departmental productions of Barker texts included *(Uncle) Vanya* (1995),[13] *Ursula* (2004) and *Gertrude – The Cry* (2007), while Lurking Truth offered my English-language premiere production of *A Wounded Knife* (Aberystwyth, 2009). David Hodgson offers his experience as an audience member attending the 2007 Aberystwyth production of *Gertrude – The Cry*:

> I first discovered Barker through just reading about his work, and from this distance I was intrigued. His words and thoughts resonated quietly with my teenage self. They seemed potent, vital, and this was before I even saw anything on stage. I felt I had a grasp on it, that I 'got' Barker. Of course, I was totally wrong. This comfortable introduction didn't prepare me enough. On stage *Gertrude* hit so hard I felt bloodied up, assaulted by it. I left the theatre stunned and disturbed. I couldn't be sure of what I had seen. Then something happened that I didn't expect; part of me began to feel more vulnerable than a couple of hours before. The Catastrophe left a hidden part of me exposed, and didn't apologise for it. What was worse is that I didn't understand what I had witnessed, at least not fully. Barker talks of an audience divided, but in this instance I felt as if I was the one that was disconnected, my understanding of what I had seen being so splintered and conflicting. I could tell you that this feeling disappeared and that I came to a grand conclusion as I pulled the pieces together, though that would be a barefaced lie. I never completely put the pieces together, not entirely. To me, this is the crux of why I enjoy immersing myself in Barker's work so much; the potency of what is presented extends beyond the immediate. It still gnaws at my guts in ways I couldn't have prepared for.[14]

Pot of Thieves, 2011–12

Phoebe Patey-Ferguson relates how she was drawn, by the work, to the place:

> A chance encounter with The Wrestling School's production of Barker's *The Seduction of Almighty God* in 2006 while it was touring changed the course of my life. I was a 16 year old fine art student and I stumbled out of that production with all of my perceptions altered and boundaries exploded. I had never seen anything so painful, cruel or beautiful. I took to theatre, to the art of theatre. I applied to Aberystwyth University. Initially, I was disappointed that not every student shared my enthusiasm for challenging, strange and contemporary drama. However, a small group of us were magnetically drawn to each other and Pot of Thieves Theatre Company was created. Like 'The Lurkers' in whose tradition we consciously followed, we became a close group tied together through the enormous difficulties of tackling the text together and the ecstasy of performing it.[15]

Pot of Thieves staged *Five Names* (an unpublished script generously released for performance by Barker), chosen for its fractured narrative and mythic characters, and *Slowly*, chosen for its rhythmic vocal power and all-female cast; both plays were performed several times in Aberystwyth and Cardiff, and *Five Names* was also taken to the 2012 International Student Drama Festival in Sheffield 2012, where, Patey-Ferguson reports, 'it played to an international audience and divided opinions fiercely'; thereafter, Pot of Thieves trained with other Barker texts, work which 'fed closely into the studies of all students involved, and what we studied we experimented with in rehearsals',[16] leading to work-in-progress showings of both *Acts (Chapter One)* and *Lot and His God* at Aberystwyth Arts Centre in 2012. Patey-Ferguson recalls: '*Acts* was a text that nearly destroyed us as a company, and thus made our bonds to each other even tighter'.[17] This comment will be reverberative for many practitioners, engaged in exploring Barker's theatre, because of how the work often prevents conventional cohesion by throwing into relief the differences of all involved; if these differences can be negotiated into specific strengths, harnessed by a tightly focused aesthetic framework, the 'ecstasy' of performance, of (self-) overcoming, may prove binding.

Jonathan Patton (who performed in *Five Names, Lot and His God* and my second production of *The Forty*) notes how 'although a recognised figurehead in the canon of British text based theatre, Barker has lived a precarious existence in the periphery, a fringe position has been consolidated by his radical ideas on what theatre should be and his theatre's subversion of established theatrical paradigms'; however:

> The resilience of Barker's work amidst an adverse cultural environment seems rooted in certain groups' reverence of it: particularly those within the realm of theatre academia. This seems to be anticipated by the words of Barker's letter of encouragement to Rabey on his arrival at Aberystwyth, how universities might be 'safe houses, like old monasteries, where not only cant, but a few truths, may lurk'. Like monasteries, drama and theatre departments in particular might provide an academic habitus from which students' dispositions are allowed to emerge in near freedom from the creative hindrances to which theatre in its mainstream manifestations is subjected: the restrictive forces of commercialism and economic viability as well as the insatiable need for accessibility and public approval which accompany it.[18]

Patton observes further: how the performer, who is 'required to approach the text instinctually and embrace its irrational quality', 'acts as a conduit for the language and the intricate nexus of extreme emotion which underpins it'.[19] Here, Patton's experience reflects and echoes that of Lynch; the second production of *The Forty* would bring them together.

The Forty (Few Words): 'In mid-wickedness'

Patey-Ferguson recalls her work as assistant director on the first performances of Barker's *The Forty*, a departmental advanced production project in 2011, her final year as an undergraduate: how 'three months of "few words" at times nearly drove us to madness, the sobering cold of Aberystwyth's Theatr y Castell perhaps being the only thing that saved us'; and yet *The Forty* 'is the Barker text that most pervasively haunts me, each gesture and every movement of those around me becoming highly charged and acquiring monumental importance (I have never let myself glance at another person in an art gallery since . . .)'.[20]

Lara Kipp similarly observes from her perspective as a performer in both productions of *The Forty*, on how this is an 'example of Barker's work to which I feel compulsively drawn back time and time again':

> It is notable that, in this instance, the spoken lines don't present the greatest difficulty – as one might very well expect of a Barker text. Here, we are instead confronted with platitudes that sit alongside evocative, choreographic stage directions. It is these, which actors and directors have to extricate first; to find the right arrangement of bodies in space, let alone the intricate, expressive gestures, takes a highly conscious engagement with the potentials that reside in the empty space between people. I'm tempted to compare the plays in *The Forty* to black holes: their presence and vast energetic potential is only known by the force they exert on their visible (and audible) surroundings.[21]

Kipp, Patey-Ferguson, Patton, Gritzner, Owen, Lynch (who had recently directed a production of Barker's *I Saw Myself* for Lurking Truth, Cardiff, 2012) and others returned to *The Forty* as Lurking Truth in a special 2014 co-production between the company and the Department of Theatre, Film and Television Studies at Aberystwyth, in celebration of the Department's fortieth year.[22] Kipp, from the experiences of her additional roles as associate director (alongside Patey-Ferguson and myself) and costume designer in the 2014 production, reflects on the further tensions of determinacy and indeterminacy offered by this most distilled example of Barker's art of theatre:

> One of the immense logistical challenges which the plays present, when played continuously back-to-back with a cast of twelve and minimal expenditure, is the necessary extension of stage space. The stage design requires the malleability of a black box studio to accommodate the wide range of places present in the script; it has to be equally suited

to be a morgue, a cliff top and a queen's chambers. Consequently, the costumes attain special significance: it is through them that we gain a sense not only of who these characters are (regarding details such as age and status) but perhaps more importantly of their 'where and when'. The latter is always resolutely ambiguous in Barker, though necessarily historical, affording a distance to current everyday reality. Similarly, the where is uncertain, particularly in these short plays, which often do not have a place descriptor at all; yet the costumed body of the actor conjures spectres of known times and places, achieving a sense of approximate 'likeness': this time is somewhat like the 1930s or 1940s, this place is perhaps like Beachy Head, and so on. This layering of a social, collective memory as construed by dominant historical discourses with individual memory gives a sense of incomplete recognition, inviting the spectator to identify the known, yet thwarting the completion of that process. It may be 'like' something familiar, but ultimately it is not familiar after all. Costumes give the actors a body where there is no classically discernible character; the audience recognise this body as amalgamation of multiple collective and individual histories that enables original figures to emerge.[23]

Devon Baur reflects on her experiences as a performer in this production:

> On first reading, *The Forty* struck me as a collection of exquisite and gruesome stories, not unlike the Grimm Fairy Tales. This collection of stories, or scenes, does not pose any lessons or preach morality, but rather poses questions to (and of) humanity through an examination of beauty and horror. I recalled Barker's words: 'All my plays as I say are hypotheses and most fairy tales are hypotheses. The trouble with the word fairy tale is it makes everything sound effete and silly. But the great fairy tales go right into the psychosis of society and human nature.'[24] With this quotation ringing in my ears, I approached the text considering the role of the hypothesis. Given a particular set of circumstances, society conventionally expects a predictable outcome; however, Barker's characters often break from the expected, questioning preconceived notions of 'humanity', and so dive right into the 'psychosis of society and human nature'. Dreamlike and abstract

in nature, the playlets demand a certain level of unbalance from the actors, as they teeter on the edge of a moral dilemma or a dangerous hypothesis. As a performer, the most significant and influential note I received from Rabey was to explore actively, and remain on, the peripheries of physical balance: persistently responding to this note, in my embodiments, allowed me to manifest physically any tension, impulse or desire, as opposed to merely analyzing the expected 'human' response. Playlet 19 in *The Forty* is a particularly striking examination of beauty and horror: the model enters the scene exuberantly, in celebration of her own beauty. Caught up in exquisiteness and 'inebriated with her own divinity' she impulsively and selfishly breaks the expected hypothesis. Like the fairy tale character there is no sense of contemplation but rather a heightened moment of unbalance. After her erotic urge has ceased, the stage is still; all parties are stunned and the stage is tarnished with echoes of horror. Finally the photographer punishes her and the old man, before leaving them both alone. Upon her resolve the model marches off alone, sobs concealed and hair back into place . . .[25]

Emily Dyble-Kitchin writes, from the perspective of one of two current undergraduates who joined *The Forty '2'* as performers:

I am struck by what feels an overwhelming artistic or perhaps aesthetic sensibility within Barker's dramatic work. It seems to converse with the senses in vivid, urgent hues. Perhaps, this is not surprising; the practices of playwright, poet, and painter seem equally innate to Barker as means of creative expression: As Morel observes, 'Barker's triple creation operates a centripetal triangulation [. . .] the paintings and the poems may allow one to read the plays more effectively'.[26] While Barker's work often appears to evade familiarisation (indeed, can be considered notorious for doing so), I still find myself striving to slip his work into an environment of familiarity. Despite its regular hints at temporal or locational settings, *The Forty* seems to exist freestanding, emancipated from any settled placement, chiefly because it wrenches timeless things, things that have forever embodied people with particular pain or unexplainable tension, to the surface. Barker turns characters inside out, peeling away superficiality by dissecting or abandoning what appear systems of societal construction, such as colloquial speech. He seems to negate the thin veil of taboo with which we attempt to numb our terror of what feels unknown or uncontrollable. From inevitable aging to destructive desire, *The Forty* speaks, often through silences, of futility innate to being our singular selves, paradoxical entities desperate to escape isolation, yet running, also, from collective responsibility.[27]

Patey-Ferguson recalls that the convocation of individuals and (anti-) histories under the banner of Lurking Truth for the 2014 performances of *The Forty* was 'an experience that escapes expression'; but she attempts a possible expression, in conscious imitation of the stage directions of *The Forty*'s playlet 22:

> *The woman is still. She seems to recollect the years. She throws her head back, smiling with fond memories. She sniffs. She wipes her face with his sleeve. She laughs. She shakes her head. She falls silent again. The woman, charmed, continues her journey.*[28]

When I approached rehearsals for the second production of *The Forty*, I had recently heard Phillip B. Zarrilli, in a lecture,[29] suggesting the possibility of considering performance in terms of dynamic feedback loops which shift awareness to bring performers (and audience members) 'out of the ordinary' and into a sense of being 'in the moment'. This made me remember Gerrard McArthur's succinct description of many situations and process of consciousness involved in performing Barker – junctures of enquiry: 'What is this new HIM/HER that is happening to HIM/HER'.[30] This further prompted me to develop the formulation of a dynamic feedback loop of character (and performer) interaction in kernel moments of tensile confrontation, which might be explored psychophysically in rehearsals and performances of the second production of *The Forty*:

1. What is this new her/him that is happening to her/him?
2. What is this new her/him that is happening to me?
3. What is this new me that is happening to me?
4. What is this new me that is happening to her/him?

This idea of a mutually informing 'loop' between (physical) gesture and internal (imaginative) imagery in performance is supported by Rebecca Loukes's considerations of Roberta Carreri's acting process, in which gestures 'create internal images which inform the way she continues to make movement',[31] and by Loukes's citation of Andy Clark's observation that gesture 'continuously informs and alters verbal thinking, which is continuously altered by gesture (i.e. the two genuinely form a coupled system)'.[32] This might be extended to being applied to most of the dramatic encounters within *The Forty*, moments in which characters/performers hear themselves speaking, and feel and see themselves performing gestures and actions, surprisingly, in relation to others: the consequences of which are explored in a predominantly silent time (perhaps in some ways akin to that which has been identified in Ōta Shōgo's theatre, in which 'stark images of divestiture, wandering and bare survival are presented in their unrelenting entirety').[33]

Inconclusion: 'I will say it and go'

Returning to my theme of 'hinge moments', this tour of images and voices seems (like so much exploration of Barker's work) to mark, and perhaps demand, a point of transition: the end of one era, in work and life, to open up another. Barker's theatre has a *funereal* quality, not only when it fictionally depicts the social ritual of valediction (as in *The Loud Boy's Life, Victory, Gertrude – The Cry, A Wounded Knife, The Fence*): in wider senses, it ritualizes severance and the melancholy of inevitable, irrevocable loss, where the *gravitas* is nevertheless shot through with heightened senses of resurgently vivified sexuality, eruptions of embarrassment, surprising laughter, all of which are thrown up by an unusually full confrontation with death, and therefore with the still-raging possibilities of life. Last words, to the youngest student represented here, Emily Dyble-Kitchin: with observations inspired by *The Forty* which again ultimately resonate more widely, through all the events mentioned in this essay:

In production, *The Forty (Few Words)*, appeared to me somewhat like the staging of a live art exhibition. The text seems a collation of potential performed images, a collection of living paintings embryonic in their written form, for which Barker is both creator and curator. He selects snapshots of existence, amalgamating themes and motives so that, as in any large gallery, subjects constantly recur in different guises. Limitation of spoken dialogue seems to heighten a sense of journeying in a gestural landscape. Whether laughing, sobbing, touching, concealing, revealing or simply walking in space, Barker's drama regularly revisits landmarks of emotive response. Each gestural recapitulation invokes involuntary relocation to a renewed frame; it is in the context of the whole display that we may make complex, possibly deeper subliminal connections towards and within the forces of expression that we witness. The gallery of images grow thus, through collaboration, and so avoid the custody of their frames.[34]

Notes

Introduction

1. The Wrestling School, '21 for 21', http://www.thewrestlingschool.co.uk/21for21.html (accessed 15 August 2014).
2. Colin Chambers, interview with James Reynolds, Kingston, 13 March 2013. All subsequent references to Chambers refer to this interview.
3. Kenny Ireland, interview with James Reynolds, Teddington, 24 July 2013. All subsequent references to Ireland refer to this interview.
4. Kenny Ireland archive, 24 July 2013. The ideas presented in this release may also have been used in the company's first Arts Council application. It is titled 'SOME NOTES TOWARDS A CHANGE OF METHOD IN PERFORMANCE AND TEXT'.
5. Chris Corner, telephone interview with James Reynolds, 11 August 2014. All subsequent references to Corner refer to this interview.

Chapter 3

1. Andrew Haydon, 'Thursday, 6 May 2010, *Slowly* – Riverside Studios', *Postcards from the Gods*, http://postcardsgods.blogspot.co.uk/2010/05/slowly-riverside-studios.html (accessed 13 August 2014).
2. The Stolen Generations, 'Breeding Out the Colour', Auber Neville, cited by Robert Manne in 'The Stolen Generations', *Quadrant* (January–February 1998), p. 59, http://www.stolengenerations.info/index.php?option=com_content&view=article&id=140&Itemid=109 (accessed 13 August 2014).
3. Mary Mazzilli, 'London Reviews, January–May 2010, *Slowly*', *Fringe Review*, http://www.fringereview.co.uk/fringeReview/3360.html (accessed 13 August 2014).

Chapter 4

1. Howard Barker, *The Last Supper*. London: Calder, 1988.
2. Howard Barker, *The Gaoler's Ache for the Nearly Dead*, in *Collected Plays 4*. London: Calder, 1998.

Chapter 5

1. Howard Barker, *Arguments for a Theatre: Third Edition*. Manchester: Manchester University Press, 1997, p. 186.
2. Ibid., p. 88.
3. Ibid., p. 110.
4. Ibid., p. 111.
5. Ibid.
6. Howard Barker and Eduardo Houth, *A Style and Its Origins*. London: Oberon Books, 2007, p. 41.
7. Barker, *Arguments for a Theatre*, p. 160.
8. Ibid., p. 185.
9. Ibid., p. 48.
10. Ibid., p. 79.
11. Ibid., p. 149.
12. Ibid., p. 150.
13. Ibid., p. 76.
14. Ibid., p. 85.
15. Barker/Houth, *A Style and Its Origins*, p. 118.
16. Ibid., p. 71.
17. Barker, *Arguments for a Theatre*, p. 53.
18. Ibid., p. 136.
19. Ibid., p. 74.
20. Barker/Houth, *A Style and Its Origins*, p. 109.
21. Ibid., p. 48.
22. Ibid., p. 106.
23. Ibid.
24. Ibid.
25. Ibid., p. 64.

26 Ibid., p. 32.
27 Barker, *Arguments for a Theatre*, p. 134.
28 Barker/Houth, *A Style and Its Origins*, p. 42.
29 Ibid., p. 24.

Part Two: Introduction

1 Howard Barker, *Arguments for a Theatre: Third Edition*. Manchester: Manchester University Press, 1997, p. 9.

Chapter 6

1 Friedrich Nietzsche, cited in Susan Sontag, *On Photography*. London: Penguin Books Ltd, 1977, p. 84.
2 Duane Michals, cited in Robert Hirsch, *Seizing the Light: A History of Photography*. New York: McGraw-Hill, 2000, p. 371.
3 Howard Barker, letter to the author, 10 July 2014.
4 Hereafter referred to as TWS.
5 Michel Morel, 'Howard Barker's Paintings, Poems and Plays: "in the deed itself", or the Triple Excavation of the Unchangeable', in David Ian Rabey and Sarah Goldingay (eds), *Howard Barker's Art of Theatre*. Manchester: Manchester University Press, 2013, p. 183.
6 Charles Lamb, 'Reading Howard Barker's Pictorial Art', in David Ian Rabey and Sarah Goldingay (eds), *Howard Barker's Art of Theatre*. Manchester: Manchester University Press, 2013, pp. 180–2.
7 Howard Barker, introduction, *Landscape with Cries*, published by The Wrestling School, 2006.
8 Referred to as *ASIO* from now on in the text.
9 Lynda Haverty Rugg, *Picturing Ourselves*. Chicago: Chicago University Press, 1997, p. 13.
10 For the purposes of this chapter, when referring to the author of *A Style and Its Origins*, it will be Houth as the predominant voice as Barker is spoken about in the third person.
11 Howard Barker and Eduardo Houth, *A Style and Its Origins*. London: Oberon Books, 2007, dust jacket.

12. Ibid., p. 41.
13. Ibid., p. 45.
14. Ibid., p. 10.
15. Lyn Gardner, *The Guardian*, 18 April 2008.
16. Lyn Gardner, *The Guardian*, 20 October 2003.
17. Ian Shuttleworth, *The Financial Times*, October 2003.
18. See Mark Brown, 'Barker, Criticism and the Philosophy of the "Art of Theatre"', in *Howard Barker's Art of Theatre*, pp. 94–104.
19. Howard Barker, letter to the author, 10 July 2014.
20. Howard Barker, programme notes, The Wrestling School, *Und*, 1999.
21. Howard Barker, programme notes, The Wrestling School, *A House of Correction*, 2001.
22. Howard Barker, programme notes, The Wrestling School, *Dead Hands*, 2004.
23. Howard Barker, letter to the author, 10 July 2014.
24. Sontag, *On Photography*, p. 15.
25. Donald Rayfield, *Anton Chekhov: A Life*. New York: Henry Holt and Company, 1997, p. 203.
26. Andy W. Smith, '"I am not what I was": Adaptation and Transformation in the Theatre of Howard Barker and The Wrestling School', in David Ian Rabey and Karoline Gritzner (eds), *Theatre of Catastrophe: New Essays on Howard Barker*. London: Oberon Books, 2006, p. 43.
27. Howard Barker, letter to the author, 14 August 2014.
28. 'Barker sometimes wrote for actors . . . his favourite actors led him from one phase to another, a classic instance of mutual infatuation both in the artistic and the private sphere . . .' Barker/Houth, *A Style and Its Origins*, p. 39.
29. Ibid., p. 10.
30. Eléonore Obis, '"Not nude but naked": Nakedness and Nudity in Barker's Drama', in *Howard Barker's Art of Theatre*, p. 75.
31. Barker/Houth, *A Style and Its Origins*, p. 110.
32. Ibid., p. 109.
33. John Pultz, *Photography and the Body*. London: Calman and King Ltd, p. 67.
34. Obis, *Howard Barker's Art of Theatre*, p. 78.
35. Ibid., p. 68.
36. Modernist photographers of the body include André Kertész, Imogen Cunningham, Tina Modetti and Margrethe Mather.

37 Barker's original photographs are often cropped for the programme covers, along with changes in the tone and colour of the original to the final programme image.
38 Julien Levy, cited in Gerry Badger's *Eguene Atget 55*. London: Phaidon Press, 2001, p. 54.
39 Ian Walker, *City Gorged with Dreams: Surrealism and Documentary Photography in Interwar Paris*. Manchester: Manchester University Press, 2002, p. 88.
40 Ibid., p. 95.
41 Ibid.
42 Barker/Houth, *A Style and Its Origins*, p. 84.
43 Ibid., p. 71.
44 Howard Barker cited in Mark Brown (ed.), *Howard Barker Interviews 1980–2010, Conversations in Catastrophe*. Bristol: Intellect, 2011, p. 190.
45 Barker/Houth, *A Style and Its Origins*, p. 116.
46 Howard Barker, letter to the author, 7 April 2003.
47 T. S. Eliot, 'Hamlet and His Problems', in *The Sacred Wood: Essays on Poetry and Criticism*. London: Faber and Faber, 1997, p. 86.
48 The same photograph is used on the front cover of the publication of *Gertrude – The Cry* by Calder Press (2002).
49 David Ian Rabey, *Howard Barker: Ecstasy and Death: An Expository Study of His Drama, Theory and Production Work, 1988–2008*. Basingstoke: Palgrave Macmillan, p. 171.
50 'Gertrude is bound to Claudius by an exquisite crime or the play hardly hangs together'. Barker, programme notes, The Wrestling School, *Gertrude – The Cry*, 2002.
51 The position of the body and the constructed *vérité* style of the photograph bring to mind the extraordinary photographs of Weegee in New York City in the 1930s and 1940s, chronicling the underbelly of the city, appearing at murder scenes and photographing the gruesome consequences of car accidents.
52 Pulzt, *Photography and the Body*, p. 33.
53 Rugg, *Picturing Ourselves*, p. 13.
54 Howard Barker, *Gertrude – The Cry* in *Plays Two*, Oberon, 2006, p. 174.
55 Sontag, *On Photography*, p. 17.
56 Geoffrey Batchen, *Burning with Desire: The Conception of Photography*. Cambridge: MIT Press, 1999, p. 10.

57   Sontag, *On Photography*, p. 16.
58   Barker/Houth, *A Style and Its Origins*, pp. 83–4.
59   Barker, letter to the author, 10 July 2014.
60   Ibid.
61   Barker/Houth, *A Style and Its Origins*, p. 82.
62   http://www.eduardohouth.co.uk/biography.htm (accessed 29 July 2014).
63   The credit '*Progress*. Eduardo Houth, 1923' again placed the photograph in a historicized, fictional context. *The Fence* is also notable for its character names *Photo* and *Camera*.
64   Barker/Houth, *A Style and Its Origins*, p. 118.
65   Hirsch, *Seizing the Light: A History of Photography*, pp. 380–1.
66   Sontag, *On Photography*, p. 14.
67   Roth cited in Steve Finbow, *Allen Ginsberg*. London: Reaktion Books, 2012, p. 7.
68   Barker/Houth, *A Style and Its Origins*, p. 16.
69   Rugg, *Picturing Ourselves*, p. 18.
70   Barker/Houth: '. . . so English in appearance, he nearly parodied it with his high forehead and narrow jaw . . .', *A Style and Its Origins*, p. 115.
71   Ibid., pp. 18–19.
72   Andrei Tarkovsky, 'Nostalgia's Black Tone', interview with Hervé Guibert, *La Monde*, 1983. Re-printed in *Andrei Tarkovsky: Interviews*, John Gianvito (ed.), Jackson, MI: University Press of Mississippi, 2006, p. 86.
73   Barker/Houth, *A Style and Its Origins*, p. 118.

Chapter 7

1   David Ian Rabey, 'Raising Hell: An Introduction to Howard Barker's Theatre of Catastrophe', in David Ian Rabey and Karoline Gritzner (eds), *Theatre of Catastrophe: New Essays on Howard Barker*. London: Oberon Books, 2006, p. 27.
2   Aleks Sierz, *Modern British Playwriting: The 1990s*. London: Methuen, 2012, p. 54.
3   Ibid.
4   See the chapters 'Ye gotta laugh', 'Theatre without a conscience', 'The theatre lies under a shroud', and 'The idea of promiscuity in the Theatre

of Catastrophe' in Howard Barker, *Arguments for a Theatre: Third Edition*. Manchester: Manchester University Press, 1997.
5   Howard Barker, *Women Beware Women* in *Collected Plays, Volume 3*. London: Calder, 1996, p. 180.
6   Aleks Sierz, 'Beyond Timidity? The State of British New Writing', *Performing Arts Journal*, Vol. 81 (2005), p. 55.
7   Graham Saunders, 'Kicking Tots and Revolutionary Trots: The English Stage Company Young People's Theatre Scheme 1969–70', in Mireia Aragay and Enric Monforte (eds), *Ethical Speculations in Contemporary British Theatre*. Basingstoke: Palgrave Macmillan, 2014, p. 204.
8   David Edgar, 'Unsteady States: Theories of Contemporary New Writing', *Contemporary Theatre Review*, Vol. 15, No. 3 (2005), p. 297.
9   See Chris Megson, '"England brings you down at last": Politics and Passion in Barker's "State of England" Drama', in David Ian Rabey and Karoline Gritzner (eds), *Theatre of Catastrophe: New Essays on Howard Barker*. London: Oberon Books, 2006, pp. 124–35.
10 Howard Barker, 'Barker's Bite', interview in *Time Out*, 17 February 1988.
11 See 'The Idea of Promiscuity in the Theatre of Catastrophe', in *Arguments for a Theatre*, p. 119.
12 Quoted in Jacqueline Bolton, 'Capitalizing (on) New Writing: New Play Development in the 1990s', *Studies in Theatre and Performance*, Vol. 32, No. 2 (2012), p. 216.
13 Ruth Little, and Emily McLaughlin (eds), *The Royal Court Theatre: Inside Out*. London: Oberon Books, p. 286.
14 Jacqueline Bolton, 'Capitalizing (on) New Writing: New Play Development in the 1990s', p. 217.
15 Jacqueline Bolton, 'Looking Back, Looking Forward: Literary Management at the Royal Court', *Contemporary Theatre Review*, Vol. 18, No. 1 (2008), p. 137.
16 Jacqueline Bolton, 'Capitalizing (on) New Writing: New Play Development in the 1990s', p. 222.
17 Aleks Sierz, '"Art Flourishes in Times of Struggle": Creativity, Funding, and New Writing', *Contemporary Theatre Review*, Vol. 13, No. 1 (2003), pp. 36–7.
18 Ibid., pp. 35–6.

19. Ibid., p. 33.
20. Ibid., p. 36.
21. Ibid., p. 45.
22. Ibid., pp. 44–5.
23. Aleks Sierz, 'Beyond Timidity? The State of British New Writing', p. 56.
24. Ibid.
25. Harry Derbyshire, 'The Culture of New Writing', *Contemporary Theatre Review*, Vol. 18, No. 1 (2008), p. 131.
26. Mary Luckhurst, *Dramaturgy: A Revolution in Theatre*. Cambridge: Cambridge University Press, 2006, p. 201.
27. Jacqueline Bolton, 'Capitalizing (on) New Writing: New Play Development in the 1990s', p. 219.
28. Ibid., p. 220.
29. Speaking on this topic at the University of Lincoln on 23 March 2012, Max Stafford-Clark discussed the circumstances surrounding the receipt of Dunbar's script: 'Very early on in my time at the Court, we had a young writers' festival and I thought I ought to get involved with that. And indeed there was this one play that came in written in green ink in very childish handwriting in a school exercise book. And it was life on what we would describe as a sink Bradford housing estate [. . .] *The Arbor*, by Andrea Dunbar. So I thought, "let's get in that straight away". And we produced that immediately after *Hamlet* with Richard Eyre directing with Jonathan Pryce. So it seemed like a declaration of intent, to put *The Arbor* by a fifteen-year-old unknown schoolgirl right jam up against *Hamlet*. But again I think *The Arbor* is a first hand report from that kind of life.'
30. Graham Whybrow, interview with Jacqueline Bolton, London, 19 November 2007.
31. David Lane, 'A Dramaturg's Perspective: Looking to the Future of Script Development', *Studies in Theatre and Performance*, Vol. 30, No. 1 (2010), p. 128.
32. Quoted in Jacqueline Bolton, 'Capitalizing (on) New Writing: New Play Development in the 1990s', p. 217.
33. Theodor Adorno and Max Horkheimer, *Dialectic of Enlightenment*, trans. by John Cumming. London: Verso, 1997, p. 120.
34. Howard Barker, 'On Naturalism and Its Pretensions', *Studies in Theatre and Performance*, Vol. 27, No. 3 (2007), p. 289.

35 Howard Barker, *Arguments for a Theatre: Third Edition*. Manchester: Manchester University Press, 1997, p. 23.
36 Ibid., p. 142.
37 Ibid., p. 111.
38 Howard Barker, 'On Naturalism and Its Pretensions', p. 291.
39 Ibid.
40 Ibid.
41 Howard Barker, *A Style and Its Origins*. London: Oberon Books, 2005, p. 86.
42 Ibid., p. 105.
43 Tim Walker, interview with Howard Barker, *The Daily Telegraph*, 1 October 2009, http://www.telegraph.co.uk/culture/theatre/theatre-news/6252056/Howard-Barker-the-playwright-says-the-Arts-Council-is-Stalinist.html (accessed 10 January 2011).
44 Howard Barker, *Death, The One and the Art of Theatre*, p. 86.
45 David Edgar, 'Unsteady States: Theories of Contemporary New Writing', p. 308.
46 Mary Luckhurst, *Dramaturgy: A Revolution in Theatre*, p. 213.
47 Graham Saunders, 'Introduction', in Rebacca D'Monté and Graham Saunders (eds), *Cool Britannia? British Political Drama in the 1990s*. Basingstoke: Palgrave Macmillan, 2007, p. 3.
48 Ken Urban, 'An Ethics of Catastrophe: The Theatre of Sarah Kane', *Performing Arts Journal*, Vol. 69 (2001), p. 40.
49 See Graham Saunders, *'Love me, or kill me': Sarah Kane and the Theatre of Extremes*. Manchester: Manchester University Press, 2002, p. 19.
50 Ken Urban, 'An Ethics of Catastrophe: The Theatre of Sarah Kane', p. 40.
51 Sanja Nikčević, 'British Brutalism, the "New European Director", and the Role of the Director', *New Theatre Quarterly*, Vol. 21, No. 3 (2005), p. 263.
52 Graham Saunders, 'Introduction', *Cool Britannia? British Political Drama in the 1990s*, p. 7.
53 Sarah Kane quoted in Dan Rebellato, 'Sarah Kane: An Appreciation', *New Theatre Quarterly*, Vol. 15, No. 3 (1999), p. 280.
54 See Dan Rebellato, 'Performing and Globalisation: Towards a Site-Unspecific Theatre', *Contemporary Theatre Review*, Vol. 16, No. 1 (2006), p. 112.
55 Karoline Gritzner, '(Post)modern Subjectivity and the New Expressionism: Howard Barker, Sarah Kane, and Forced Entertainment', *Contemporary Theatre Review*, Vol. 18, No. 3 (2008), p. 340.

56 Graham Saunders, 'Introduction', *Cool Britannia? British Political Drama in the 1990s*, p. 7.

Chapter 8

1 Howard Barker, *The Ecstatic Bible*. London: Oberon Books, 2004, p. 168.
2 Howard Barker, *Death, The One and the Art of Theatre*. London: Routledge, 2005, p. 2.
3 Howard Barker and Mark Brown (eds), *Howard Barker Interviews 1980–2010*. Bristol: Intellect, 2011, p. 192.
4 Howard Barker and Eduardo Houth, *A Style and Its Origins*. London: Oberon Books, 2007, p. 116. Barker describes himself as 'probably' an atheist in: Mark Brown (ed.), *Howard Barker Interviews 1980–2010*. Bristol: Intellect, 2011, p. 191.
5 Howard Barker, *The Love of a Good Man; All Bleeding*. London: John Calder, 1980, pp. 7, 53.
6 Ibid., p. 54.
7 Barker, cited in Charles Spencer, *Daily Telegraph*, 3 January 1990.
8 Howard Barker, *Arguments for a Theatre: Third Edition*. Manchester: Manchester University Press, 1997, p. 216.
9 Ibid., p. 222.
10 Ibid., p. 173.
11 The exception is the play *Judith* (1990), which dramatizes the climatic moments of the apocryphal book of the same name. The four episodes from *Genesis* are: *Rome: On Being Divine* (1993) from *Genesis* 22; *Lot and His God* (2012) based on the destruction of Sodom and Gomorrah in *Genesis* 19; *I Saw Myself* (2008), which includes monologues that explore Eve's transgression in Eden in *Genesis* 3; and *All This Joseph* (written 2000), an unpublished play based on *Genesis* 39. 7–9, and considered by David Ian Rabey in *Howard Barker: Ecstasy and Death*. Basingstoke: Palgrave Macmillan, 2010, p. 166.
12 Ronald Hendel, *The Book of Genesis: A Biography*. Princeton: Princeton University Press, 2013, p. 17.
13 Ibid., p. 18.
14 Ibid., p. 23.

15. In *Lot and His God* (2012), an Angel, Drogheda, is sent to warn Lot and his wife, Sverdlosk, to leave Sodom before it is destroyed. Later in the play God himself possesses a waiter in order to speak directly to Lot.
16. Howard Barker, *The Castle; Scenes from an Execution*. London: John Calder, 1985, p. 9.
17. Ibid., p. 8.
18. Lamb, *The Theatre of Howard Barker*, p. 97.
19. Howard Barker, *The Castle*, pp. 20–1.
20. Michel Foucault, *The Use of Pleasure: The History of Sexuality, Volume 2*. London: Penguin, 1992, p. 14.
21. Barker, *The Castle*, p. 21.
22. Ibid., p. 22.
23. Lamb, *The Theatre of Howard Barker*, p. 125.
24. Barker, cited in Laurence Marks, *Observer*, 22 February 1988. In *The Guardian* on 10 February 1986, Barker's '49 Asides for a Tragic Theatre' opens with a declaration that (tragic) art is the necessary response to the perceived crisis on the left, 'We are living the extinction of official socialism. When the opposition loses its politics, it must root in art', Howard Barker, *Arguments for a Theatre*. London: John Calder, 1989, p. 11.
25. Barker, *The Castle*, p. 30.
26. Seyyed Hossein Nasr, *Science and Civilisation in Islam*. Chicago: ABC International Group, 2001, p. 148.
27. Tony Dunn, 'Interview with Howard Barker', *Gambit International Theatre Review: Howard Barker Special Issue*, Vol. 11, No. 41 (1984), pp. 33, 33–44.
28. Barker, *The Castle*, p. 37.
29. Lamb, *The Theatre of Howard Barker*, p. 96.
30. Barker, *Death, The One and the Art of Theatre*, p. 2.
31. *Exodus* 20. 3, *The Revised English Bible*.
32. *The Europeans* was originally written in 1987 although significant changes were made before its publication in 1990. See David Ian Rabey, *Howard Barker: Politics and Desire* (revised edition). Basingstoke: Palgrave Macmillan, 2009, p. xviii.
33. Barker/Houth, *A Style and Its Origins*, p. 33.
34. Barker, *Arguments for a Theatre*, 1989, p. 91.

35 Barker, cited in Lindesay Irvine, 'Podcast: Howard Barker Talks', *The Guardian*, 6 December 2006, http://www.theguardian.com/stage/theatreblog/2006/dec/06/podcasthowardbarkertalks (accessed 27 May 2014).
36 Howard Barker, *The Europeans; Judith*. London: John Calder, 1990, p. 44.
37 The Christian apocalypse is initially a place dominated by images of death and chaos: 'There as I looked, was another horse, sickly pale; its rider's name was Death, and Hades followed close behind. (. . .) There was a violent earthquake; the sun turned black as a funeral pale and the moon all red as blood.' *Revelation* 6. 7, 12, *The Revised English Bible*.
38 John Gray, *Black Mass: Apocalyptic Religion and the Death of Utopia*. London: Penguin, 2007, p. 207.
39 Žižek in Doug Henwood and Charlie Bertsch, 'I am a Fighting Atheist: Interview with Slavoj Zizek', *Bad Subjects*, Issue #59, February 2002, http://bad.eserver.org/issues/2002/59/zizek.html (accessed 27 May 2014).
40 Barker, *The Europeans*, p. 31.
41 Ibid., p. 15, emphasis his.
42 Ibid., p. 15.
43 Barker/Houth, *A Style and Its Origins*, p. 116.
44 Oliver Davies, *God Within: The Mystical Tradition of Northern Europe*. London: Darton, Longman and Todd, 1988, p. 4.
45 Meister Eckhart, *The Essential Sermons, Commentaries, Treatises, and Defense*. New York: Paulist Press, 1981, p. 78. This was one of 17 articles that were formally considered by the medieval church to 'contain the error or the stain of heresy', p. 80.
46 Meister Eckhart and Reiner Schürmann, *Wandering Joy: Meister Eckhart's Mystical Philosophy*. Great Barrington: Lindisfarne Books, 2001, p. 6.
47 Eckhart in John D. Caputo, *The Mystical Element in Heidegger's Thought*. Ohio: Ohio University Press, 1978, p. 13.
48 Meister Eckhart, *The Essential Sermons, Commentaries, Treatises, and Defense*. New York: Paulist Press, 1981, p. 286.
49 Arthur Schopenhauer, *The World as Will and Representation, Volume II*. New York: Dover Publications Inc, 1966, pp. 613, 610.
50 Howard Barker, *Death, The One and the Art of Theatre*, p. 20.
51 Ibid., p. 10.
52 Barker uses both the terms 'the one' and 'one-ness' in the text: 'The evidence of *one-ness* lay precisely in the vehemence with which she tried

to demonstrate she was not *the one* at all . . .', Barker, *Death, The One and the Art of Theatre*, p. 47, emphasis his.
53 Ibid., p. 21, emphasis his.
54 Ibid., p. 66, emphasis his.
55 Ibid., p. 32.
56 Although sexual desire was absent from Eckhart's conception of the divine, this was not the case for the two female mystics who influenced his theology. As Amy Hollywood observes, 'Mechthild and Porete bring together the understanding of God as love with courtly images and themes in which God is represented as the male lover, in contrast to the female soul', Amy Hollywood, *The Soul as Virgin Wife: Mechthild of Magdeburg, Marguerite Porete, and Meister Eckhart*. Notre Dame: University of Notre Dame Press, 1995, p. 7.
57 Barker's poem *Sheer Detachment* (2009) clearly refers to this Eckhartian concept, where an encounter with a hermit leads to a process of complete detachment from previous notions of self: 'I knew my habits would reveal me and my few / Truths fall in on me as palaces crush / Their proprietors smothering them in stones: / I said my name and he repeated it as if he / Might clean it with his spit and sell it on as new: / His sheer detachment', Howard Barker, *Sheer Detachment*. Cambridge: Salt Publishing, 2009, p. 71.
58 'Infant sacrifice was widely practised in Canaan and in the Phoenician colonies of N Africa (. . .) in critical times as a way of diverting divine wrath', Raymond E. Brown, Joseph A. Fitzmyer and Roland E. Murphy, *The New Jerome Biblical Commentary*. London: Geoffery Chapman, 1990, p. 26.
59 Howard Barker, *Collected Plays, Volume 2*. London: John Calder, 1993, p. 205. When the followers of Moses degenerate into idolatry it is a golden bull-calf they create (Exod. 32. 1–4).
60 Ibid., p. 207, emphasis his.
61 Ibid., p. 207.
62 Ibid., p. 229.
63 Ibid., p. 234.
64 Ibid., p. 204.
65 Ibid., p. 210.
66 Ibid., p. 237.
67 Ibid., p. 268.

68 Barker in Karoline Gritzner and David Ian Rabey, *Theatre of Catastrophe*. London: Oberon Books, 2006, p. 34.
69 Barker, *Collected Plays, Volume 2*, p. 269.
70 Ibid., p. 269.

Chapter 9

1 Gay McAuley, *Space in Performance*. Ann Arbour: University of Michigan Press, 2000, pp. 29, 23 and 33 respectively.
2 The Wrestling School, exhibition booklet, *Landscape with Cries: Howard Barker Painting, 1996–2006*, 2006, p. 1.
3 Howard Barker, seminar with David Ian Rabey and students, Aberystwyth University, 26 January 2007.
4 McAuley, *Space in Performance*, p. 24.
5 Howard Barker, *A Style and Its Origins*. London: Oberon, 2007, p. 39.
6 Howard Barker, interview with Nina Rapi, *Brand Literary Magazine*, No. 6 (Spring 2010), pp. 73–7, 76.
7 Howard Barker, cited in Ann Jellicoe, *Community Plays*. London: Methuen, 1987, pp. 6 and 18 respectively.
8 Howard Barker, letter to Kenny Ireland, undated, circa 1990/1.
9 Colin Chambers, interview with James Reynolds, Kingston, 13 March 2013.
10 Colin Chambers, *Inside the Royal Shakespeare Company*. London and New York: Routledge, 2004, p. 93.
11 Ibid., p. 131.
12 Chambers, interview.
13 Chambers, *Inside the Royal*, pp. 131 and 137 respectively.
14 Chambers, interview.
15 Colin Chambers, *Other Spaces*. London: Methuen, 1980, p. 78.
16 Chambers, interview.
17 Richard Boon and Amanda Price, 'Maps of the World: "Neo-Jacobeanism" and Contemporary British Theatre', *Modern Drama*, No. 41 (1998), pp. 635–53, 646–7 and 645 respectively.
18 Chambers, interview.
19 Robert Shaughnessy, 'Howard Barker, TWS, and the Cult of the Author', *New Theatre Quarterly*, Vol. 5, No. 19 (1989), pp. 264–71, 265.

20 Chambers, interview.
21 Max Stafford-Clark, letter to Kenny Ireland, undated, circa 1990/1.
22 Howard Barker, letter to Kenny Ireland, undated, circa 1990/1.
23 The first use of this I can locate is in the flyer material for TWS's 1998 production of *Ursula*.
24 Kenny Ireland, interview with James Reynolds, Teddington, 24 July 2013.
25 Howard Barker, programme note, The Wrestling School, *Blok/Eko*, 2011, p. 3.
26 McAuley, *Space in Performance*, p. 32.
27 Roger Owen, 'Demolition Needs a Drawing, Too', in David Ian Rabey and Karoline Gritzner (eds), *Theatre of Catastrophe*. London: Oberon, 2006, pp. 184–97, 195.
28 Bert O States, *Great Reckonings in Little Rooms*. Berkeley and Los Angeles: University of California Press, 1987, p. 54.
29 The Wrestling School, exhibition booklet, *Landscape with Cries*, pp. 9 and 1 respectively.
30 Nick Wood, 'Flatness and Depth: Reflections', in Alison Oddey and Christine White (eds), *The Potentials of Spaces*. Bristol: Intellect, 2006, pp. 61–5, 65.
31 States, *Great Reckonings*, p. 64.
32 Stanton Garner, *Bodied Spaces*. Ithaca: Cornell University Press, 1994, p. 162.
33 Howard Barker, interview with Nina Rapi, p. 74.
34 Boon and Price, 'Maps of the World', pp. 645, 648 and 650, respectively.
35 *Silva Rhetoricae*, 'Quintilian (35–100 C.E.) – Rhetorical Terms', iws.collin.edu/grooms/cr2sp13quintq.pdf (accessed 28 July 2014).
36 Howard Barker, interview with David Ian Rabey and Karoline Gritzner, 'Crisis Is the Essential Condition for Artforms', in Mark Brown (ed.), *Howard Barker Interviews: 1980–2010*. Bristol: Intellect, 2011, pp. 123–4, 123–30.
37 States, *Great Reckonings*, p. 48.
38 McAuley, *Space in Performance*, p. 25.
39 David Shearing, 'Scenographic Landscapes', *Studies in Theatre and Performance*, Vol. 34, No. 1 (2014), pp. 38–52, 50 and 51 respectively.
40 Howard Barker, interview with Nina Rapi, p. 74.
41 Shearing, 'Scenographic Landscapes', p. 47.
42 Michael Evenden, 'No Future without Marx', *Theater*, Vol. 29, No. 3 (1999), pp. 100–13, 109–10.

43 Karoline Gritzner, '(Post) Modern Subjectivity and the New Expressionism: Howard Barker, Sarah Kane, and Forced Entertainment', *Contemporary Theatre Review*, Vol. 18, No. 3 (2008), pp. 328–40, 332.
44 Barker, *A Style*, p. 83.
45 Karoline Gritzner, '(Post) Modern Subjectivity', p. 334.
46 Howard Barker, interview with Nina Rapi, p. 75.
47 Adrian Curtin, 'The Art Music of Theatre: Howard Barker as Sound Designer', *Studies in Theatre and Performance*, Vol. 32, No. 3 (2012), pp. 269–84, 271.
48 Alan Thomas, 'Howard Barker: Modern Allegorist', *Modern Drama*, Vol. 35, No. 3 (1992), pp. 433–43, 435 and 436 respectively.
49 Aniela Jaffe, 'Symbolism in the Visual Arts', in Carl Jung (ed.), *Carl Jung: Man and His Symbols*. London: Picador, 1964, pp. 255–322, 316–17.
50 Vadge Moore, 'Chthonic Awakening', www.vadgemoore.com, 2004, http://www.vadgemoore.com/writings/beast_to_godhead.html (accessed 6 August 2014).
51 Barker, *A Style*, pp. 16, 118 and 116 respectively.
52 McAuley, *Space in Performance*, p. 29.
53 Barker, *A Style*, pp. 32 and 14 respectively.
54 The Wrestling School, production flyer, *13 Objects*, 2003.
55 Barker, *A Style*, p. 84.
56 Garner, *Bodied Spaces*, p. 90.
57 McAuley, *Space in Performance*, p. 31.
58 Thomas, 'Howard Barker', p. 440.
59 Barker, *A Style*, p. 73.
60 Evenden, 'No Future', p. 108.
61 States, *Great Reckonings*, pp. 70, 71 and 69 respectively.
62 Barker, *A Style*, p. 74.
63 Ibid., p. 63.
64 Julia Tarnoky, cited in David Ian Rabey, *Howard Barker: Ecstasy and Death*. Basingstoke: Palgrave Macmillan, 2009, p. 254.
65 Gerrard McArthur, cited in David Ian Rabey, *Howard Barker's Art of Theatre*. Manchester: Manchester University Press, 2013, pp. 4, 258–9 and 5 respectively.

66　Howard Barker, *Found in the Ground*, in *Collected Plays, Volume 5*. London: John Calder, 2001, p. 286.
67　Ibid., p. 287.
68　Howard Barker, programme note, 'Eating the Dead', The Wrestling School, *Found in the Ground*, 2009, p. 3.
69　Barker, *Found in the Ground*, p. 353.
70　Ibid., pp. 327 and 317 respectively.
71　Ibid., p. 365.
72　Ibid., p. 362.
73　Ibid., p. 333.
74　Ibid., p. 287.
75　McAuley, *Space in Performance*, p. 33.
76　Howard Barker, 'On Naturalism and Its Pretensions', *Studies in Theatre and Performance*, Vol. 27, No. 3 (2007), pp. 289–93, 291 and 293 respectively.

Chapter 11

1　Howard Barker, *The Castle/Scenes from an Execution*. London: John Calder, 1985, p. 47.

Chapter 12

1　I refer to Barker's Wrestling School texts as those that are identifiable in their style from a turning point in the original production of *Ursula*. As Rabey argues, the 'physical and scenographic aesthetics would be developed in Barker's subsequent directing work, but they emerged and came together in *Ursula* [. . .] The play and production constituted confident new benchmarks in Barker's theatrical achievements' (David Ian Rabey, *Howard Barker: Ecstasy and Death, An Expository Study of His Drama, Theory and Production Work 1988–2008*. Basingstoke: Palgrave Macmillan, 2009, p. 101). This is significant to consider as I argue that the refinement of this 'style' is a direct result of the relationship between Barker the writer and TWS actors.

2. Howard Barker and Eduardo Houth, *A Style and Its Origins*. London: Oberon Books, 2007, p. 102.
3. *Ursula: Fear of the Estuary* was performed at the Gallery Space in the Riverfront Theatre, Newport with students from University of South Wales's BA (Hons) Performing Arts Degree in January 2014.
4. Barker first outlined his description of 'Humanist Theatre' in *Arguments for a Theatre*, first published in 1989. Manchester: Manchester University Press, 1993, p. 71.
5. Julia Tarnoky, cited in David Ian Rabey, *Howard Barker: Ecstasy and Death: An Expository Study of His Drama, Theory and Production Work 1988-2008*. Hampshire: Palgrave Macmillan, 2009, p. 254.
6. Ibid.
7. James Reynolds, 'Barker Directing Barker', in David Ian Rabey and Karoline Gritzner (eds), *Theatre of Catastrophe: New Essays on Howard Barker*. London: Oberon Books, 2006, pp. 56–69.
8. Melanie Jessop, in Rabey, *Howard Barker: Ecstasy and Death: An Expository Study of His Drama, Theory and Production Work 1988-2008*, p. 258.
9. Gerrard McArthur, 'Appendix One: Testimonies by Barker Actors', in Rabey, *Howard Barker: Ecstasy and Death*, p. 258.
10. Ibid., p. 260.
11. Charles Lamb, *The Theatre of Howard Barker*. Routledge: London, 2006, p. 15.
12. Anne Bogart and Tina Landau, *The Viewpoints Book: A Practical Guide to Viewpoints and Composition*. New York: Theatre Communications Group, 2005, p. 7.
13. Italics are author's emphasis.
14. Bogart and Landau, *The Viewpoints Book*, 2005, p. 20.
15. Ibid., p. 23.
16. Anne Bogart, *A Director Prepares: Seven Essays on Art and Theatre*. London: Routledge, 2001, p. 91.
17. *Studies in Theatre and Performance*, Vol. 32, Issue 3, 2012.
18. Lorna Marshall, *The Body Speaks: Performance and Expression*. Hampshire: Palgrave Macmillan, 2001, p. 293.
19. Ibid.
20. Howard Barker, *Death, The One and the Art of Theatre*. London: Oberon Books, 2005, p. 35.
21. Howard Barker, *Ursula Fear of the Estuary* in *Plays Three*. London: Oberon Books, 2008, p. 111.

22 Bogart and Landau, *The Viewpoints Book*, 2005, p. 49. Author's emphasis.
23 Deborah Solomon, *Lillian Bassman: Women*. New York: Harry N. Abrams, Inc., 2009, p. 7.
24 David Ian Rabey, 'Raising Hell: An Introduction to Howard Barker's Theatre of Catastrophe', *Theatre of Catastrophe New Essays on Howard Barker*, p. 13.
25 Jean Baudrillard cited in Charles Lamb, *The Theatre of Howard Barker*, p. 43.
26 Ibid., p. 49.
27 Bogart and Landau, *The Viewpoints Book*, 2005, p. 15.
28 Solomon, *Lillian Bassman: Women*, 2009, p. 7.
29 Rabey, *Howard Barker: Ecstasy and Death*, p. 101.
30 *Across the Restaurant* was originally printed in 1949 and was reprinted in 1994. The image can be seen in Solomon's publication, p.16.
31 Rabey, *Howard Barker: Ecstasy and Death*, p. 101.
32 Barker, *Ursula*, p. 88.
33 Barker discussed the principles of his use of stage directions in a workshop for The Wrestling School Summer School at Exeter University in 2010. The reference *(He Frowns)* was made to his 2010 play *Hurts, Given and Received* and a stage direction relating to the character Biro.
34 Barker, *Ursula*, p. 87.
35 Ibid.
36 McArthur, *Howard Barker: Ecstasy and Death*, p. 260.
37 Barker, *Ursula*, p. 129.
38 Ibid., p. 129.
39 Ibid., p. 117.
40 Solomon, *Lillian Bassman: Women*, p. 7.
41 Ibid.
42 Barker, *Ursula*, p. 146.
43 Ibid., p. 153.
44 Barker/Houth, *A Style and Its Origins*, p. 19.

Chapter 13

1 Hodgart first directed *Victory* at the Royal Scottish Academy of Music and Drama in 1986.

2. The RSAMD, having expanded its curriculum to cover dance and film, renamed itself the Royal Conservatoire of Scotland in 2011.
3. Produced by Joint Stock theatre company in 1983.
4. Having performed in Joint Stock's 1983 production, Ireland went on to become a founder member of Barker's theatre company, The Wrestling School (for which he both acted and directed), in 1988, and artistic director of the Royal Lyceum Theatre, Edinburgh, from 1993 to 2003.
5. A role which the actor reprised in the Royal Lyceum, Edinburgh's critically acclaimed production, directed by Kenny Ireland, in 2002.
6. Mark Brown (ed.), *Howard Barker Interviews 1980–2010: Conversations in Catastrophe*. Bristol: Intellect, 2011, p. 151.
7. Howard Barker, *Arguments for a Theatre*. Manchester: Manchester University Press, 1997, p. 19.
8. Howard Barker, *Plays One*. London: Oberon, 2010, p. 69.
9. Kenny Ireland's production for the Royal Lyceum Theatre, Edinburgh, 2002.
10. Karl Marx and Friedrich Engels, *The Communist Manifesto*. London: Penguin, 1985, p. 83.
11. Barker, *Plays One*, p. 80.
12. Howard Barker, *Collected Plays, Volume 4*. London: Calder Publications, 1998, pp. 5–9.
13. Hodgart was an associate director at the Royal Lyceum Theatre, the major repertory theatre in Edinburgh, between 1984 and 1993.
14. Teatr Pieśń Kozła (Song of the Goat Theatre) is a Polish company whose work develops upon the principles and practice of the theatre master Jerzy Grotowski. The company is based, as was Grotowski's Theatre Laboratory, in the city of Wrocław, Poland.
15. Russian filmmaker Andrei Arsenyevich Tarkovsky, 1932–86.
16. The Biblical Jewish leader.
17. Brown, *Howard Barker Interviews 1980–2010: Conversations in Catastrophe*, pp. 188–9.
18. A reference to a conversation, at an earlier time, between Hodgart and Brown regarding some of the work of live artists which involves them cutting themselves, draining blood from their bodies etc.
19. Włodzimierz Staniewski, founder of the Grotowskian Gardzienice Centre for Theatre Practices in the Polish village of Gardzienice. Grzegorz Bral and Anna Zubrzycki, founders of Teatr Pieśń Kozła, were members of Gardzienice.

Chapter 14

1. Howard Barker, 'To the Aberystwyth Students', in *Gary the Thief/Gary Upright*. London: John Calder, 1987, pp. 86–7.
2. Caitlin Moran, *Moranthology*. London: Ebury, 2013, pp. 195–7.
3. Roger Owen, in David Ian Rabey and Karoline Gritzner (eds), *Theatre of Catastrophe: New Essays on Howard Barker*. London: Oberon Books, 2006, pp. 184–97.
4. Richard Lynch (Aberystwyth 1984–7), e-mail to the author, 2014.
5. Ian Cooper (Aberystwyth 1984–7), e-mail to the author, 2014.
6. Ian Lucas (Aberystwyth 1985–8), e-mail to the author, 2014.
7. Eric Schneider (Aberystwyth 1985–8), e-mail to the author, 2014.
8. Aliya Whiteley (Aberystwyth 1992–5), e-mail to the author, 2014.
9. Schneider, e-mail to the author, 2014.
10. Ibid., 2014. Schneider's words, on the held and decaying gesture, on the power of ellipses, resonate forwards for me, into recent experiences of, and deductions from, my two productions of Barker's later text *The Forty*: 'Chasing the Ellipses: Staging Howard Barker's *The Forty (Few Words)*', *Studies in Theatre & Performance*, Vol. 32, No. 3 (2012), pp. 285–304.
11. Ibid., 2014.
12. Ibid.
13. Andy Cornforth and David Ian Rabey, 'Kissing Holes for the Bullets: Consciousness in Directing and Playing Barker's *(Uncle) Vanya*', in *Performance and Consciousness*, Vol. 1, No. 4 (1999), pp. 25–45.
14. David Hodgson (Aberystwyth 2005–8), e-mail to the author, 2014.
15. Phoebe Patey-Ferguson (Aberystwyth 2009–12), e-mail to the author, 2014.
16. Ibid.
17. Ibid.
18. Jonathan Patton (Aberystwyth 2010–13), e-mail to the author, 2014.
19. Ibid.
20. Patey-Ferguson, 2014.
21. Lara Kipp (Aberystwyth 2009–12, 2012–13, 2013–), e-mail to the author, 2014.
22. Thanks to the crucial support of Dr Jamie Medhurst, then Head of Department.
23. Kipp, 2014.

24 Barker in Maddy Costa, 'The Curious Romance of Howard Barker', 2 October 2012. *States of Deliquescence*, http://statesofdeliquescence.blogspot.co.uk/2012/10/the-curious-romance-of-howard-barker.html (accessed 2 June 2014).
25 Devon Baur (Aberystwyth 2010–13), e-mail to the author, 2014.
26 Michel Morel, 'Howard Barker's Paintings, Poems and Plays: "in the deed itself", or the Triple Excavation of the Unchangeable', p. 183, in David Ian Rabey and Sarah Goldingay (eds), *Howard Barker's Art of Theatre*. Manchester: Manchester University Press, 2013, pp. 183–91.
27 Emily Dyble-Kitchin (Aberystwyth 2011–14), e-mail to the author, 2014.
28 Patey-Ferguson, 2014.
29 Zarrilli, 'The actor's work on attention, awareness and active imagination: between phenomenology, cognitive science and practices of acting', Aberystwyth University Department of Theatre, Film and Television Studies, 12 March 2014.
30 McArthur, quoted by Rabey, in Rabey and Goldingay (eds), *Howard Barker's Art of Theatre*. Manchester: Manchester University Press, p. 4.
31 R. Loukes (2014) in P. B. Zarrilli, J. Daboo and R. Loukes, *Acting*. Basingstoke: Palgrave Macmillan, p. 219.
32 Clark, quoted by Loukes, ibid., p. 219.
33 Boyd, quoted by Zarrilli, ibid., p. 148.
34 Dyble-Kitchin, 2014.

Index

Aberystwyth 205, 225–40
Ackerman, Vanessa 54, 59–60
acting 37–50, 175–88, 215–24, 225–40
Adelaide Festival 12
Adorno, Theodor 123
Alexander, Bill 37–8
Almeida, The 6, 67
Animal Farm 34
Army, Bill 192
Arts Council England 7, 14, 21, 23, 117, 119, 124–5, 153, 155
Atget, Eugène 103
Avedon, Richard 101

Barbican, The 5, 13, 151–3, 162
Barker, Howard,
  21 for 21 5
  alter-egos 95–112
  in America 189–98
  Arguments for a Theatre 79, 86, 89–90, 115, 122, 126, 137, 192, 197
  Death, The One and the Art of Theatre 90, 141–3, 145, 146
  on discipline 79–87
  Exordium 75–6, 84, 158–9
  on influences 87
  interdisciplinary 87
  Landscape with Cries 96, 156
  the naked body 99–107, 184–5
  painting 45, 49, 95, 155–6
  photography 95–112
  puppets 85
  radio plays 15, 151, 181, 182–3
  in Scotland 215–24
  student performances 199–213, 215–24, 225–40

A Style and Its Origins 5, 17, 79, 87, 95–112, 124, 212
Theatre, The 80–2
Theatre of Catastrophe 79, 80, 96, 115, 122, 123, 138–9
works,
  13 Objects 107–8, 163
  Acts (Chapter One) 233
  Animals in Paradise 13
  The Bite of the Night 33, 128, 151, 153, 160, 162, 220
  Blok/Eko 14, 34, 155, 163
  The Castle 5, 10, 12, 36, 39, 40–2, 87, 134–6, 151, 157, 162, 175, 188, 190, 192, 194, 195, 196, 197, 227–8
  Crimes in Hot Countries 5, 21, 151
  Dead Hands 108, 157, 164
  Downchild 5, 21, 151
  The Dying of Today 157, 164, 219
  The Ecstatic Bible 12, 71, 73, 76, 165
  Ego in Arcadia 159
  The Europeans 5, 10, 12, 26, 39–40, 66, 71, 136–9, 152, 158, 190, 192, 194, 195, 229–31
  The Fence in its Thousandth Year 14, 110, 164, 239
  Five Names 233
  The Forty 76, 205, 234–40
  Found in the Ground 52, 97, 110, 165–7
  The Gaoler's Ache for the Nearly Dead 75
  Gary the Thief 190
  Gertrude – The Cry 43, 105–7, 108, 164, 192, 196, 197, 232
  Golgo 9, 39
  That Good Between Us 5, 151
  The Hang of the Gaol 37–8, 152

A Hard Heart 6, 190, 196
Hated Nightfall 7, 10–12, 66, 162
He Stumbled 164
A House of Correction 44, 76, 102, 104, 157
Hurts Given and Received 53
I Saw Myself 14, 42, 51, 157, 164, 235
In the Depths of Dead Love 15, 163
Judith 12, 66, 76, 79, 154, 157, 158, 162
The Last Supper 6, 8, 27, 30, 63, 66, 69
Lot and His God 233, 234
The Loud Boy's Life 5, 239
The Love of a Good Man 132, 151, 162
No End of Blame 190–1, 192
Plevna 190, 192, 193
The Poor Man's Friend 150
The Possibilities 6, 215, 218, 221, 223
The Power of the Dog 6, 22
The Road, The House, The Road 163, 164
Rome: On Being Divine 143–7
Scenes from an Execution 6, 13, 27, 35, 114, 151, 162, 175–88, 190–1, 192, 194, 196, 197
The Seduction of Almighty God 110, 233
Seven Lears 9, 31, 39–40, 64, 66, 71, 151, 153, 160, 162, 164
Sheer Detachment 253n. 57
Slowly 51–61, 233
To the Aberystwyth Students 225–6
(Uncle) Vanya 12, 66, 67–8, 75, 100, 154, 192, 232
Und 101, 110, 157, 162, 164
Ursula 34, 43, 44, 73, 87, 100, 154, 164, 199–213, 232
Victory 5–6, 10, 11, 12, 21, 22, 24–5, 26, 28, 39–40, 66, 71, 83, 87, 128, 152, 153, 157, 162, 175, 190, 192, 194, 196, 215, 218, 219, 221, 230, 239
Women Beware Women 39, 41, 115
A Wounded Knife 232, 239
Wounds to the Face 154, 162, 223
Barlow, David 192
Bassman, Lillian 207
Batchen, Geoffrey 107
Baudrillard, Jean 208
Baur, Devon 236–7
Bechtler, Hildegard 35, 178, 180
Beckett, Samuel 53, 176–7, 221
Benjamin, Walter 104, 109, 111
Berrigan, Hanna 51–61
Bertish, Jane 23
Bible, The 132–3, 136, 144, 250n. 11, 252n. 37
Birtwistle, Harrison 34
Bogart, Ann 200, 202, 203, 205, 208
Bolton, Jacqueline 117, 120
Bond, Edward 215
Boon, Richard 152–3, 158
Boyd, Michael 22
Boyle, Danny 6, 22
Bradley, Jack 122
Brantley, Ben 196
Brassaï 111
Brecht, Bertolt 115, 124, 176–7, 208
  Mother Courage and Her Children 177
Brenton, Howard 114
Brink Productions 12
Brook, Peter 192
Brown, Joe 195
Brown, Mark 104
Bull, Paul 7, 73

Cairns, Tom 175, 179–80
Chambers, Colin 4–5, 36, 151–3
Chekhov, Anton 100, 154, 164, 218, 220, 222
chorus 23, 33–5, 52, 54

Index

chthonic 149, 160–8
Clyde, James 40–2
Communist Manifesto, The 219–20
Cooper, Ian 228
Cooper, Suzy 48–50, 54
Corner, Chris 5, 8–15, 27–8, 63
Curtin, Adrian 160

Davis, Oliver 139
Derbyshire, Harry 119
Dior, Christian 108, 207
Don, Robin 66, 67
Draper, Alex 192
Dunbar, Andrea 120, 248n. 29
Dyble-Kitchin, Emily 237–8, 239–40
Dyer, Chris 39
Dykes, Stephen 192

Edgar, David 116, 125
Eliot, T. S. 105
Emmet Lunney, Robert 192
Engels, Johan 12, 39, 66
Europe 136–9
Evenden, Michael 159, 164
Expressionism, New 129
Eyre, Richard 24, 28

Faraone, Cheryl 189–98
Ferguson, Sally 60
Foucault, Michel 134
Francis, Matthew 28
Franks, Philip 38–40
Friedlander, Lee 110–11
Frost, Roger 6, 23, 31

Gardner, Lyn 98
Garner, Stanton B. 157
Gaskill, William 21, 116
Glasgow Citizens 64
Gray, John 138
Greenwich Theatre 9–10, 28, 154
Grey, Pamela J. 192
Gritzner, Karoline 129, 159–60
Grotowski, Jerzy 208

Hall, Megan 54
Hall, Peter 34
Hare, David 114
  Slag 190
Harold, Madd 217
Harper's Bazaar 100, 207, 211
haute couture 207
Haverty Rugg, Lynda 97, 106, 111
Haydon, Andrew 58, 61
Hayes, Dermot 66
Hendel, Ronald 133
Hodgart, Hugh 215–24
Hodgson, David 232
Houth, Eduardo 95–112
Hunter, Kathryn 13
Hytner, Nicholas 24

Ibsen, Henrik 222
Innes Hopkins, Robert 66
In-Yer-Face Theatre 118, 127
Ireland, Kenny 5–11, 38, 39–40, 42, 63, 64, 65, 71, 153–4, 215
irony 43, 46

Jellicoe, Anne 150
Jessop, Melanie 31, 81, 101, 201
Jung, Carl 160, 168

Kaiser, Billie 97, 99, 107, 108
Kane, Sarah 128–9
Kent, Nicolas 22, 26
Kipp, Lara 235–6

Lamb, Charles 95, 134, 201, 208
Landau, Tina 200, 201, 203, 208
Lane, David 121
Le Prevost, Nicholas 23, 28, 31, 37–8
Leathers, Megan 192
Leicester Haymarket 8–10, 12, 154
Leipzig, Tomas 60, 97, 98, 99, 107
Les Miserables 5, 152
Levy, Julien 103

Lewis, Edward 60
Lichtenfels, Peter 8, 10
Little, Ruth 117
Loukes, Rebecca 239
Lucas, Ian 228
Luckhurst, Mary 119–20, 125
Lurking Truth/Gwir sy'n Llechu 227–30, 232, 235, 238
Lyceum, Edinburgh, The 10, 22, 26, 66, 220
Lynch, Richard 227

McArthur, Gerrard 53–4, 75, 165, 201, 211, 238
McAuley, Gay 149, 159, 162
McCarron, Ace 12, 60, 63–77, 163
McDiarmid, Ian 6–7, 10, 30
McGhie, Penelope 53
McIntosh, Jenny 28
McLoughlan, Emily 117
Mala Nocha 13
Manchester Evening News Awards 10
Maxwell, Jan 191–2, 194
Mazilli, Mary 60–1
Medea 183–4
Megson, Chris 116
Meister Eckhart 132, 139–47
Melvin, Jules 44–5
Michals, Duane 95
modernism 102, 110
Mondello, Bob 195
Morel, Michel 95

Nasr, Seyyed 135
National Theatre, The 27, 28, 34, 35, 53, 114, 122, 153, 175, 182, 187–8, 218
Naturalism 30, 31–2, 34–5, 38, 82, 86, 87, 115, 118, 121, 124, 126, 154, 158, 163, 164, 168, 193–4, 219, 223
Neo-Nihilist 126, 127
Neville, Auber 58–9
New Brutalist 126

New Labour 125
New Writing 113–29
Nietzsche, Friedrich 95
Nikčević, Sanja 127
Nunn, Trevor 5, 151

Obis, Eléonore 101–2
objet trouvé 110
O'Brien, John 229
O'Callaghan, Sean 42–3
Odéon Théâtre de l'Europe 155
Overlie, Mary 202
Owen, Roger 151–6, 227

Pakhuis Seventeen 67
Patey-Ferguson, Phoebe 205, 233–4, 238
Patton, Jonathan 234
Phillips, Andy 63–4
picaresque 221
Picasso, Pablo 186
Price, Amanda 127, 152–3
Print Room, The 15
PTP/NYC 189–98
Pultz, John 102, 106

Rabey, David Ian 105, 110, 165, 207–8, 209
Ravenhill, Mark 126, 127, 129
religion 131–47
Reynolds, James 201
Richards, David 195
Riverside, The 10, 52, 53, 154
Romagnoli, Richard 189–98
Rose, Lloyd 195
Roth, Philip 111
Royal Academy of Dramatic Art (RADA) 14, 42
Royal Conservatoire of Scotland 215
Royal Court, The 6–12, 21–2, 63, 84, 113–14, 116–17, 122, 127, 153–4
    Joint Stock 21–2, 71, 84, 116, 124

Royal Shakespeare Company, The 4–7, 21, 35, 36, 84, 151–3
The Warehouse Theatre 5–6, 21, 36, 38, 113, 151–3
Russell Beale, Simon 41

Saunders, Graham 115, 125, 129
Scarfe, Gerald 190
Schneider, Eric 229–31
Schopenhauer, Arthur 141
Scott, Matthew 7, 25, 27, 63, 72
Sezno, Paula 97
Shakespeare, William 53, 54–5, 65, 74, 81, 105, 117, 150, 176, 183, 185, 216, 217, 220, 222
Shaughnessy, Robert 153
Shaw, Fiona 175–88
Shearing, David 159
Sheffield Crucible 9, 22, 154
Shentang, Caroline 97
Shuttleworth, Ian 98
Sierz, Aleks 117–18, 127
Smith, Rae 39, 66
Soho Theatre 118, 127
Solomon, Deborah 207–12
Sommers, Pamela 195
Song of the Goat/ Teatr Pieśń Kozła 222–3, 224
Sontag, Susan 99, 107, 111
Sowerby, Georgie 68
Stafford-Clark, Max 21, 83, 120–1, 153, 248n. 29
Staniewski, Wlodzimierz 224
Stanislavski, Konstantin 122, 208, 216
States, Bert O. 155, 159
Steed, Maggie 6, 23, 41
Stieglitz, Alfred 102
Strabo 59
sub-text 41, 46–7
Surrealism 103–4, 110

Tarkovsky, Andrei 83, 112, 223
Tarnoky, Julia 165

Théâtre de Complicité 64, 66
theatre space 28–9, 35, 70, 149–68
Thomas, Alan 160
TMA Regional Theatre Awards 10, 13
tragedy 137–43, 149, 156, 159–60, 168, 187, 251n. 24
Tramway, Glasgow 12

uncanny, the 109
Urban, Ken 126

Viewpoints 193, 199–213
violence 128
Vogue 208, 211

Walker, Ian 103–4, 109
Wallace, Neil 12–13, 34, 67
Warehouse Theatre, The 5–6, 21, 36
Weegee 245n. 51
Whistler in the Dark 198
Whitely, Aliya 229–30
Whybrow, Graham 117, 121
Wicks, Victoria 30, 31, 45–8, 81, 209
Wilson, Snoo 189, 190
Wood, Nick 156
Wrentmore, Stephen 10
Wrestling School, The,
    acting 31, 37–50
    directing 29, 42–3, 51–61
    history 15, 21–36, 150–6
    lighting design 63–77
    programmes 95–112
    sound design 25, 27, 29, 60, 72, 73–4
    style 26–7, 29, 30, 32, 35, 60, 79–87
Wright, Nicholas 22

Zarrilli, Phillip 238
Žižek, Slavoj 138